JACK MINER
AND THE BIRDS

JACK MINER HIMSELF

Photo by his friend
Frank Scott Clark,
Detroit

Jack Miner and the Birds

AND

SOME THINGS I KNOW ABOUT NATURE

By

JACK MINER

CHICAGO
THE REILLY & LEE CO.

FIFTH PRINTING

Printed in the United States of America

All Rights Reserved

CONTENTS

CONTENTS—*Continued*

ILLUSTRATIONS

INTRODUCTION

MY REASON, dear reader, for writing this book, I will assure you is not to expose my A, B, C education, but simply because my many friends have requested me to put into book form at least a portion of my interesting experiences.

For years I have simply ignored such requests; but the more I thought about it, the more seriously it appealed to me. So this morning I loaded up chair, stove, tent, etc., and made my way to the woods, where I am at home, and away from the wires of communication and the honk of the automobiles, and even the enquiring voice of my little boy. I have run away from them all and have pitched my tent in the woods.

As I was out gathering wood for the camp-fire I quietly looked around, and a few remnants of old stumps are still visible where I helped to cut the virgin timber, the forest that provided a home and shelter for the raccoon that I once hunted by night, and the birds, from quail to the wild turkey, that I hunted by day. About one hundred yards to the east of where I am sitting is where I split my big toe with a nine-pound broad-axe while hewing railroad ties when I was but fourteen years of age. But Nature is helping me to replace a little, and the second-growth trees are from thirty to fifty feet high.

A hawk has disturbed the Bob-Whites that are increasing in numbers very rapidly, and the sweet tones of their familiar voices are making this old spot fairly ring. In fact the very atmosphere seems so full of cheer that when I entered the tent and sat down to write, I first whispered a few words of silent prayer of thankfulness, and asked God to guide my untrained hand so that you will understand my meaning.

Let me assure you I will be as brief as possible. And while I am very thankful to my many friends who have offered to write it for me if I would only dictate it, yet I firmly believe the majority of readers will enjoy these facts right from the awkward hand of Jack Miner better than if they were polished too much. While it may read very unreasonable, yet please don't forget that outside of a little joke I may attempt to crack, the rest is all facts gathered from personal experience and observation, and I assure you these views are not second-hand, as I am a very poor reader and have never read a book through in my life.

—J. M.

NOTE TO UNITED STATES EDITION

AFTER privately publishing this book in Canada, I am pleased to say the sales so far exceeded my expectations that I am hustling out a second edition.

I feel that I have passed through the experimental stage and that my bird sanctuary is at last a success. Men who once chuckled with laughter at my foolish idea now grasp my hand and pour out congratulations.

In the spring of 1924 I fed fully 25 per cent more feed to the visiting birds than on any previous spring, and the aluminum tags, which in years past I placed on the legs of wild geese and ducks, are now being mailed back to me nearly every week of the year, bringing in more and more information concerning the wandering habits of our wild fowls.

During the year 1923 I made several trips to Niagara Falls to study the wild swans. Mr. William Hill ("Red" Hill, the riverman) and I concluded that if the swans were fed and protected near Kingsville, Ontario— nearly 200 miles away—it might be that these beauties would learn to stay there and not be meeting their death in the Niagara rapids.

When the first bunch of swans arrived at our lake shore in the spring of '24, I wired J. B. Harkins, of Ottawa, for help. In a few hours two mounted policemen arrived and patroled the shore, forbidding anyone to throw stones at the swans or in any way frighten them. The swans came closer and closer, hundreds of them, and in time the little town of Kingsville, Ontario, with a population of 2,000, learned to boast of having 15,000 people there in one day to see the wild swans. But best of all, not a swan went over Niagara Falls that spring.

One Sunday I drove over to see them and the bank of the lake was lined with people for over a mile, and out in the water were hundreds of these lovely white swans.

I got out of the car to drink in the sight, but I soon withdrew and came home, for men of all classes came rushing towards me, pouring out their congratulations; some saying, "Jack, it wasn't a dream after all." One man even thought of the fact that this would increase property value!

Years ago their sneering jokes put me on my mettle, but on that day their kind and loving remarks really melted me. After all, I couldn't see that I had really done anything of my own self, but that it was the fulfillment of God's promise—"Let man have dominion over all."

J. M.

Kingsville, Ontario
February, 1925

PREFACE

L ONG and intimate acquaintance with the author of this book must be my apology for attempting to write a brief introduction. Meeting Jack Miner for the first time in 1888, I was at once impressed with his striking personality. I found myself instinctively attracted to him, and a cordial friendship sprang up between us, which grew in intimacy as the years passed. Although lacking in academic culture, his manner was decidedly urbane, and it was not long before I discerned beneath his rough exterior an enshrined soul.

Inheriting, as I did, a passion for dog and gun, I cultivated his friendship, and many delightful days have we spent together afield. I was a novice in woodcraft; he taught me to hunt and shoot. Many a bird fell to his gun for which I took full credit in those early days, until, on one occasion, when I had made, as I thought, a particularly clever kill, I glanced over my shoulder as I heard him say: "Good shot, Doctor!" only to see him hurriedly slipping a shell into the smoking breech of his gun. I said: "Did you shoot, Jack?" and his face betrayed guilt as he replied: "Take more time, Doctor. If you hit a bird fair at that distance, you will have nothing to pick up!" I was shooting too soon, and of course missing. He had got on to my time, and was now and then dropping a bird, apparently to my gun, to give me confidence.

What impressed me most, perhaps, in the days of my novitiate was the determination with which he pursued a wounded bird. He would spend an hour ferreting out a cripple rather than leave it to die in misery, or become the prey of its natural enemies, owls, hawks or vermin. He invariably repiled the logs and brush he had dislodged in his efforts to retrieve a wounded bird. And this is but one evidence that a keen sense of justice, a full regard for the rights of all living creatures, are conspicuous traits in Jack Miner's character.

Years passed. Until now he had held aloof from church and social life in the community. Then trouble came. Trouble, that so often floors the weak man, is the strong soul's opportunity to reveal itself. Thus it proved in Jack Miner's case. Death robbed his family circle of three of its members in a comparatively brief period of time. Of an exceptionally emotional and sympathetic nature, his grief was overwhelming. Something had to move, or break. Gradually he came over to the allies, and became active in social and Sunday-school work. All his dormant virtues seemed bursting with life, and latent genius sprang into activity. He pursued his hobby of making friends with the birds with a zeal, as it were, begotten of despair. Steadily he plodded on in the face of financial burdens, in spite of the discouraging indifference of the many, and in defiance of the more malignant opposition of the few.

Ultimately he secured possession of the entire Miner homestead. He procured thousands of evergreen trees from the Government, and using native trees as well, prosecuted his work of beautifying his surroundings, until he had transformed what was an ordinary farm of two hundred acres, without one attractive feature, into a place which would arrest the attention of the passer-by, and which formed a veritable paradise for birds and waterfowl. Inheriting a love of the beautiful from his mother, he has developed his home surroundings into a bower of lilacs and roses. I venture to say that there is no spot in Western Ontario, if indeed in the entire Province, that attracts to itself, season after season, the thousands of visitors— distinguished men and women of Canada and the United States— that come to see the Miner Bird Sanctuary.

As a lad, however, he did not see exactly eye to eye with his mother. Of what use was an old, battered spoon, the sole surviving member of a set of pewter, that had been in the family for generations? He would convert it into smooth, round bullets, and make it contribute to the upkeep of the table. So one night the spoon went into the melting-pot, to appear in a few days on the table in the form of savory venison steak, and Mrs. Miner was left guessing what had become of her precious heirloom.

Jack Miner has built an enduring monument to his patient toil and his unfaltering confidence in an over-ruling Providence, that will stand for all time. That this untutored man of the woods is able to entertain and interest vast concourses of people in our college halls throughout Canada and the United States, being recalled season after season to our educational centres as well as to our towns and villages, to deliver his lectures, is convincing evidence that he has a world message and can deliver it with compelling force.

I have read "Jack Miner and the Birds" in manuscript form. It is a remarkable book, by a remarkable man. While it makes no pretensions to literary excellence, it is free from faults of egotism and verbiage, often present—almost laconic in style. It contains much valuable information, expressed in trite and witty language, and will prove a valuable addition to our works on bird lore.

Of more interest, perhaps, to the average reader will be a brief narrative of a few episodes in the life of Jack Miner. With characteristic self-effacement, he has refrained from incorporating in his book any incident in which he might seem to figure as the hero. Nevertheless his life has not been without tragic experience and thrilling adventure.

No sketch of his career, however brief, will do him justice without reference to his elder brother, Ted, whom Jack regarded with the profoundest respect and reverence. They played together—if work can be called play—hunted together, slept together, and lived with and for each other. As boys they practised shooting with a rifle at snowballs thrown into the air, at twenty-five yards rise, until they became so expert that they could break forty-six out of fifty.

In 1898, when the brothers were hunting with a friend in Northern Quebec, Ted was killed instantly, shot through the head by the accidental discharge of his companion's gun, as he was dropping on one knee to dispatch a wounded and charging bull moose. Imagine the situation, if you can! Jack came running down the ravine through which he had driven the moose, confident that the boys had made a kill, only to meet his friend running toward him, his face pale as death, frantically shouting: "I have killed Ted!" Though dazed by the shock, Jack nevertheless realized the necessity of submerging his emotions, for the occasion demanded sane judgment and prompt action, and the friend was helpless by reason of his grief. They were twenty-five miles from the nearest railway station; help must be procured promptly and—it was up to him. Washing the blood from his dead brother's face, and pressing a kiss on his pallid brow, he covered his body with snow, lest the smell of fresh blood might attract a band of prowling wolves before he could return, and, leaving him within a dozen feet of the big bull moose he had shot as he pulled the trigger for the last time, Jack set out for help. He ran thirteen miles to the nearest settler's cabin, where he procured the aid of an old man and his boy. On returning to the scene of the accident, a litter was improvised on which the body was placed, but the absence of all trail, and the deep snow, made it impossible to proceed except in single file, and so Jack took his brother, who weighed 202 pounds, across his shoulders as he would a dead deer, and carried him almost the entire distance of thirteen miles, while the other three men cut brush and broke trail. Arriving at the lake they placed Ted's body in the bow of a home-made punt, and Jack paddled twelve miles down the lake in the face of a blinding snowstorm, making the entire distance in twenty-four hours. From this terrible strain he has never fully recovered.

Many times he has rescued men lost in the woods. Indeed he has never once failed to bring his man out alive, although in some cases he had nothing human to guide him, all trail having been obliterated by heavy snowfall. For this signal success he takes no credit to himself, but attributes it to Divine Guidance in answer to his petitions.

On one occasion he was gone from camp forty-eight consecutive hours without sleep or rest, and with little food, tramping through snow up to his knees, in search of two men who had strayed in entirely opposite directions. He brought them both to camp, his hands being frozen during his adventure.

On another occasion, when hunting moose in Northern Quebec, at about three o'clock in the afternoon, he heard in the distance signal shots of distress. It gets dark early and suddenly in the North in November, but Jack immediately broke into a run, never stopping until, just at dusk, he came up to a young guide, standing guard over a man fallen in the snow. This was a well-to-do gentleman who had joined a hunting party, but was overcome by the strain of the unusual fatigue. His clothing had become saturated with the wet snow, his limbs lost all sense of feeling, and he fell, unable to move hand or foot. Jack Miner gave the rifles to the guide, hoisted the man, who weighed 185 pounds, on his shoulders, and carried him to an old lumber camp five miles distant in less than two hours. Other members of the party arrived, a fire was made, and hot coffee, hot flannels, and much rubbing, eventually brought feeling into the benumbed limbs. By morning the man was able to walk. As so often happens, the most solemn occasion is not without its spark of humor. When all immediate danger seemed to have passed and enquiry was made as to the whereabouts of the rifles, the guide, with the utmost sangfroid, said: "I left them stacked back in the woods at the scene of the tragedy!" Since no one but Jack would brave the dangers of the dark and the swollen river which had to be crossed on a fallen tree, it was up to him to retrieve the guns, and he did it.

He was never so happy as when studying the lives and habits of the wild creatures, whether it was the timid field mouse or the lordly moose, the socially inclined chickadee or the elusive Canada goose. Thus did he lay the foundation of the success he has achieved as a hunter and naturalist.

In traversing the forest his sense of location and direction is akin to that of the denizens of the woods. When an Indian caches his game, intending to return for it at some future time, he blazes trees and breaks twigs to guide him back. Jack Miner was never known to blaze a tree nor break a twig for the purpose of locating a dead moose or a beaver-trap. He can follow a trail all day long to every point of the compass, and at nightfall turn his face directly toward camp. If on the following day he wishes to return to any spot visited the day before he will go to it with a directness and accuracy almost uncanny.

Years before he ever set foot in the northern woods he and Ted planned annual hunting excursions. They were the pioneers of big game hunting in Essex County, and while it is true that Jack Miner has killed car loads more game than any other man in Western Ontario, it must be remembered he never wasted a pound of meat, nor kept more than perhaps ten per cent. of his kill for his own use, but gave it away to rich and poor alike. He organized moose dinners for charitable purposes, even buying meat on one occasion when he had not enough of his own to supply the tables.

So did Jack Miner, the boy dreamer, become Jack Miner, noted naturalist, popular lecturer and Canada's Famous Birdman.

—J. Earle Jenner, M.D

TAME ENOUGH FOR WILD GEESE

I LOVE THE BIRDS AND THEY HAVE COME TO ME

Jack Miner and the Birds

CHAPTER I.

Who is Jack Miner?

NOW, as you have this book in your hands and have looked at the name of the writer, and possibly flipped over a few pages, glancing at the interesting illustrations, etc., I imagine I can see you raise your head, as your eyelids come down for an instant. "Who is Jack Miner? Who is Jack Miner?" This thought repeatedly flashes through your mind.

Well, let me assure you of this fact, that Jack Miner is not Old Bill Miner, nor Jesse James, and although I have been raised in the woods, that is no evidence that I have split feet and antlers. But I will admit there has been many a time in my life that if you could have seen me you would have thought you were looking over Esau's line-fence.

However, just who I am is a question I am not prepared to answer, as it is not a history of my life I am supposed to be writing; but in a few brief words will say that my dear mother's people that are in America are a good, self-sacrificing, respectable, God-fearing people. And my father never had but one full sister; yet, he said, where he lacked in quantity he made up in quality. Father and mother were both born in Leicestershire, England. As to my father, I know he was a truthful, honest man, and, according to his own story, he was raised on the toe of a step-father's boot. A few years after he graduated from this lofty position, he followed mother and her people to America, and eventually overtook them in the good old State of Ohio, and on the 10th day of April, 1865, I was born, barefoot. According to my oldest brother's statement, father was at that time quite down-hearted over the fact that his old favorite yellow tom-cat had been coming home absent for about two weeks, and he had given up all hope; but as soon as I arrived and he saw my complexion, he took me out and laid me in brother's arms, and as he raised up he clapped his hands together, quite cheerful, and said, "Ted, we'll call him John Thomas." John Thomas it really is. Fortunately, my friends have shortened it down to just Jack.

We were very poor financially, and as I was second oldest boy in a family of ten children, I had to put a shoulder to the wheel and help roll the bread-wagon.   The result is I was educated for ditching, cutting cord-wood, and splitting rails.   In the spring of 1878 father

LOOKING OVER ESAU'S LINE FENCE AT THE WRITER
Photograph taken in 1907 while on a Moose Hunt.

decided to migrate, and at the age of thirteen I was liberated here in Canada, a sportman's paradise.   I took to the woods as naturally as a park hare, and I know I was father's favorite because he always called me to build the fire in the morning, and when the other boys would lodge a tree I have often heard him shout, "Come out and come away from it! You'll get 'urt! Leave it w'ile Jack comes; 'e'll go hunder and cut it down." If we were splitting rails, father always set the wedges, permitting me to handle the maul.

Father and mother enjoyed life together nearly sixty years and put up with the mingled enjoyment and annoyance of us ten children. How some of father's teachings still ring in my ears! When I have gone to him with complaints about others he has often said, "Shut up; I don't want to 'ear it. But if you have some of your own failings to tell, let's 'ear 'um." Yes, he was always short but to the point. One piece of advice that he gave us boys I have always tried to practice; that was: whenever we grabbed hold of anything and found it was red-hot, to drop it.

But now let me lay these smiling facts aside for a few seconds and close my introduction to you in real earnest. For, outside of un-avoidable sadness, my life has been one continuous round of enjoy-ment made up of failures and disappointments and dark, stormy clouds, which have been completely trampled out of existence by success that in every case exceeded my expectations, and has caused the sun to shine so brightly that it has illumined my path clear up to the Great Divide, and given me an imaginary glimpse of the beautiful Beyond

CHAPTER II.

My First Pets.

WELL, the first pet I can remember having was a young blue jay. I was, of course, very anxious that he should live, so I filled him to the top with fish worms. The next morning the blue was there, but the jay was silent.

The next I have any recollection of was when father took our pet 'possum by the handle and wound it around the corner of the old stable, to settle a quarrel which arose between my brother and myself over its ownership.

I remember I started one spring with a pair of white rabbits, and when fall came, I had every box on the premises full; even father's old wagon-box was turned up-side-down with a snarl of rabbits under it, and when he used the box my troubles were many. As I knew how to set traps around my rabbit pens I am strongly of the opinion that some of the neighbors' cats haven't got home yet.

How well do I recollect seeing the wild geese, and hearing their "Honk! Honk!" as I strained my young eyes to see them 'way up there, often having to look twice before seeing them, as they passed, in spring and fall, over the good old State of Ohio on their migrating trips. Oh, how I used to stand with clenched hands and wish I were a man so I could follow them somewhere and secure one, but not until I got to Canada did the real fun begin.

All kinds of game, and such a variety of pets as I had; squirrels, coons, foxes, crows and ravens, and I even got a nest of young hen hawks and kept them until father found it out. You know in those days there was one day in the week that we did not work, and I made every minute count; and although I had miles and miles of woods to roam through, night and day, yet my ambition was a little higher. So I secured a pair of tree-climbers, and then there was no tree high enough for Mrs. Crow or Mrs. Hawk to raise her young so as to be out of my reach.

Well do I remember shooting my first deer, and how I burglarized the top shelf of the pantry to get one of my mother's old pewter spoons. This spoon had a great handle to its history, being handed down from somewhere this side of Noah. I pounded it, to remove the ancient look, melted it and ran seven small bullets, while my un-

suspicious mother looked on at the operation of melting and mould-
ing. By daylight the snow had ceased falling, and I put the seven
balls in the "thumb-hand" barrel of the old shot-gun and started
on my first deer hunt. By noon I was back with a fine deer, and
if I had had a melted spoon in the other barrel I surely would have
killed two.

CHAPTER III.

Market Hunting.

AS QUAIL and grouse were so very plentiful and good warm clothes were scarce, the second fall we were here my brother and I started to hunt for the market. This caused us to study the nature of game. I soon found myself practising the call of Bob White. I would call early in the morning, when the country was silent, and listen to the echo come back from the woods, until I could call Bob right up to me from as far as he could hear the faintest sound of my imitative note. Yes, many a time during the nesting season have I called five or six male birds up near where I was sitting, then see them have a scrap. I tell you they are gamey little fellows. And what fun it was to be back in the field, hid in a bunch of goldenrod, with my old slouch hat tucked in my pants pocket, allowing my long hair and freckles to blend with the surroundings, and watch these plump little beauties come together in battle, sometimes striking each other so hard they would go fully six feet in the air and come down facing each other. I have had them so close I could almost feel the breath of their wings; and possibly three or four rods away was another one, picking the earth sidewise, apparently challenging the fourth who was sitting on a stump as if he were refereeing.

I tell you, life in the country was so sweet to me I would have agreed to stay here longer than it would take a raft of detectives to find my great-grandmother's pewter spoon.

But the grouse was a hard fellow to call. This, however, did not prevent our success; for as soon as we got one we would examine its crop and find out just what it was feeding on; if it contained budst then what kind they were, etc. And you could rest assured thas ninety per cent. of the grouse in that country were feeding on thi, same variety of food. Then as we would walk through the woods with the dogs at our heels and our faces as nearly on the tops of our heads as possible, the grouse became very easy. I have shot five out of the tiptop of a cotton-wood tree where nine out of ten men would never think of looking. But if the crop contained seeds from the ground, the dogs were put to work where these seeds grew. As practice makes perfect, we soon became expert shots and the result was we left a bloody trail behind us.

6

We would walk miles away in the morning and start in so as to be near home at night with our heavy loads. Once or twice a week we would box our game up, and when the road was fit we would wheel it on a wheel-barrow up to the old stage line.

For at least five miles around, these birds appeared to fear us, and fly and scream as though Satan himself was after them. Brother and I often remarked: "Why did they just fly over the fence from the farmer, and ten minutes later, when we arrived, fly a mile or more from us?"

During the summer months these same birds seemed quite tame; in fact, they did not seem to be a bit more frightened of us than they were of the other residents of the county.

However, we soon found that every grain of sport had vanished, and we were in a financial business. So, speaking from actual experience, I know that market-hunting is not sport; that it is murder in the first degree, and no principled sportsman will practise it. For one successful market-hunter will deprive twenty-five real sportsmen of their enjoyable recreation and outing.

I am pleased to say that we two boys soon outgrew this murderous practice, and hunted for pleasure only. And as we kept two well-trained dogs, many pleasant hours' recreation have we enjoyed with some of the best gentlemen this earth can produce, returning home with an appetite for anything and stomachs that would almost digest railroad iron; then about nine p.m. we would roll in and sleep a hole right down through the bed.

Next morning, when you awake after such an experience, you will usually find your eyes are open, and more in focus.

CHAPTER IV.

Our Faithful Dogs.

WHILE I would not advise any person to keep a dog unless he needs one, yet one of the most faithful animal friends man can have is an educated dog. Our two bird dogs were full brothers and though my brother and I were always together, yet the dogs knew us apart. If I went to the barn alone, my dog would follow me; yet if we boys walked to the road together, both dogs would follow us and would not come farther unless they were invited. If we threw our coats down, each dog would lie on or near his master's coat.

I never knew Set ("Set" was my dog's name) to disobey orders but once; that was when he was about eighteen months old. Brother and I had started from home before daylight to walk about eight miles, to hunt deer. When daylight came we were about five miles on our way, and I looked around and here was Set following. I at once gave him a right down good scolding, and told him to start for home, but he hesitated. That minute, a snarl of "just dogs" came yelping out from a settler's buildings, and Set took leg bail for home with this bunch pow-wowing in pursuit. Just then brother looked at his watch and it was fifteen minutes past seven. When we arrived home at night my first question was "What time did Set get home?" Mother looked over her glasses and said, "He got here just at seven o'clock." Now I knew he was going some, by his actions, but just where he gained the fifteen minutes still remains a mystery.

On one occasion three sportsmen came and wanted a hunt, but I could not go; so I introduced Set to them, and as they had guns he eventually consented to go along. In about an hour he pointed a large bevy of quail in a weed field. The three sportsmen lined up and pressed forward, and as the birds buzzed up in front of them, bangety-bang! went six shots, right out in the open. And not a bird was touched. Dear old Set looked around in disgust, turned, and came straight home.

Well, it wasn't long before our faithful dogs were getting a year older every twelve months, but still they clung to us, though life had become a burden. Dear mother, unbeknown to us, got a man to chloroform them. When he started to dig their graves we caught on, and both of us, men, stopped work and made a box and laid our faithful friends—friends who had never deceived us—side by side in one coffin and buried them under a shade tree on the old homestead. As we pushed the earth on the box I felt ashamed to look up at brother, but when I did I found there were tears in his eyes, too.

CHAPTER V.

Bob White Quail.

NOW as I had grown from boyhood to man and had become the father in a little "home, sweet home," my responsibilities naturally caused me to take life a little more seriously. But, as a boy loves to go bare-foot and play marbles in the spring of the year, when fall came my whole body and soul seemed to reach out for just one sup of pure, unadulterated nature, and many and many a morning, after I have been over to the factory and built a fire under the boiler, have I taken a stroll by twilight, before breakfast, and stepped up into a fence corner, leaned against the old rails and stood and breathed the pure air of a new-born day. Possibly the swish-sh-sh-sh of a flock of small wild ducks might be heard overhead as they darted their way southward; the note of the wood-thrush might also be noticed, and the flutter of the dear old woodcock's wings have sometimes almost caused me to flinch. Then as the last stars were closing their eyes for the day and the white frost of the early-October morning became visible on the top rail, away to the east would come the faint call of the quail. That voice would hardly die out before the father of another family would start calling the roll, right in the next field; then one to the south; another bevy, near the woods, to the north; and again to the west would come these cheerful notes; until the frosty air would fairly ring, all around me, with the melody of Bob White's roll call, the head of the family calling and each member answering. And if all is well, and none is missing, in about three minutes all is still and one would not know there was a quail in the country, unless a hawk happened to dart among them; then a shrill alarm is given, and all buzz for cover.

Now it is said that there never was a tribe of heathen discovered that did not worship some kind of idol. This I am not prepared to prove. But I will say this: That no intelligent man can live in this great, great out-of-doors and study the creatures that occupy it before man has any control over them, combined with the regularity of the sun, moon and whispering stars, without being compelled to believe that there is an over-ruling Power. And although I had not read a word on the value of our quail, this thought often presented itself to me: "What did God put them here for?" Yes, I can recall time and time again, when, after I had emptied the quail out of my hunting-coat pocket I have gone to the kitchen door and thrown out by the handful the weed-seed that had worked out of their bursted crops; and how often, in the summer, I have seen them picking insects, as they strutted by my hiding place! Now, I am proud to say, I have not shot a quail in nearly twenty years, and I am still prouder to say that I have this much confidence in humanity, that to-day there wouldn't be one quail shot where there are five, if these shooters would first consider their cheerfulness, beauty and value while alive. For one Bob White sitting on the top rail, sounding his beautiful note, brings more gladness and more cheer to more people than twenty-five will in a bloody game-sack.

Now about the only argument the quail shooter has to put up is that the wire fence has taken the place of the old rail and weedy fence row, and has destroyed their cover, and that if he didn't shoot them the quail would only fight, one among the others, and would not nest. I am not here to say that this man has no brains, but I will say that the itching of his trigger-finger to shoot something has got control of his brains; and when I hear him blowing off this stuff I take father's advice, and "drop it." For the positive fact is that the old fence row is, and always was, the worst death trap that quail ever took shelter in. The height of a sportsman's ambition is to see them alight there; and the prowling house-cat has a great advantage there; and when March comes, that is just the place to look for a bunch of dead quail—quail that sought shelter there during the winter months, were drifted under, and died. All thinking men will admit that when quail are in real need of shelter, this old fence row is nothing but a fence drift. The only drawback quail have in Western Ontario, and in Ohio as well, is the disappearing of the woods that sheltered them from the drifting snows. Not that he gets any of his living there, but just flies there for shelter during the severe storms of winter.

As to them becoming so numerous as to quarrel and not breed, quail do not nest or breed in the woods. When we came to Canada in 1878 there were twenty-five where there hasn't been one during the last ten years. I am sure I have seen one hundred and fifty quail on an ordinary farm; and this change is not because the wire fence has taken the place of the rail, etc. All these excuses are false and without foundation.

Now here is the positive fact: The great mistake the sportsmen have made is that they have directed all their attention on the death-dealing weapons, as to how to destroy the quail. The breech-loader has taken the place of the old muzzle-loader; the six shot pump gun has taken the place of the double-barrelled breech-loader; the quick, nitro explosives have taken the place of the slow black powder; and thus we have gone on and on for the last thirty-five years, to my personal knowledge, thoughtless and ignorant of what we were doing, not taking into consideration at all the increasing number of shooters, year by year, until at last we have waked up to find that our birds have decreased over ninety per cent. during that time.

Has the wire fence destroyed the ducks, the beautiful trumpeter swans, our mourning doves, the woodcocks and meadow-larks? These migratory birds have decreased the same as our Ontario quail have, and God-given intelligence, wrongly directed, is responsible for it all.

SELF-SERVING FEED-RACK FOR QUAIL THAT GAVE FAIRLY GOOD SATISFACTION

Now just picture North America if, during the last thirty-five years, we had paid as much attention to the protection and increase of our birds as we have to these death-dealing weapons. What a cheerful difference it certainly would have made!

About ten years ago I started to protect the quail in earnest. I made eight feed-racks, the same as shown in illustration.

The boxes are eight inches square and four inches deep. The cover is about three feet wide and almost one foot from the feed. If a little snow does drift in, it is very light and the birds will scratch and get the feed, as no sleet or rain can reach it.

The quail soon found the food and I was agreeably surprised to see the number of tracks around these racks the first time I went to visit them; but when I returned three or four days later there was scarcely a quail to be seen. On investigation I found that the hawks had apparently struck the Klondyke of their lives, and it was almost sure death to Bob to go near the feed, as Mr. Hawk was always watching.

Then I bought a few No. 1 jump traps and cut three poles, fifteen or twenty feet long and from four to five inches through at the butt. I then drove three or four small nails in the butt end of each pole, to stay the trap and keep it from blowing off, but leaving it free

HAWK AND OWL TRAP

This photograph shows a mistake in that the Clog got fastened and is hold-ing the Hawk up. This will scare other Hawks and make them shy of the place.

enough so that when it caught its victim he could fly up and raise the trap off the top of the pole. A small brush-clog was fastened to the end of the chain and a nail was driven in the side of the pole about a foot from the trap, to hang the clog on. About six or eight small staples were driven in around the pole, near the trap, to put frag-ments of weed and grass in so as to disguise the trap, making it appear like an old sparrow's nest. Then I stood the pole, with the butt up, beside another small tree so that the boughs of the tree would project a foot or so above the trap; then wired the pole to the tree. When a hawk or owl gets his toe in such a trap there is nothing solid for him to jerk against, but he can fly down with the trap and clog, and isn't apt to jerk out. Moreover, when hawk number two comes along, number one is not up there, flapping, to scare him and make him shy of this pole. I have known them, time and again, to alight on the same pole and then fly down and kill and eat the hawk below who was flapping around with the trap and clog.

In these three traps I caught seventeen quail-destroyers the first month I put them up, and I also got the toe of another hawk, and the following winter I got the rest of that hawk.

As proof that birds visit the same places, I will say that I haven't caught over fifteen hawks and owls down there in any one winter, in those three traps, since.

SHELTER AND FEEDING PLACE FOR QUAIL

Well, the feed racks did not seem to fill the bill in every way, so in a year or so I decided to try another scheme. I loaded up all the old junk lumber I could find and hauled it to the woods, and in one day another man and I completed ten little bungalows-in-the-rough. They are about one foot high in the rear, and four to five feet high in the front, with from five to six feet ground space, as shown in the illustration herewith.

Then, to complete my experiment, I begged ten bags of weed seed from a neighbor who was hulling clover. I threw a bagful in each house, and then threw in, on top of the weed seed, corn, wheat and buckwheat. In less than a week the birds visited every house, and on a cold, zero day I believe I have seen as high as fifty quail buzz out of one of these little, unpatented shacks. And best of all, they scratched right down through the grain and ate the weed seeds first. I soon found I had made a hit, as the shacks furnished the birds shelter as well as food in the time of need, and a certain amount of protection from their natural enemies.

But these birds down in the woods remained quite wild. So I got several quiet bantam hens and kept them ready, and when any neighbor farmer disturbed a quail's nest I had a place for the eggs. In this way I have had some enjoyable experiences.

I first set the hen in a small box on the ground, on a nice cushion of soft grass, pet her lots and let her eat from my hand; I push her feathers forward and pepper her just full of Prussian insect powder, and sprinkle a little in the nest, also. Now I am all ready for some one to phone that they have disturbed a quail's nest.

SHELLS OF QUAIL EGGS AFTER HATCHING

If you take eggs from a nest that is not disturbed, never, never take them until the bird has finished laying and has started to set, for if you take the eight or ten she will build another nest and finish laying, then put in her valuable time with only half a brood, whereas if she has started to set she will only lay off a few days, then will build a new nest and raise a full brood. A quail will lay from fifteen to twenty-two, and sometimes as high as twenty-five, eggs.

Quail eggs all hatch, and hatch very suddenly. One year I looked at a nest at ten o'clock and there was nothing doing, and when I came by at twelve o'clock the old hen scolded, so I took another peep; all hands had apparently opened the door at once, and the cluster of pure-white eggs had changed so that they resembled a live bumble-bee's nest.

Quail have no trouble hatching, like some of our domestic fowl; they just simply open the door and jump out. See the illustration.

Pat once asked a little boy what he came for. The little chap in his bashful way replied, "Oh, nothing." Again Pat took his pipe from between his teeth, as he said, "Well, you'll find that in the jug behind the door, where the whiskey was." So we can say the same about this illustration; it is where the little quail were. Notice the neat, uniform way in which they opened the door from the inside.

When they are about to hatch, shut the door of the box so as to keep the tiny pets in. When they are from twenty to thirty-six hours old, move all hands to a dry coop near the garden, or in the back yard near shrubbery. The coop should be from eighteen to twenty-four inches square inside, built with a shed roof ten to twelve inches high in the rear and eighteen to twenty inches high in the front, with a board floor so that the old hen cannot scratch and be on damp ground. Now take three boards about one foot wide and two feet long, tack them in front of the old hen's coop for a play-ground for the quail. Leave the hen in the coop and she will put her head out and talk to her family, who cannot get over two feet away from her. Feed them a little custard (one egg to half a cup of milk; no sugar). Feed tiny bits five times a day, always tapping the tin with the spoon as you go near them. In three or four days they will accept the hen as their step-mother, and you as their step-parent. Now draw the two nails (which are only partly driven in) and pull the three boards quietly away, leaving the hen in the permanent coop, but giving the quail their liberty. See illustrations.

Now don't run after them if they run away; just tap the tin a little, as you drop a little custard in front of their mother so she can call them.

Let me say right here: Never try to drive any bird. They can hide where you can't, and experience has proven to my entire satisfaction that they can fly faster that I can run. Always throw feed and kindness at them, and watch results.

In about a week, let the hen out a few minutes before sundown, so she hasn't time to stray far from home and will go back into the roost. In about another week the hen can run all the time with her family. Feed at the back door, or any place you want the quail to come, and your pets will be there. Remember that it is the human race that is wild, not the birds. Birds are wild because they have to be, and we are wild because we prefer to be. Any creature that is intelligent enough to fly or run from you for self-preservation, will come to you for food and protection from all other enemies.

YOUNG QUAIL JUST FOUR WEEKS OLD
Notice one in Baby's hair.

EATING FROM THE HAND THAT ONCE HELD THE GUN

As to the value of quail, I know this, that they are the farmer's friends; that they cannot live in the dense wilderness and that they do follow up the pioneer's axe where climate will allow; and that fully seventy-five per cent. of their diet consists of weed seed and insects that are injurious to the production of food stuffs for the human race. The small amount of wheat they eat is 'most all gathered from the stubble field, and as for the few kernels of corn, this is mostly taken during the winter; and we all know that a farmer who makes a practice of leaving his corn out, is an undesirable heavy weight and possibly has no appreciation of Bob White's beautiful note ringing in the country, and the sooner he moves to town and joins the "Retired Failures' Association" the better for the country.

CHAPTER VI.

Raising English or Ring-necked Pheasants in Canada.

HAVING often heard father speak of the English pheasant as a beautiful game bird, and as I was overly anxious to pay Canada back some of the birds I had murdered in my younger days, I decided to try these pheasants.

In 1895 I sent to Pleasant Ridge, Ohio, for two or three settings of English pheasants' eggs. I felt sure this climate would agree with them as they were exactly the same breed as I was, English buck-eyes! However, I was smart enough not to ignore my mother's kind offer, and I let her have one setting to hatch for me. I paid particular attention to the two hens I set, scarcely allowing them to get off the nest; and here is where I now believe I made the mistake. Not one egg hatched. But dear mother signalled me to come over and I was right there. Her old hen had hatched eleven. Mother smiled and gave them to me, hen and all, but told me to leave them with her until the next day. Then I moved them, and raised nine to the size of quail, when a dog killed four, leaving the old hen and me with only five. Four of these proved to be males and a cat owl killed the hen. March, 1896, found me with four beautiful male birds only.

I had now learned that a gentleman in London, Ontario, had English pheasants for sale, and as my experience had proved that an English buck-eye hitched up to a Canadian was a joyous, satisfactory cross, with the human race, I wrote this man and secured two hens which were undoubtedly English-Canadians. I liberated three of the four male birds and put the two hens in with the one male; and from this trio we hatched sixty-two pheasants. Then I enclosed four acres with a wire fence seven feet high. Along one side I made several brood pens about two rods square, each. I put one male bird with every five hens, putting plenty of gravel and grit in each pen so as to secure good digesting powers. I also gave the birds plenty of shade.

Our pheasant hens laid from thirty-five to fifty eggs each between April the 15th and June the 15th. By giving the old birds lots of grit, the egg shells were very hard. I used Wyandotte hens for mothers, putting from twenty to twenty-five eggs under each hen and setting them on the damp ground as much as possible. The eggs, like quail eggs, hatch in twenty-four days. I pursued the same course, all through, as I have described for raising quail, only the nest and coop are one-quarter larger. I used the insect powder by the pound. I usually set four or five hens at a time; keeping a record of the same, I knew when to prepare for a hatch. I penned them in front of her for two or three days, the same as with the quail.

When raising pheasants, I never let hens out of the coops. When birds are from six to eight weeks old I take the hen away but leave the coop there. Coops may be set around like bee-hives, two or three rods apart. I painted my coops, some white and some red; the little fellows will know their own coops and will not forget them.

Remember, I have experimented with a great variety of pheasant foods. I have raised flies by the tens of thousands to feed to them. To do this I would take a piece of meat, say of beef's liver, allow the flies to blow it, and a few hours later throw the meat in a barrel; the barrel would be partly filled with rotten sawdust and the top of it would be covered with a screen, with a hole left about an inch in diameter. In a few days the maggots would have the meat all eaten up, and would have disappeared into the sawdust below. In about two weeks the barrel would be simply full of flies. I would now put a small flytrap over the hole, darkening the rest of the screen: the flies would come to the light, get into the trap, and when in the small trap could be either scalded or drowned. I have also fed the pheasants the maggots. But to raise either flies or maggots is not as desirable for the nose as it might look from the eye and both are unnecessary. Feed a little custard, and when about two weeks old, add corn-meal to it. Keep them hungry and let them hunt for insects. Exercise is what they need and what they must have. When birds are three months old, they should be caught and shipped.

The high fence for young is unnecessary, for your birds will know you and will be just as tame as chickens. In this way I made my pleasure self-sustaining, and I would often let an old hen and fifteen or twenty go. The finest brood I ever saw was out of two poor hatches. I put twenty-five with one hen and in about a week I let hen and all out. They roamed all over the premises, but of course like spiteful deeds and chickens, they came home to roost. I fed them just enough to give them a sweet taste in their mouths, and the hen raised twenty-three of them. How they did grow! Finally she left them and they went to the woods about one-half mile away.

In this way I stocked this township so I could have shot a two-bushel bag full in half a day. Two miles north of my place there were twenty-eight seen dusting in the road at one time. But to-day

I doubt if there is one left in the township. Men came for miles and miles around. Yes, I have seen them come twenty-five miles to hunt rabbits in this neighborhood! Now I don't want to insinuate that all rabbit hunters were hunting pheasants, but what I really want to say is that all pheasant hunters were hunting rabbits!

CHAPTER VII.

The Natural Enemies of Our Birds.

NOW we come to the most serious question that the bird-lovers of America are up against; and until this great question is settled, we shall continue to pull against each other.

At a sportsmen's show in Michigan I once saw one-half dozen mounted hawks in a glass case, and there were thousands of school children looking at them. The label read: "These are all valuable hawks." Another man will say, "Protect the cat-owl, or great horned owl," and possibly this same man will advocate the destruction of the wild house-cat, when the positive fact is that this owl is nothing but a wild house-cat with the advantage of wings, and for cruel, blood-thirsty, murderous depredations he has got the house-cat chased right out of the slaughter-house, for he will kill and eat a great variety of adult birds and animals I have never known a house-cat to destroy, such as turkeys, wild geese, peacocks, all kinds of hawks and all other owls, and animals such as skunks, muskrats, groundhogs, minks, weasels and hares. Now, although I have no personal knowdlege of this, yet a gentleman farmer who lived near the woods told me (and I believe him, or I would not repeat it) that his bunch of house-cats which were about half grown, were in the habit of climbing upon the roof of the house and sitting near the chimney to keep warm during the winter months; these horned owls came and took away every one of the cats. However, I have no positive proof of this last statement. But this I do know: There is nothing roosts high enough or sleeps low enough to be out of reach of this heartless cannibal. One regrettable fact to me is that I have never seen where another bird or animal ever killed a great horned owl, although they have lived in the township with me all my life.

A particular friend of mine was dissecting a shrike. This shrike is a bird about the size and color of a blue jay, known to a great many people as the butcher bird. I said to those standing by, "He is a bad one; always shoot him on sight." My friend stopped for a moment and said, "Beg your pardon, Jack, but you are wrong; this is not the big northern shrike you have reference to." "No, no, my dear fellow," I replied; "I mean the very one you are skinning, and again I say, shoot him on sight." My friend smiled and replied in a kind, cheerful manner, "Jack, I am surprised at you." Now, dear reader, here were two natural born naturalists right opposite each other, one advocating the protection, the other the destruction, of the same bird. I had watched this shrike in Ohio when I was a kid. I had often found his nest and knew what he fed his young upon. I have caught dozens of them, right in the act, in Canada, and they are always searching for birds, chiefly the small fly-catchers. Well, we dissected this fellow, and found two little birds' legs, and they were not mates. Last fall I saw a shrike follow a snow bird fully five hundred feet high, but the snow bird won out.

I said to another man, "The crow and bronze grackle take the robin's eggs." "Why," he said, "I don't understand that; there is a robin's nest within a rod of my door, and the woods are full of crows." Why, bless your life, that is just the reason why the robin built there, it simply came to him for protection.

Now first of all we must not lose sight of this fact: That there never was but one perfect Manager stood on this earth, and He put these creatures all here. So let us roll back the pages of time and take a look at nature before man interfered. Likely you have read the history of America; I haven't; but I doubt if there is any account known of the clouds of birds that once hovered over this continent. The settlings in the bottom of the little artificial pond near my house, caused from the wild goose and duck droppings, are exactly of the same material that we find in our marshes, and which is from three to ten feet deep in the average marsh. I will not attempt to mention the number of birds I have seen in one day, because the average boy of the present would not believe it; but I will say that I firmly believe I have seen more birds in one day, before I was ten years of age, than the average ten-year-old boy of the present day has seen in all his life. Time and time again during my life have I seen a wounded bird lag behind as the flock flew to cover; and often have I seen a hawk dart at them, and he never failed to get the wounded one. And some wounded quail have been stolen from me by hawks before I got to where they lit, and if it were not for the snow I wouldn't have known what had happened as I did not always see the hawk.

Once in my life I had a flock of about thirty young wild ducks. There were two little runts that appeared to want to die, but I rebelled and kept patching them up. Finally one took with a sore eye disease, and in a few days the other little scab had it, and both died, but not until they had introduced these sore eyes to the rest of the ducks and all my nice, healthy ducks started drooping. When I eventually got this disease checked I had only seven ducks left. Now, according to my own experience, if a hawk had come along he would have picked up the weak ones and prevented this disease. So, after all my life's study I am fully convinced that these cannibal birds were put here to destroy the weak and sickly and prevent contagious disease, letting the strong and healthy survive. But man has interfered. He has paid all his attention to the destruction of the food birds and has almost annihilated them and let what we now call their enemies go; or, in other words, we human beings have combined our forces with the food birds' enemies.

Now Point Pelee marsh is about fifteen miles from where I am sitting. Point Pelee is the most southerly part of mainland in Canada, and the hawks cross there by the thousands every fall; yet I never knew of a hunter going purposely to shoot them. But if there were twenty-five ducks in a pond down there and twenty-five men knew it to-night, there would likely be fifty guns there to-morrow morning. Yes, I honestly believe there are as many hawks and owls in America to-day as there were thirty years ago.

Last fall, when the hawks were migrating, in October, they started roosting in our woods, and in less than a week there were thousands upon thousands coming there. So I took a flash-light and the .22 rifle and went down and I am sure as high as twenty-five would fly out of one little tree every time I shot. It was a bright moonlight night, and they soon took the hint, and I only killed fifteen or twenty. But to hear their wings as they hovered around, over the woods, would cause one to wonder where they came from and where they were going. However, once was enough; the rest took the hint for the next night not one was seen going there. So don't let us blame the Great Provider; it is man's mistake, that is all; we have gone wrong.

"Oh, but say, Jack Miner, do you pretend to say that there were once birds enough in America that the old and the delicate, crippled, maimed and diseased would supply all these hawks and owls with food?" Yes, that is just exactly what I want to say, yet I have no proof of it. I only know that the hawks will take a cripple every time and let the strong and healthy go. "Well," you say, "how about a flock of little ducks? He could take any one of them." Not so easily. Wild ducks at six hours old will dive like a lot of frogs, but a delicate one cannot; he will possibly just put his head under, and his body will stick out like a bloated toad. Yes, I believe that less than one hundred years ago there were more of the above class of birds for the hawks, each year, in America, than there are altogether, now. So, after having a lifetime of experience raising birds, instead of doctoring the sickly ones and petting the droopies and sore-eyes, I just take the hawk's plan and destroy them.

While I would not like to see these cannibal birds become extinct, yet I would be pleased to see them decreased the same as our other birds have become during the last forty years.

CHAPTER VIII.

Some Things I have Known Cannibal Birds to Do.

NOW, dear reader, I am well aware of the fact that my book would be more popular if I left these questions out. I am like yourself, I wish I had nothing to say but good about every bird, for I love to see them. But remember, what I am telling in this book is what I know about nature, so please don't jump on me with both feet for telling the truth.

First of all let me say that the larger the hawk, the more anxious the majority are to shoot him. This is a mistake. It is the medium-sized hawk that is the worst. The sparrow-hawk is the smallest. and he is hard on fledglings such as bobolinks and song sparrows, Yes, I know they will eat grasshoppers, but these are usually eaten by the young birds; the adult sparrow-hawk lives chiefly on mice and small birds.

When I raised pheasants I always made a "hide" where I could lay for the little chicks' enemies. One day I fed my chicks at one p.m.; when I returned at four-thirty I tapped the tin to call them and only seven out of the seventeen little beauties came and they were on their tiptoes, shy and frightened. My first thought was, "a weasel," but when I saw Mrs. Hen turn her head sidewise and look up, I called to my boy to bring the shotgun and a couple of loads of No. 6. I soon was in the "hide," and the boy had scarcely got to the house when I heard the old hen say "k-tt-tt-tt," meaning "lie low," so I took her advice, and in about five seconds a sparrow-hawk came down out of the heavens like a bullet—too fast for me. Before I could get the gun on him he was on the ground. He saw me and missed his bird; and when he was about four feet in the air again I just lifted him with a load of shot. The next morning we went over to the woods and destroyed the other old one and the young, and found remnants of some of the young pheasants. Now this hawk killed and carried away ten of these little chick pheasants in less than four hours. These little pheasants were about ten days old. After pheasants get to be the size of a small quail or mourning dove, sparrow-hawks will not take them. Many a small hawk have I fooled by taking a little dead pheasant and running a wire through him, standing up in a natural position on a steel

25

trap, letting Mr. Hawk come down out of the air and help himself. I have often caught owls in this same way.

I could go on and on, relating such experiences until you got hungry. But remember, the sparrow-hawk is only one. The worst are yet to come, the Cooper's, the sharp-shinned, and the goshawk; these three are just like bullets in the air. But while the pheasants are tiny the sparrow-hawk is the worst, because it is more numerous. To any person who might think of raising pheasants for profit let me say that unless you first study how to destroy weasels, barn rats, stray house cats and cannibal birds you had better give up the business a week or so before you start. Remember, when hawks are driven to it by hunger they will kill and eat each other, and owls will do the same; I have known dozens of cases of this in my life.

There are two large hawks I never destroy, the Red Tail and the Red Shoulder. They are too big and clumsy to be very destructive on our birds. When these two varieties get in my traps I usually label them with an aluminum band and let them go; but, strange to say, I have never heard from one of these in my life. I know they will kill a clumsy barnyard fowl or so, and they will also kill snakes; so I say of them as Pilate said, "I find no fault" with these fellows.

I spend a lot of my life burning brick and draintile at night, and during the summer months it is very interesting to see the toads come before the light of the fires and catch insects. The snakes that these big hawks eat, kill the toads; and I don't like snakes, even if they are not in my boots.

Now this innocent-looking little screech-owl! Just last summer I went over to the martin house one morning to see what was wrong with them, and here were three or four helpless fledglings flapping on the ground, and the old ones hovering at the house as if it were a bees' nest. Well, to be brief, we killed nine screech-owls in less than two weeks, but not until they had killed and driven all our martins away for that year. At a screech-owl's nest I once found my hat-full of remnants of blue-birds' wings, young robins' wings and feet, and quail, song-sparrow and English sparrow feathers. In another case a screech-owl went through the two-inch mesh wire netting and killed a golden pheasant hen for me and ate her throat out. This owl only weighed three and one-half ounces. A doctor in the town of Leamington once called me in to see what had killed his golden pheasant hen that was setting on twelve eggs. The pen was made of two-inch mesh netting. I at once said it was a screech-owl and showed him how I knew. He then told me he harbored screech-owls in and around his barns to kill the English sparrows.

Another man I knew kept a screech-owl in his barn to kill the sparrows, and he was puzzled to know what killed his tame pigeons.

The screech-owl is just a miniature horned owl, both in looks and habits. But I have never had my wits tried more with any bird than I have with the Great Horned Owl. On one occasion one of these winged brutes came and apparently just got his toes pinched in a trap; and night after night he sprung the traps and took a hen pheasant. This went on until he had taken twelve. Then I put on fur coat and made a bed of robes out in the "hide" which I always kept ready in the enclosure; and there I lay in that bright moonlit, stinging-cold, zero night. At last I saw an owl hovering over the ground, and fortunately for me he got fooled; he came to examine the decoys near me and while his attention was rivetted on them I raised up and fired, and he never knew what hit him. When I went to the house it was three a.m. I usually catch twelve to fifteen of these owls every winter.

Remember, when he comes and gets a bird he will eat what he wants of it, and come back the following night for a new one.

But how these cannibals locate other birds for miles and miles across the country is a mystery. Yet if we go down in the field and kill a beef on a hot summer's day, the turkey buzzards will be here in less than one-half hour. Where did these vultures come from? You perhaps have not seen one for a month. How did they know you were killing a beef? This question may be just as much in place as: How do the hawks and owls find their prey?

The great horned owl nests in the winter or early, early spring, building in a cavity of a tree or a crow's or hawk's nest. They lay two pure white eggs, round like a turtle's eggs, about the size of an ordinary barnyard fowl's or a shade smaller. I have got the nest as early as the first day in February, when old Mrs. Owl was setting. The female horned owl is larger than the male; she will weigh about four pounds and has a wing-spread of fully fifty inches.

Now I know there are a lot of people who protect these cannibal-birds because they kill mice. Yes, they do kill mice. But it takes dozens and dozens of our insectivorous and weed-destroying birds to raise one owl. I claim that the good one robin or quail does, in one day, overbalances the harm a dozen mice will do.

Now we come to the crow and bronze grackle, the largest blackbird. These two birds raise their young chiefly on the eggs of other birds. Why this is, I won't pretend to say, nor will I attempt to throw a ray of light upon it, but will frankly confess I do not understand. Possibly it has come about through man's interference with their natural habits.

The crow was the first bird I hunted in Canada, as we thought they pulled our corn. I went to the woods and located their nests, and soon I became wise enough to imitate the call of the young; then I had Mr. Crow beaten. I would first destroy the young if possible, then hide in the green bushes and caw quietly as I had heard the young do, and dozens of crows have brought their food to the wrong baby. Yes, I have even gone so far as to call them right down into the small trees so as to make a very light load of ammunition do the work, as it cost money to buy powder and shot in those days. Now comes more of what we don't want to hear. What were these crows feeding their young on? Crawfish, polly-wogs, small frogs, grubs, etc.; but seventy-five per cent. of the food that these old crows would vomit up as they struck the ground was eggs. It was these old black rascals that taught me what to raise fledglings on, and it is just as easy for me, now, to raise a young bird on custard as it would be to raise a row during a political campaign.

I am going to tell you some pitiful things. I have seen young, unhatched robins spewed out of a dying crow's mouth, and the little things were still alive. Whether the eggs were broken in her throat before I shot her or not, I do not know, but they were broken when thrown up. Yes, they will take blackbirds' eggs just as quick as they will the robins', and other, weaker birds' if they have the op-portunity; but the robin does seem to be their choice, possibly be-cause he does not conceal his nest better. Yet I was hunting the crows because they pulled our corn! In all my life I never knew a crow to bring corn to her young. Yes, I have shaken as high as seven little, unhatched birds out of a gasping crow's mouth, and any one of these creatures, if left to mature, would do as much good as a crow. If you want to trap a crow use hens' eggs for bait, but bear in mind he is cute, and you must conceal the trap very carefully.

The bronze grackle is nothing only a small crow; his habits are exactly the same. He will drop on a tree and look around; seizing an opportunity he will come down and go through a bush where there is likely to be a song-sparrow's nest just like a ferret will go through a stone pile after a rabbit. I have known him to take the young birds after they were hatched. But so many men who know the habits of these birds will say they think they do as much good as they do harm! Why they make this statement I don't under-stand. And if you throw this book across the room and never pick it up, I cannot help it, for I am telling you the truth: These crows and grackles are the worst nest-robbers in America. They do ten times more harm than good. Remember I am not writing just to please the reader, but to give you facts gathered from personal ex-perience and observation, and my beliefs founded thereon; and I

am sure that fifty per cent. of the eggs and young of our song, insectivorous and game birds in Ontario are devoured by these cold-
blooded, nest-robbing cannibals, the crow being the worst of all.
He will take young mourning doves out of the nest when they are
as large as sparrows; the quail, and kildeer, and dozens of other such
beautiful mothers are perfectly helpless and can no more keep him
off than a human mother's naked hands could keep a vicious lion
from tearing her baby into fragments.

By the way, I am now perfecting a trap whereby I can catch
crows by the hundreds during the winter months. These crows
will be handed over to gun clubs for trap-shooting purposes. And
although he is a black murderer we must treat him fair, and give
him a chance for his life; therefore, my request will be to shoot them
from five unknown traps at twenty-five to thirty yards rise. The
shooter will not be charged for the crows he kills, but will be fined
for every one he allows to escape; in addition to the above fine he
will be liable to any other punishment a good, cheerful bunch of
trap-shooters see fit to impose upon him, such as rail-riding him
around the club-house for allowing one of these black murderers
to get away. The shooters will be fined according to their shooting
ability. These fines will be used for buying up old, faithful horses
which will be humanely destroyed and used for bait to decoy more
of these old, black Pharaohs to their just doom. Thus what is now
the crow nuisance will be turned into a sport.

The hawks and owls are worst on the adult birds, the screech-
owl is not so innocent as he looks, but there is none can compare
with the great horned owl, and I just wish you knew the annoyance
he has caused me by taking my choicest pets. Yes, it seems he
delights in taking the nearest and dearest. But now let me give
my horn a toot: Never did a horned owl take a bird from me but
what paid the penalty.

About the only argument you hear in favor of the hawks and
owls is "mice." But when a bunch of successful farmers meet at my
tile factory, never in my life have I heard them complain about
mice, and I know mice seldom bother clean, shrewd farmers. But
I have heard them complain about worms until I could almost feel
myself crawling. The cut-worms were cutting their corn, or the
wire-worms were destroying their oats, the army worm was working
north, and so forth. Personally I have never had any experience
with worms, but field mice I have often carried in my pockets, and
if it wasn't for some youth practising the same sport, how I would
like to tell you some of the fun I have had with them when I was a
lad. For the death of each mouse by hawks and owls possibly we
lose several birds which would destroy thousands and thousands of
worms each year. I know there is a type of farmer who is much

more easily annoyed by mice than others.   You will usually find him down town, sitting on a soap box, smoking in the time, now and then getting up and moving his seat around and possibly turning it end for end to keep it from 'getting tired; his stock at home are of the rainbow variety, with long whiskers, and when they see him coming they don't know whether to come or go, and the one or two razor-backed, South Carolina, thistle-digger hogs don't care whether or not they get out of the steaming manure heap, to be disappointed; the remnant of scrubby apple trees in the field, which some one else planted, have been fleece-grown with cut grass ever since he got possession of the farm, that, of course, was handed down to him.

If your orchard is stubble or clover sod, go through it in the early fall.   By being careful you can determine whether there are any field mice there by the little runways that criss-cross on the ground. If so, take about one-half bushel of grain and thirty or forty bundles of corn fodder; throw a handful or two of grain on the ground and two bundles of fodder side by side over it, making a nice mouse cover. Refuse hay, or clover chaff will do, but I prefer the corn fodder. Fifteen or twenty of these little harbors are sufficient in an ordinary orchard.   In ten days or two weeks all the mice in the orchard will be under these covers.   Now take the six- or eight-pronged pitch-fork, scratch around these little harbors to destroy their road of retreat, then throw the cover off quickly; the light striking their eyes so suddenly, they are apparently blinded for a second, giving you just time enough to give them a side whack with your fork; if you study what you are doing, you will kill seventy-five per cent. of them the first time 'round, always placing the cover back ready for next time.   If you don't care for this sport, just introduce a bunch of school boys to your plan and you will soon find your annoyance turned into sport and education for the neighbor boys.

In case you haven't the above-mentioned material to make these mouse covers, old junk lumber thrown on the ground will answer the same purpose.   But if you leave these mice and depend on the hawks and owls to destroy them, some of your trees will be girdled, as the mice seem to have a sort of human appetite, and appear to like the apple tree bark equally as well as the human race likes the apple tree juice.

The mouse question always reminds me of a story told on the other fellow.   It is said that he saw an advertisement: "How to kill potato bugs!   Full directions sent on receipt of one dollar."   This of course was a cheap opportunity, and he enclosed a dollar at once. In reply he received a small box containing a little block and mallet· the directions were: "Put him on No. 1, and hit him with No. 2."

CHAPTER IX.

Weasels, and How to Destroy Them.

NOW, as a field-mouse destroyer we have come to the king of them all. I have found as high as twenty-seven adult field mice stored in a weasel's winter home. Yet of all the four-legged enemies our birds have, I know of none to compare with the weasel. But if I were to ask the experienced hunters of America if they know the weasel all would be disgusted, because the weasel is so common throughout this country. I was once in that class myself; I thought I knew all there was to be known about them. I had shot them out of the tops of trees, and dug them out of the ground; I had called them into the tile shed and even into the engine room; I had sat here in the woods and called them so they would come up and smell of the ends of my fingers; I had seen dozens of the little rascals in Northern Ontario when I had been hunting moose, and had sat down and called them across the creek to me. Yes, I thought I was well acquainted with them.

Now, when I come to think of it I am always reminded of a middle-aged, corpulent gentleman who once came to our tile yard. After he had his wagon loaded he climbed down over the wheel; as he struck the earth, he took both hands and pulled his loose trousers up over the dome of his constitution; then pushing his right hand down into his pants pocket he pulled it out full of what looked to be tobacco, Canada thistles and milk-weed chaff; after pouring this from one hand to the other and blowing the coarse gravel out, he tipped his mouth on top of his face, and raising his hand above, he let this junk roll into the cavity, just like throwing garbage into a skunk-hole. Then he turned and said, "Mr. Miner, do you know Mr.——?" calling his neighbor by name. "Yes," I replied, "I am well acquainted with him." "Well," he said, as he raised one hand and came towards me, "that is just where you are mistaken. Now, Mr. Miner, you think you know him, but you don't." Then raising both hands, he continued, "Now let me tell you who he is, Mr. Miner. He is a limb of the devil," and he continued coming closer and going from bad to worse, saying nasty, unclean things about his neighbor until this combination in his mouth was all churned into a dirty froth, with the over-splush slopping out the corners and running down his chin like tar boiling out of a hotbox on a manure-spreader. So I excused myself: The engine in the factory needed my attention.

So now, whenever I think of this man's conversation I always think of the weasel, as I was sure I knew him. To prove I didn't, the third year I raised pheasants these innocent-looking little vermin took over two-thirds of what were hatched. You talk about worms bothering the farmers' crops; they weren't in it. Really, these weasels bothered me more than the heavy mortgage that held my buildings down and took care of my insurance policy.

I watched them day and night. I shut the birds in so tight that they smothered in their pens, and yet the weasels got them. I sat on the fence and blew several into fragments with a load of shot, and would go to the house quite light-hearted; next morning likely I would find ten or fifteen more dead pheasants. I put traps everywhere and caught as many pheasants as weasels. I used all kinds of bait, and failed. I tried to call them, but no, no. I took young, live birds and put them in a small mesh wire cage and set traps on the outside, but nothing doing. At last I brought the pheasants near the house and all hands watched them, and even then we lost some. I studied weasels night and day, but I was beaten. Where did they come from?

> For there were weasels in the door-yard,
>   Weasels in the barn,
> There were weasels in the hen-house,
>   Weasels all over the farm;
> There were weasels in the engine-room.
>   Weasels in the shed,
> And when I went to sleep at night
>   There were weasels in my head.
>
> I could see weasels on the bare ground,
>   Weasels in the weeds;
> I could see weasels in the pheasant-coops
>   Doing their bloody deeds;
> I could see weasels coming across the road;
>   I could see weasels in the lane;
> And in the morning when I awoke
>   I had weasels on the brain.

For in spite of all my determined efforts the weasels were increasing by leaps and bounds. Not that they were getting more numerous throughout the whole country, but they were simply attracted here by the pheasants, and it was no use, as there would be more and more next season. I thought I would have to give in, beaten. But Mr. Weasel had run up against a determined fellow to kill, and I was dying hard; and while it is not my intention to preach a sermon, yet I want to tell you what happened.

A few years previous to this, a dear little boy whom God lent to me for a short time climbed upon my lap, and putting his little arms around my neck with his sweet face looking into mine, pleaded with me to go to Sunday school with him and mamma. I unclasped his little arms one at a time, and told him to get down and go along as it was all right; but he insisted, stating it looked lonesome to leave me at home all alone. His sincere request took such a hold on me that I could not resist, and the very next Sunday found him and his father, hand in hand, on their way to the little old red school-house. And although against my will, as I had no schooling, but finally to my delight, in about three months I was teaching a class of boys. They, of course, did the reading, but I was general manager and furnished the brute force if required. It took us several Sundays to get acquainted, and when we read the 26th verse of first Genesis we were very much encouraged to know that we were given "Dominion over all." Now, dear reader, lest I forget I want you to know His promise in this verse is the foundation of a great percentage of my success in taming and controlling these so-called wild creatures during the last twenty years. Although the weasel had me beaten, yet my mind kept drifting back on His words, "Let man have dominion over all."

Eventually I thought, "Why did the weasel take the remnants of pheasants over to the rail pile, nearly one hundred yards away?" Yes, it was plain enough he was over there and knew that hiding place before he got the birds. Well then, if I had had a trap over there I would have headed him off. So I would reverse my plans, and instead of destroying their homes I would build them some as perfect as I knew how. So with bright prospects and a light heart I went at it again and built three weasels' houses as follows:

For each one I took four pieces of two-by-four scantling, three feet long, laid them down on the level ground, pointing these scantling east, west, north and south, but leaving them about six inches apart in the centre—just room enough to set a No. 1 or 1½ jump trap. Then I covered the top with old lumber and nailed it fast, leaving a hole in the centre about a foot square, right over the trap, which I covered with a loose board. See illustration.

Now I had a weasel house, complete, six or seven feet square, the cover just two inches from the ground, with all the runs leading to the trap like the spokes lead to the hub.

I placed these three platforms around in the most likely places, two in the enclosure and one on the outside. I then threw pieces of stumps, rails, or anything I could find, around to make a complete weasel harbor. Then I scratched a hole out about an inch deep in the centre and put in a handful of soft hen feathers, and placed trap down on them, setting the trigger of the trap very light. Then I dropped two or three light feathers on top, making it appear like a perfect mouse-nest. I now put the loose board cover over. I set the traps early in the spring, but weasels did not come until I put the pheasants out. Then the real fun began, for I caught three in

UNDER SIDE OF WEASEL TRAP AND HARBOR

one trap in one day; this was in the trap on the outside of the enclosure. To prove to your satisfaction that my weasel story is not exaggerated, I caught fifty-seven weasels the first summer, and they only got four pheasants; for three seasons in succession I got over fifty weasels each year. But now they are so nearly exterminated that we only keep one weasel platform, as we call them, and catch two or three weasels a year.

Please let me ask you to excuse me for writing so much to say a little, but I want you to understand just how to head off this pest, as one weasel will kill as high as twenty or thirty young fowl in one night, and to know how to catch him the night before, instead of the morning after, is worth the price of this book a good many times a year if you have had a taste of my experience. And the great beauty of it is you cannot help yourself without helping your neighbor.   Previous to my exterminating over ninety per cent. of the weasels in this neighborhood, some of my neighbors were almost discouraged trying to raise young turkeys, and, in fact, any domestic fowl, but to-day these complaints seem to be a thing of the past and the weasel annoyance, ancient history.

CHAPTER X.

Robins.

NOW I have tested your staying qualities, giving you the worst first, and we have come to the bright side of what the birds have taught me. After all, I have a lot to thank the cannibal birds for, as there is about thirty acres in this piece of second-growth woods where I am now sitting, and during the summer months I take a stroll down here at least once a week. This is the most perfect place for robins to build that one could find in a day's travel, yet the last four or five years I haven't seen five of their nests down here; but just one-half mile away, at my home, there were seventeen nests last summer, all within one hundred yards of the house, and outside of the thirteen maples that shade our door-yard the shrubbery is very young. All thinking humanity must admit that they come there for protection from their natural enemies, as there is usually a crow's nest hidden away in this or the neighboring woods. But remember a crow knows better than to venture near my house. And the robins know it.

The chief reason the robins leave us early in the fall is because their choice food, the worms, have gone into the ground for the winter; but as soon as the worms start coming to the surface again the robins come back; and the beauty of it is they come to the same homes, and perch on the same limbs of our trees, sounding their cheerful notes to brighten the dark spots in our paths. Between songs they drop down on the lawn and hop and listen; all at once they start pecking at a grub in the grass; as soon as they have pecked him out and turned him into a robin they either listen for more, or jump up and give us another song. By catching so many mothers of the season's grubs they render us tens of dollars worth of service.

Then about July the first the grubs that are not destroyed are under the hard, dry soil, and the robin has its second family to support; and Shame! Shame! Shame! on the man who claims to be intelligent who will slip out and shoot him because he took two cents' worth of sour cherries that possibly were not worth picking. Has this man got a heart? If so, let him go under the tree where the little starving young robins are calling, "Mamma! mamma! mamma!" That's the exact interpretation of these three chirps that are getting fainter and fainter. Now, my brother, let me ask you again: Have you got a heart? You love your little baby brother or your darling baby boy, and the very thought of King Pharaoh makes you wicked within; but remember, as cruel as he was, he never demanded that a baby boy should die a lingering death as these dear little robins have to do through the fact that you shot their mother. Personally, I hate to shoot a crow or a grackle, as bad as they are, during the nesting season, on that account.

Now it would not be fair for me to pass the robin by without giving you a taste of our enjoyable experience, as while I know that at times robins will annoy fruit growers by congregating there in hundreds, yet to be fair we must consider the most good for the most people. So let us take the average farm, occupied by the cleanest of farmers, with his corn, potatoes, tomatoes, cabbages, and other crops too numerous to mention, all coming up through the clean, fertile soil. And now, like a sneaking thief in the night, the annoying cut-worm crawls out like a snail, cuts down the promising plant and then passes on to another and repeats his destructive doings. Then when he has gorged himself to the limit he will just dig himself in under the soil near the stump of the last plant he has destroyed. I have known fully one-fourth of the plants in a field to be destroyed by cut-worms in less than five days. Not that there are so many of them, but, like the weasel, each one is so destructive. Now just think of the expense and drawback to this farmer, having to replant. Moreover, the second planting never produces the same crop as the original one would have done. Here is only one of the valuable points I could explain for Robin Red Breast. For long before the average farmer is out of bed, he is in the field, hopping from one plant to another in search of these worms; and when he gets two or three in his throat he flies across to his family, and in less than three minutes he is back again.

Yes, I know there are men who will tell you the robin will not eat cut-worms and that his song is no better than that of a warty toad. One of these statements is just as true as the other. The robin will eat about all kinds of worms I have ever seen excepting the dirty tobacco worm, and we must give him credit for that. Last summer I saw a young robin not over six weeks old, picking up ants at the rate of sixty per minute. What does this mean to your lawn?

Some years ago a boy was passing my house carrying a .22 rifle. I heard him shoot, so I went out to the road and investigated; went and picked up the old robin that was fluttering, a few rods away, and as she gasped her last, two cut-worms spewed out of her mouth and a third was squirming on the ground near where I picked her up. After this boy and I had had a heart to heart talk about the matter we separated, but that afternoon I found another robin with a bullet in its back.   The next day was Sunday, and at ten a.m. I was sitting near the window trying to read, and as I glanced out I saw a young robin, dying, under the fir tree.   I soon found a nest above it, and two larger ones were still alive, but cold.   We brought them in, nest and all, and when they got warm I dropped a little custard in the mouth of the larger one.   This caused number two to realize that there was some to be had and he, too, awoke from his slumber, and apparently put all his strength into his neck and jaw bones, for he opened his mouth so wide that it seemed to split his head completely in two.   The little bits they choked down them immediately gave them strength to want more, and as soon as they were satisfied, we covered them up with good warm flannel.   When we returned from church about an hour and a half later and uncovered them, one hopped right up on the edge of the nest and just squealed for more custard, and in two days they were out, hopping around us for their feed.   In fact I have never had robins accept us as their step-parents so quickly as these two did.   Possibly when they were in their unconscious state they forgot their original parent to a certain extent.   In two weeks they were flying all over the premises, but always came to the back door and chirped when they got hungry, and would stay until some one fed them.   Finally they would follow us men over to the factory and often have I seen them sitting on the mill, watching the stream of clay run out, now and then turning their heads sidewise as if they doubted their best eye.   Once or twice I saw them alight on a hot gas pipe; this always made me laugh, because they got off long before one had to tell them.   The next one might see of them they would be out at the clay bank, watching the man dig clay, now and then picking out an earth worm. But they never went near any stranger that happened around, and this point alone brought us a lot of satisfaction, just to know that these two innocent robins, that had scarcely been acquainted with us a month, knew every person that worked around the premises.

These two stayed with us until October and disappeared.   But they taught me one good lesson: What a great mistake I had made, through life, by keeping my pets shut up, as one bird having its liberty to go and come at will is worth a hundred in a cage.

Well, that is some years ago, but we have had pet robins ever since.   The last seven or eight years, strangers have been coming here by the thousands, and all want to feed our robins; we, of course, let them, and sometimes I will not feed them myself for days.   But I often see them come flying when a bunch of strange people arrives. Why?   Just because they are fed so much by strangers; that is why.

A laughable thing happened last summer.   I heard the lady of the house scolding and shooing with the broom; I found that little Jasper had left the screen door open and three of his pet robins had flown in and roosted on his mother's choice picture that hangs in the cold storage room, or parlor, as some call it. When Jasper found what the noise was about he just took the feed tin and went in, gave the pan a few taps with his spoon, and the birds at once flew down into the pan, the boy walked out with it and ended all confusion.

JASPER FEEDING THE ROBINS

In 1917 we had twenty-one pet robins, and I have often seen little Jasper start for school and have to come back and feed his pets to keep them from following him away.

The way we get them is when some neighbor gets afraid his cats are going to kill the young robins around his place, we get them. If you want to try it, keep them warm, in a small dry-goods box. When you have had them about six hours, open their mouths and slip a little custard in them. The second day they will open their own mouths and in about three days they will accept you as their step-mother and you can let them out. Be sure and keep them good and warm, and feed often.

We put tags on some of our robins, and odd ones returned the next spring, and they are always more wild; in fact when they return they will not let you near them. This fact I do not understand.

My last experiment was to take two robins out of a nest of four where the parent birds were the tamest of any I knew; then I went and got one out of a nest of two, with exceptionally wild parents. The birds were all taken the same hour.   But the two were tamer in two days than the one was in four.

SNOWBALL

This reproduction of a photograph will introduce to you Miss Snowball, our pure white robin with pink eyes and cream-colored beak and feet.   Snowball was hatched in a nest with three others, but like the parents, the other three were just common robins.

CHAPTER XI.

The Bluebirds.

TO THE average middle-aged person of America, this bird needs little or no introduction, but to the young people they are now quite rare. In fact I was speaking to a young lady quite recently, and she has camped out every summer for the longer part of her life (but of course, like all other girls at her age, she has just passed sixteen; passed it coming back, of course) and she told me she had never seen a bluebird. They have decreased over ninety-five per cent. the last forty years, but when I was a boy they were as common as the robin is to-day. They usually arrive the same day in the spring, bringing with them their beautiful note that no musician has ever been able to imitate correctly.

In 1908 I put up three or four nests for them and in 1909 a pair came and built in one.   These nests were made of wood; so it occured to me possibly they would build in tile houses, and I set to work and made six or eight different varieties of drain-tile, and to my surprise and delight the wrens and bluebirds both took to the tile houses and have never built in the frame one since. Last summer I put a wren house up on Monday and the very next morning Mrs. Wren had her nest half built; or in other words, the tile house had hardly gotten cold before she started carrying in sticks.

I had one pair of bluebirds raise their first family for three successive years in the same house. So last summer I made about two hundred bluebird houses, taking this, their choice house, as a pattern. This pair of birds I know raised three families one summer, but they usually raise two. The same house does for both wrens and bluebirds; if the wrens use it, they will stop the large hole up with sticks so the English sparrows cannot get in, but of course leaving door-room enough to get in themselves, as they are so much smaller. This is my experience, but whether these birds will take to tile houses away from here, where they are not accustomed to seeing red tile and a red man, remains to be proven.

In case they do not, there are several remedies. The houses could be painted any color in order to get them coming. But first of all, leave it to the birds, as they seem to know whom it was put there for. So, knowing that the birds prefer them, and as the tile house can be made for about one-fourth of the cost of the wood and, like Pat said about the stone coffin "Sure it will last a lifetime," I know I have secured a home run for the birds.

The removable top can be left off all winter if preferred. The wet and frost will rid the house of mites and so forth, which sometimes kill fledglings. By the use of these little fireproof bird dwellings around our home, the wrens have become far more plentiful than English sparrows, as the latter know they are not wanted. Although we have four or five pairs of bluebirds each year, yet they do not

TILE BIRD HOUSES

The house to the right is the old original that the birds picked out, and the one to the left is the duplicate I made with the removable top.

seem to multiply as rapidly as the wrens; I believe this is due to the wrens' cunningness in barring the door against these cruel "flying rats." This experience has compelled me to believe that the sparrows are responsible for the decrease of our lovable bluebird. I say "lovable," and so will any person who is acquainted with the blue-bird, for they expose their love for humanity by preferring to build their nests near our dwellings so they can rely on our protection.

We usually toe-nail their houses on top of the fence posts around our premises. I have never tagged the bluebirds, therefore I have no positive proof the same one returns year after year; yet I am like the Scotchman who said he was open to conviction but he would like to see the man who could convince him otherwise, for we have several old birds any one of which will permit us to climb up the fence post and remove the roof from her house, and when we peep in she will sit there on her eggs, within eight inches of our eyebrows, and, turning her head sidewise she will cover our whole face with her one little eye as much as to say "Beg your pardon, sir, but you should have rapped before you opened the door." If a stranger is permitted to do this, she will fly out, every time, though after I have taken the top off she will permit him to look in and will not fly out.

"WHY DIDN'T YOU KNOCK BEFORE YOU OPENED THE DOOR?"

The chief cause of the decrease of the bluebird is English sparrows. One of man's great mistakes was when he introduced this little, domineering Bolshevik into America. Not that he doesn't destroy insects enough to counterbalance the amount of grain he takes, but here is my charge against him: He is doing all in his power to exterminate several varieties of birds that God put here, and any one of these birds will destroy more insects in a day than he will in a week.

Last summer when I awoke one Sunday morning I heard the voices of sparrows and bluebirds fighting at the bluebird house, which was about one hundred feet from my open window; but as I knew the young bluebirds were hatched, I just rolled over and had another

snooze.   About an hour later I saw that the English sparrows had
possession.   So I went over, and found five young bluebirds lying
dead at the foot of the post.   Now I did not see the sparrows throw
them out.   I only know that the old bluebirds were chirping and
hovering around the nest and were driven back by the sparrows,
and that the little dead birds were still warm.   In fact, one was just
gasping its last when I picked them up, and each showed marks where
it had been pecked.   I pinned the five little murdered babies to a
piece of cardboard and hung them out and took their picture, which
is shown herewith.

THE ENGLISH SPARROWS' VICTIMS

CHAPTER XII.

Woodpeckers.

NEAR where this tent is pitched is a soft maple tree with a decayed limb in its top, and about one-half dozen downy woodpeckers are making their home there. This morning there is about four inches of snow, and the air is still, so that I could hear these little God-given helpers at work. So I took the ax and went and cut some samples to show you just what they are doing, cutting these little trees off three inches above and below the gimlet-holes made by the birds; then I split the blocks and photographed them. Of course I knew before I went what they were doing, as I have noticed their valuable work for over twenty-five years. The illustration shows gimlet holes made in the proper place by Mr. and Mrs. Woodpecker; then with their long, sharp, bearded tongues which they insert into the grub they gradually draw him out, either head or tail first, I don't know which. The life of the tree is thus saved.

Some years ago when I was cutting timber to secure lumber to build my present home, we sawed down an oak tree over four feet in diameter. The heart of this tree showed where the little woodpeckers had taken the grubs out, over a hundred and fifty years ago, as the marks were preserved there, in the heart of that tree, as plain as they are in the photograph reproduced above. And through their help, a hundred years before I was born, I am able to have nice quarter-cut oak in my home to-day.

Yes, the photograph makes me think more seriously of myself than it does of you. Is it possible that Jack Miner was ever so ignorant and cruel as to shoot one of these dear little forest-protectors just for the fun of seeing him fall!

But there is an old proverb, familiar to all, "Misery likes company." A friend of mine was telling me just yesterday how he and his man went to the back cornfield and shot the red-headed woodpecker because they were pulling his corn. After they had killed all the old birds in sight the man suggested that they cut the old stub down and destroy the fledglings. When this stub fell, the rotten nests broke up in dozens of pieces, killing the young. As the crop of each of these little birds resembled a wart on a needle, they decided to cut them open and see the amount of corn each contained;

but to their surprise they were packed full of injurious worms and bugs, and not one kernel of corn could be found.

Now these two incidents are only fair examples of the ignorance of us human beings during the past, regarding bird life. I could go on enumerating such convincing points for a week about our beautiful bobolink, meadow-lark, and the song-sparrow family, and dozens and dozens of other insectivorous birds. This is all outside their song service, and the cheerful, clear note of such as the bobolink as he flutters across the meadow, singing "Johnny why don't you mend your britches?" or of the cat-bird, who is perfectly willing to come and sing in your back yard if you will plant just a little shrubbery.

Wormhole.   Gimlet-hole made by Woodpecker.

HOW THE WOODPECKER GETS THE WORM

This calls to mind a particular friend of mine, Mr. Angus Woodbridge, whose summer home is about three miles from where I live, located on the north shore of Lake Erie. He has less than two acres, but the fifth year the shrubbery was planted there were over seventy birds' nests around this lovely home, twenty different varieties, a pair of mourning doves being so bold as to build on the window-sill and raise their young there. The brown thrasher, who has such a beautiful imitating voice, could not resist the tempation and built his home in the wild grape arbor that covers the path in the little ravine that wends its way down to the sandy beach. My chief reason for mentioning this fact is to make it plain that these beautiful creatures will come clear across the continent to you, if you will go a few steps towards them.

CHAPTER XIII

The Swallow Family.

THIS is, to my notion, the most valuable family of birds we have in America, as they live entirely on winged insects. And while I am writing on their value, I want you to keep your eye on their intelligence.

Over twenty-five years ago we built an extra large drying shed at our tile factory. It is two hundred feet long, and two stories high; then with the addition of one hundred feet of machine shed, we have over three hundred feet of the very choicest place for the old-fashioned, fork-tailed barn swallows.

Here it stood, with those windows continually open, for years; but no swallows came near.

During that time I read the first game law I have any knowledge of ever being published. I found it in Deuteronomy, twenty-second chapter, verses six and seven, which reads as follows: "If a bird's nest chance to be before thee in the way in any tree, or on the ground, whether they be young ones, or eggs, and the dam sitting upon the young, or upon the eggs, thou shalt not take the dam with the young: but thou shalt in any wise let the dam go, and take the young to thee: that it may be well with thee, and that thou mayest prolong thy days." I read, and tried to analyze the meaning, but my eyes were too weak to see the point.

Finally, to my delight, when I went over to the factory one morning here was the pair of long-looked-for swallows darting around near the south end of this shed. Now the machinery, where ninety per cent. of the work is done, is at the extreme north end of the shed; the south part is used for drying purposes only. And the next morning this pair of birds had some mud stuck up at the points of the third pair of rafters from the south end. They were building just as far from us workmen as they possibly could and still be under the same roof. How this pair of birds did keep those two verses of Scripture fresh in my mind.

Well, they had no sooner completed their house and started setting on five eggs, than along came their deadly enemy, the English sparrow, and destroyed the nest. Then I went up in the air pretty high and came down with a .22 rifle in my hand, and pointed a whole lot of my attention at this particular variety of sparrow.   And I had the pleasure of seeing those swallows rebuild and successfully raise their second brood, which is four.   Before they migrated, they got quite tame and by times they apparently came closer to us than necessary.

The next spring two pairs came back, one pair occupying the old nest, but the others built about fifty feet closer to us. I watched the sparrows closer than ever, and it seemed that the swallows called to us as much as to say "Help! Help!" whenever their enemies put in their appearance, and I always tried to be on hand like a sore thumb. That summer each pair raised two broods, making a total of eighteen young. Now we had just what we had been looking for, and these birds apparently thought the same, for every man in the factory had learned to love them and know their call when a sparrow arrived. This, too, may sound a little fishy, but I will go you one better: I know you could blindfold me and I could tell you if there was a swallow's enemy approaching them. If they looked to us to help them why surely they knew we were their friends.

The third spring they came back in goodly numbers and built five nests, and the fifth year there were no less than twenty nests in the shed. But the beauty of it all is, they simply discarded the south end, and fifteen of the nests are within twenty feet of the busiest spot on the premises where the men are all working and the steam is sometimes blowing. This proves without a doubt that these little, innocent, valuable birds came to us for protection.

I have seen three alight on the cart-horse's back, at once. I have also seen the clay digger put his hand upon the nest, and the old mother bird would simply look over the side as much as to say. "Do you like me?" But let a stranger go in the clay shed, and you will hear their sweet, alarmed voices ring out by the dozens.

Another very interesting sight is when the parent of, say nest number one, darts in at the window, fifty feet away from the nest, the hungry mouths in that nest will go up, proving that each nest of fledglings know their parents as soon as they see them at that distance.

Another great satisfaction to me is that there are now swallows' nests in about every horse-barn of this neighborhood. The great question is: What good are they? We have made a careful study of this point. I have time and again put a sheet of paper under the nest, and when these five fledglings are at their best for consuming flies there is about one-half cupful of droppings thrown overboard every twenty-four hours. I have seen our cow and cart-horse and our self-starter all three lying down in the shade of the shed, and comfortable as could be because here were a dozen swallows dipping up and down after every fly that appeared.

Now scientists tell us that these typhoid flies will carry germs. Such being the fact, when this bird catches and devours the fly that is on its way to your house with that dreaded disease, then it has prolonged your days. "That it may be well with thee, and that thou mayest prolong thy days."

There are six different varieties of swallows that visit this part of Canada. The purple martin is by far the largest, and his warbling voice should be heard around every country home in the greater portion of America, because he is so easily attracted. Thirty-five years ago there were a few in this country; they usually built their nests in old, deserted woodpeckers' holes. I knew a chestnut stub that afforded several pairs a home for the summer. But the first martin house I ever saw was on Mr. Jasperson's building in the town of Kingsville. Then a Mr. Elliott, who kept a summer hotel near the lake, built houses and had good success. This gave me the martin fever very bad, so I hooked up the self-starter and drove to the lake and saw Mr. Elliott. The dear old gentleman's voice trembled as he said, "Jack, I had twenty-five or thirty pairs around my houses, but the boys thought it fun to shoot them. They would go up the lake shore for nothing else, only to hunt my pets; and now I only have three birds left. I am going to pull the houses down because I would rather not have them come than see them shot."

The question was, how could I get them coming to my place? I am three miles from the lake and seldom ever see a purple martin out here. Finally I saw an advertisement in the little journal known as *Our Dumb Animals*, published in Massachusetts: "J. Warren Jacobs, Waynesburg, Pennsylvania, manufacturer of martin houses, shipped three carloads last week." Just then I caught myself thinking that these birds would know his houses wherever they saw them. I at once sent an order for a twenty-roomed dwelling, but when the house arrived the wild geese were continually sitting where I wanted to erect it, so to avoid frightening them I waited till they left for the breeding grounds, still farther north. On the evening of May the 2nd, 1913, I had all the boys in the neighborhood come and we raised the house on a pole sixteen feet high. The questions I was asked that evening would surely have puzzled a Philadelphia lawyer, as to "How soon would the martins come?" and so on.

The next morning, before I had my working harness sufficiently buttoned to avoid an embarrassing accident, I took a peep out the window to see what the bird house looked like in daylight, and really my breath was almost taken from me, for here was a pair of martins hovering around the house, and when the schoolboys went by they shouted, "Uncle Jack," and as they shook their little dinner pails and laughed heartily they said, "there are two blackbirds around your martin house."

In less than a month there were thirteen rooms occupied. This, of course, taught all of us children, old and young, what a purple martin was. In August I counted sixty-three hovering around the house at one time.

Now I have built two of what I call "martin castles," but it took me three years to induce the birds to come to them. To-day they have almost discarded the frame house, and are in the "castles;" the fact that the "castles" are warmer in the spring and cooler in the summer possibly accounts for this. But the brick house is altogether too expensive.

THE MARTIN "CASTLE"
Photograph taken during the absence of the birds

CHAPTER XIV.

Wild Duck Hunting.

THE FOLLOWING, I know, will sound strange to most readers. But the fact is, duck-hunting is the one sport above all others for me.

Yes, it is true I have hunted the swift, ruffed grouse, which is sometimes called partridge, and as this beautiful bird darted through the undergrowth I have downed eleven of them without a miss.

In northern Ontario I have time and again got the wind in my face and slipped up and peeped over a hill at a doe and fawn that were quietly feeding there. I have stood with the crisp breeze cutting my eyes, watching Nature in all her beauty, and presently a big fellow steps out from some concealed spot, nibbles a little browse, or perhaps walks up to a sapling and rubs his antlers. There he is, perfectly unconscious of the fact that a deadly enemy is unfolding his arms from around a clean rifle; and in the midst of life he is in death.

The lordly moose is another of our Canadian beauties (I said "beauties" when I believe I should have said "homelies") and more than once have I had an ordinary carload of these noble animals at the mercy of my rifle. There they have stood, watching their leader die, apparently unconscious of what had taken place.

I have crawled, head-first, down into an old, deserted bear den, and to my astonishment and surprise almost rubbed noses with Mr. Bruin. Needless to say I didn't require telling to back out This was in the winter, of course, when the bears were hibernating.

On another occasion, one still, frosty morning, I stood at the top of a hill and answered the howl of a timber wolf, and to my delight he replied. Then with my mouth close to the ground I again imitated that lonesome, blood-curdling sound; and in about one minute he answered back. Then in a few seconds I very carefully let out another call, and while I was examining and cocking my rifle he again answered. Now I was sure he was coming my way. There I stood, waiting, for over five minutes, with the crispy air in my favor, every nerve keyed up with anxiety. Just as I was about to turn my face to call again, I saw this monstrous, shaggy wolf break from the green cover out into a beaver-marsh about one hundred and fifty yards away, and as I pressed the rifle firmly to my shoulder a low whistle from my lips brought him to a stand, and I had the great satisfaction of seeing him give one tremendous leap in the air as that two-hundred-grain bullet blew his heart into fragments. I mention this incident because our timber wolf, the great red-deer destroyer, may be poisoned or trapped, yet, owing to his keen smelling powers, hearing, and sneaking ability, very few sportsmen—yes, very few of even the most experienced trappers—have ever had the satisfaction of stinging him with a bullet.

Yet in spite of all these experiences, which are the height of thousands of sportsmen's ambitions, I can recall no line of hunting that afforded me more real pleasure than duck-shooting over a flock of home-made decoys. And before I attempt to tell you some things that the wild ducks have taught me I want to give you a glimpse of a real duck-hunt my brother Ted and I had, way back in boyhood, muzzle-loading days, when a dollar bill would blanket a horse.

Somehow or other we had gotten our duck-boat up at a place on the north shore of Lake Erie called Cedar Creek, a distance of about five miles south-west of our home. I had whittled in nearly every night of the winter, making a flock of decoys, and brother Ted did the painting. This particular spring we were splitting rails to finish fencing in one hundred acres of bush; so one Monday morning about the first of April, father gave us a stint, to put up so much fence for the week, and at it we went. At half-past five Friday evening we had our week's work finished, ready for a duck-hunt on Saturday.

After supper we got everything ready for an early start, and as we shook the powder in the flasks and sized up the amount of shot we had in our leather pouches, the anticipation of the next day worked on us until one said, "Let's go up there to-night. We can build a fire in the cedars and sleep under the boat." Enough said; here we go! Dear mother scoffed at the idea, but she seemed powerless. "Well," she said, "if you are bound to go, I will put you up a basket of food." "No, no; we are not going to carry a basket of grub all the way up there. Just give us a small lunch to put in our pockets for breakfast."

Well, just about sunset found each of us with six wooden decoys, some in our hunting-coat pockets, others strung around our necks, and with each a pair of those old-fashioned cow-hide boots on. We started by hand over those soft, sticky, newly-built clay roads, a great percentage of it running through the unfenced forest; and by the time we got there I can assure you those twelve decoys were heavier than they were when we started. It was a beautiful night; the moon which was only a few days old, lay on its back in the south-west, those two little, sharp, bright horns almost outlining the

picture of a full moon.   To think of it, even now, calls to my memory
a sweet little song my older sister sang to me when I was but a lad:

"Oh, Mama, how pretty the moon is to-night;
   'Twas never so lovely before,
With its two little horns, so sharp and so bright—
   I hope they don't grow any more!
      If I were up there with you and my friends
        We'd rock in it nicely, you see;
      We'd sit in the middle and hang on to both ends,
        And what a nice cradle 'twould be!

We'd call to the stars to get out of our way
   Or else we would rock on their toes,
And there we would sit till the dawn of the day
   And see where the pretty moon goes.
      Oh, there we would rock, in the beautiful skies,
        And through the bright clouds we would roam;
      We'd see the sunset, and see the sun rise,
        And on the next rainbow come home."

Soon we made our way into the cedars and found our boat just
as we had left it.   Then we carried the decoys back to the lake shore
again, and as we put them down on the sand, Ted suggested we carry
old driftwood and build our "blind" ready for the morning's sport.
Even with this we weren't satisfied, but we also waded out in the
shallow water, threw out our decoys, and had the pleasure of seeing
the sinking moon glitter over the rippling waves of beautiful Lake
Erie on to the sides of our newly-painted decoys.   Then we started
back into the cedars.
In those days there were about twenty acres of this red-cedar
jungle and in some places one could not see a man over twenty-five
feet away.   The camping place we selected was about twenty feet
in diameter, partly surrounded on three sides with a bank of sand
fully six feet high, heavily capped with cedars.   Here we gathered
dry twigs and built a fire.   Then we dragged the boat over and
turned it on its side, thus filling the gap and making almost a complete circle around our fire.   After gathering armful after armful of
wood for our night's fuel and cutting lots of cedar boughs for our
bed, we sat down to rest.   The sand was dry, and as the night was
still, a very little fire kept us quite comfortable.   Then we pulled
off our cowhide boots and set them back on the opposite side of our
fire.   They made great reflectors, mine especially; for although I was
only sixteen years old, most of my growth had gone into foundation.
Ted allowed his boots were French kip; I said mine were cowhide.

This caused brother to pick at his sprouting moustache as he remarked, "Jack, to look at them from here, one would think they were cows' fathers' hides."

As I got up and dropped another stick or two on our fire, Ted spoke up quite cheerfully, "Jack, let me tell you just what this made me think of. You know the other night when I was down at that country dance, I ran across one of the sweetest French dolls it has ever been my pleasure to meet. She was a real little bird of life, and the more I danced with her the more I wanted to, and really I began to think I held a hand bigger than a foot. Finally as we were standing on the corner, awaiting our turn to swing, she nudged me and as I leaned over she whispered in my ear, 'Mr. Miner, don't you think if you were to trade your cowhide boots off for a pair of light shoes it would be easier on this man's white ash floor?'"

About the next suggestion was to eat our lunch so as not to be bothered with it in the morning. This piece of work was eagerly accomplished, only the programme was altogether too short at the one end, as I could almost feel the pieces of dead hog and hunks of bread strike the log I was sitting on. However we were compelled to be satisfied.

As we sat there watching the sparks disappear into the darkness we could hear the lonely hoot of the owl in the distance; and the swish-sh, swish-sh-sh-sh, of the small waves on the lake a few rods to the south of us; and from the slew to the north came the faint creak-k, creak-k-k-k, of the little spring frogs, as much as to say, "Go to sleep. Go to sleep." All at once Ted's voice rang out, "Wake up, Jack!" and really our surroundings were so completely covered in with Nature she had closed my eyes and I did not know it. Shortly the wind started moaning through the cedars, and we imagined we could feel a change in the atmosphere, and brother suggested we crawl in under our boat and have a sleep. So we straightened the soft cedar boughs around as best we could on the dry sand, crawled in, letting the boat down over us. We wrapped ourselves around each other very closely. The next I knew I was lying on my side with brother's warm arms around me, but my eyes were open and I imagined I could see light under the boat; so I raised it up. Ted spoke first, "Jack, look at the snow!" And really the sight almost caused one to doubt his own eyes, for everything was hanging with snow; the only bare spot was the small pile of smouldering ashes; those cowhide boots were simply snowed full. To make bad matters worse the wind was in the north and it was still snowing.

Well, we knocked it out of our boots the best we could and put them on. While I was fixing and blowing smoke in my eyes out of the fire, trying to get it started, Ted knocked the snow off his gun and went to see if the decoys were all right, and before I got the blaze going I heard "Bang!" I only thought he was trying to dry his gun out, but presently I heard "Bang!" again. Then I knocked the snow off my shooting outfit and made fresh tracks toward him. I found him quite excited. "Jack, hurry! The ducks are coming by the thousands!" There were about fifty or more in the decoys when I came. Look! Here they come again! Get in the 'blind' and keep your red head down!" and he continued pricking dry powder in the tube of his gun with a pin. As about twenty-five ducks hovered to alight we rose up and lit into them. That is, he did, and down came three; but my old gun just went "Snap! Snap!"

Ted sprang to his feet and said, "Prick some dry powder in the tubes of your gun while I go and get the boat," and just as I was in the middle of this operation brother shouted from the edge of the cedars, "Jack, get ready; here they come again." So I slipped a cap on each tube, but none too quickly, for the ducks were upon me. "Snap! Bang!" and down came a big red-headed drake. Brother fairly ran with the boat on his shoulders, a paddle in one hand; and then the real fun began, for it wasn't a case of looking for ducks, but how fast could we load those old soft-coal burners and get the fuse started. Although some of the decoys were half covered with snow, yet the ducks would alight right among them while we were standing up loading our guns; really the snowy air seemed full of them, and we had the pleasure of seeing five tumble out of one flock.

Soon our empty powder horns compelled us to stop shooting; but this did not stop the sport by any means, for there we lay low in our "blind" and watched and studied these migrating birds, as flock after flock settled down among our decoys, until I firmly believe there were over two hundred blue bills, canvas backs, red heads, golden-eyes, ruddies and so forth, within gunshot of our hiding place.

But like lots of other good times, it had to come to a close and about eight o'clock the storm ceased, it cleared off and the ducks got wise and scarce.

So we picked up the decoys and hid them in the dry sand, carried our boat to its hiding place, and about 10 a.m. we shouldered our thirty-seven ducks and started for home.

The snow was now nearly all melted on the road, leaving the clay so sticky that we decided to go home through the woods and fields. But our heavy load of ducks and the spongy fields made our travel-ling real hard work, and our progress was of the very slowest char-acter. The farther we went, the slower our gait, for our steam was gradually running down. And how we thought of the basket of grub dear mother wanted us to take! Finally we crossed the last road and the next house to become visible was ours. How high some of those old rail fences did seem, and how my stomach did gnaw for just one bit of food! Talk about Esau selling his birth-right for a plate of porridge! really there was such an aching void in me I would willingly have given my birthright, or birthwrong, for just one handful of corn-mush and pork-grease.

As we neared the house mother came to meet us. Glancing over her glasses, she said, "Are you hungry boys? Let me carry some of your ducks. How many did you get? Aren't they beauties! Now sit down, boys, and I will have your lunch ready in a few minutes." Just then the old clock said "Three." Here we had been nearly five hours coming that many miles.

But just the same, this was a real outing for your life, and as I went to bed I can remember mother and my younger sisters starting to pick ducks. When I descended the old-fashioned stairway again it was Sunday.

CHAPTER XV.

Knowledge and Ways of the Wild Duck.

IN THE previous chapter I have just given you a faint taste of some of the enjoyable hunts Providence has permitted me to have. If it were possible I would like to throw in a whiff of the home-grown savory dressing, when mother opened the old-fashioned elevated-oven door. But as I grew older, ducks, like all migratory birds, got scarcer until I seldom ever went to hunt them. Yet I have always liked to see wild ducks, both on the table and in the air.

In April, 1902, I secured some wild duck eggs and succeeded in raising three, two ducks and a drake. But it was several years before I got a pond suitable, as artificial ponds cost more than duck eggs. Then in 1905 Mr. Forest H. Conover of Leamington gave me three young black mallards that were hatched from eggs direct from the marsh. In 1907 I built my first real spring-water pond. I always kept the wings of my old birds clipped or pinioned, and the young we usually sold to sportsmen for decoys, but in 1908 I concluded that it was worth more to me to see them flying around, and that fall a bunch of the young went away. I naturally thought they had gotten out to the lake and were decoyed before some pump-gun.

The next spring several black mallards dropped in the pond and acted and looked for all the world like the ones that had gone away the previous fall, but the question was, these ducks came several days apart, and if they were the same ones they would come back together; so I just gave in, and said they were tame because they were with my domesticated wild ducks, that was all. Another point I argued with myself against their being the same ducks: These young tame ones that had left the previous fall, would be shot by the first man that ran across them, because they wouldn't know an enemy.

However, about April the 20th all the wild ducks left. One Sunday evening in June I was tapping the food tin and calling a few young wild ducks in the park when my wife's voice rang out from the house, saying, "Here are your ducks outside." As I looked up, here was an old black mallard duck and eight young ones, about one-half grown, working away to get in at the gate. For a few minutes I stood perfectly bewildered, in thought. My ducks were all around my feet; what duck was this, with eight young, trying and trying to get in at the gate? How did she know there was a gate there? At length I went and opened the gate and she withdrew to the north along the fence; the gate opened to the north but the young were to the south a few feet, and as I stepped around them they toddled, in single file, along the fence and worked their way in through the opening. As soon as the mother saw they were all through the wire netting, she just stepped back from the fence and flew over, like a crow; dropping down she spoke to her family and all walked into the water together. I then went and got my feed tin and tapped it as I usually do to call all the ducks, and sure enough, this strange duck came right up, but her family stood back; in fact, they did not come out of the water. Again I tapped the tin and she turned her head sidewise, looking at me with first one eye and then the other, as much as to say, "How long will it take you to tumble? Don't you know I am one of the ducks you raised last year, and that I returned here to my home last March, and went away to my nest about the 20th of April; and now I have brought my family here to Safety Inn."

The fact was hard for me to believe, but I was compelled to, for the very next week another black mallard, which was evidently her sister, came home, and when I got up one morning she was standing at the gate with a broken family of four ducklings as much as to say, "Will you please let my babies in?" Useless to say her request was soon granted.

In less than two weeks these old ducks and their young would all eat out of the pan; in fact I would put feed in my pockets and the old ones would climb up on my lap and put their heads in my open pocket and scatter feed to their young.

This duck story I know is beginning to sound strange to you, but remember, I have only just started telling you how they have cornered me up and made me frankly confess I didn't know anything about them. Why do these old ducks, in every case when they return with their young (that of course cannot fly) bring them around to this gate to be let in? How do they know there is an opening there? It is plain to be seen they have thinking ability enough to know that that is where we human beings enter the park and that there must be an opening there.

Another mystery is, where did they bring their young from; where did they hatch them, and so forth? In answer to this, young ducks, at three days old, can run as fast as adult Bob White quail.

Since this happened, we know of one old duck that hatched her young over four miles away and was home with them inside of a week. In another case a lady telephoned that the school children were trying to catch some little wild ducks in the ditch, and that the old duck had a tag on her leg; this was after four o'clock, and these ducks were over a mile away from here, but at six o'clock she and her family were in our north pond, scudding over the water, catching flies.

But perhaps the most interesting case I had was when a farmer phoned me to come over and help him catch a crippled wild duck that went flapping out of the clover field in front of him. He said that she could just get over the fence, but he couldn't quite catch her. I firmly believed him, because he was still out of breath when he called me up. This story sounded good to me, so in a few hours I

OLD DUCK AND YOUNG WAITING AT THE GATE
Note Aluminum tag on her leg

took a stroll around, and this wise old pet that he thought crippled was home with her family. What had she done? Why, outwitted this intelligent man by leading him to believe she was crippled; then, as soon as he disappeared, she flew back into the clover field, dropped down and gave a few quacks that brought all her family out of the grass, and they continued their journey homeward. But the fact is that if there hadn't been danger of this man stepping on some of her babies, he would never have known she was there.

About the most touching duck scene I have ever witnessed was in 1913. A wild house-cat robbed an old gray duck of her seven young. I now and then heard her squawking, but I was looking for a hawk or weasel; some men that were making hay near by saw old Mrs. Cat as she sprang upon the last ducklings. The way the old duck carried on was pitiful. She flew and squawked around for two or three days. Then one morning I missed her altogether and concluded she had gone away to the lake. But on my way from the factory to dinner I happened to think of the brood of ducks the old Wyandotte hen was about to bring out, so I jumped the fence into the park. As I neared the old hen she started scolding. I raised her up, and all had hatched, and gone, but two. Where were they? My first thought was "Weasels;" but just as I was backing away from the coop I saw the eye of old Mrs. Duck. There she sat in the weeds, about four feet in front of the coop, as still as a corpse, and I was compelled to tumble, for here was the head of a sweet, tiny duckling projecting out of her feathers near her wings. This dear old, broken-hearted mother was sitting here, stealing this hen's ducks as fast as she hatched them, and surely she knew they were not hers, for her ducklings were ten or twelve days old. As I looked at her I thought of the times I had crossed the street to meet some curly-haired little child that looked like my sweet little girl did. Well, when I went back again the old hen was alone in the coop. The other two had hatched, and Mrs. Duck was gone with the eight; and she raised them all, for that cat never came back.

Another thing worthy of notice is that this is a well-settled farming country. I am three miles north of Lake Erie and about five miles north-east of Cedar Creek, which is the nearest natural duck marsh, and some of these cute old ducks raise their families until they are nearly full-grown before they bring them home, and are seldom seen by any person, unless they happen to be in the big ditches.

A very small sportsman who stood six feet in height sprinkled corn in a living stream in order to get a shot at some of these ducks, and on Good Friday morning, 1911, he succeeded in getting a crack at a pair. As they flew up in front of him he killed the duck dead, but the drake fell with a broken pinion and ran into some rushes. After hunting for him for fully one-half hour he went for his bird dog, thus giving the drake nearly an hour to make his escape. When the dog arrived he took up the trail at once, but when he came to a ploughed field he apparently lost the scent. One week from the following Sunday Mr. Drake was at the park gate, trying to get in. Here he had been about nine days coming one mile and a half, dragging his broken wing. What handicapped him worst was a shot that had entered at the hip joint. I caught him and examined his wounds. As I let him down in the park he didn't flap away, as one would expect, but simply stood and looked for food. Fortunately for him only one of the bones was splintered and in less than six weeks he was flying again. But it took over two years for all the particulars regarding the shooting of him and the death of his mate to reach my ears.

Another fact worthy of notice is that the park gate is only thirty feet from our dining-room window, and in every case these ducks come here to look for an entrance when it isn't at all likely they ever passed through this gate themselves. Only they see us enter there. Really the way some of these birds expose their intelligence compels me to believe what I heard a farmer say at one of our Corn Growers' Conventions. This man rose up, stroking his beard; then, raising his right hand, he remarked, "I tell you, gentlemen, there are a lot of things in this world we haven't come to yet."

Another interesting fact about wild mallard ducks is the extreme difference between the faithful mother and the lazy drone of a father; for as soon as the duck starts to set, the drake deserts her entirely and he lives the life of a Brigham Young for the rest of the season. In fact he hasn't got a bit more principle than some of us men! Hence the faithful mother has to be father and mother both to her family, hatching and guarding them from their enemies, and leading them to proper feed as well as supplying the necessary shelter and warmth. Yes, she is just as faithful and true as a kind washerwoman who is compelled to bring her nursing baby with her while she scrubs the morning away and earns two dollars, but willingly takes fifty cents, and on her way back to the place called home spends it all to relieve the hunger of the three of four more darling tots that are anxiously awaiting momma's return, while the lazy, good-for-nothing father is loafing around the smoky end of nowhere, swapping garbage stories, and remarking about some lady who is passing the dirty window that is corroded with smut.

CHAPTER XVI.

Do Birds Return to Their Same Homes?

DO BIRDS return to their same homes, year after year?" This is a question that has been put to me more than any one along the bird line, and it is usually followed by: "How do you know?" Then I have had to take father's advice, "drop it," and talk about the weather or some other side line. For while I was sure of this in my own mind, yet I had no proof.

On August 5th, 1909, a wild black duck lit with my ducks in the north pond. I started cozening around her, not by going closer to her, but by letting her come closer to me. Finally she was eating out of the long-handled spoon that I had previously used for throwing little feed over to her. The spoon, of course, was on the ground, gradually being drawn towards me until it came over my left hand that was lying flat on the ground, and on September 10th of the same year this duck actually ate out of my hand. We named her Katie. In a few months Katie got so tame she would follow us in the barn where we went after the feed. So I scraped around in my hunting-case drawer and found a piece of sheet aluminum about three-quarters of an inch wide and one and a half inches long; I then took my sweetheart's best pair of scissors, and with the pointed blade I managed to scratch my post office address on it. Then I caught Katie and wrapped it around one of her hind legs. She disappeared on December 10th, and in January I received the following letter:

ANDERSON,
SOUTH CAROLINA,
January 17th, 1910.

Box 48,
    Kingsville, Ontario.

Dear Sir,—

On Friday evening, January the 14th, I was hunting on Rocky River, near this city. I killed a wild duck with a band on his leg, marked Box 48, Kingsville, Ontario. I suppose whoever sent him out wanted to hear from him, so I am writing to let you know where he came to his end. He was a very fine specimen. I must commend him for his judgment, for he came to the best County in the best

State in America.   If you will let me hear from you I will return the band I took from his leg.   So hoping you will send me his pedigree I will close until I hear from you.   Send me your address in full.

Very respectfully,

W. E. BRAY.

KATIE FEEDING OUT OF MY HAND

I at once wrote Mr. Bray and he kindly returned the tag, which is the centre one in the photograph of my collection of tags.   Mr. Bray made two distinct mistakes; one was when he called Katie "him" and another, equally as big, was when he stated that the duck came to the best spot in America, for the fact is that Essex County, Ontario, this duck's summer home, is the best spot on this beautiful earth; this, of course, will include all of North America.

In 1910 and 1911 I was so busy I didn't take the pleasure of tagging any more, but in the spring of 1912 I hatched four young mallard.   No, I didn't hatch them; I stole the eggs from a black duck that had paired off with a gray, green-headed mallard drake and set them under a domestic fowl; a few days after they were hatched they accepted me as their step-father, and this old hen and I succeeded in raising four. I always fed them in one spot on the brick wall that surrounded the pond. The fish got so they came regularly for the bits that the ducks pushed overboard; as I would tap the tin to call the ducks, I also called the fishes. I was compelled to believe this, for before I would drop a bit of food, the fishes would be right there. They were what we call bull-heads, a little, miniature cat-fish, about six inches long. To see them with their whiskers up above the water all along the wall was quite interesting, especially when I would go to the opposite side of the pond from where I usually fed them, and tap the tin. This makes me think of the Irishman who was asked the question "Do fish sleep?" He replied, "I never caught any that way."

At any rate the little ducks got all they wanted to eat, for they grew like mushrooms. I took a day off for no other reason than to go to Detroit and buy sheet aluminum and a set of stencils, and when these four ducks had their growth, each was presented with a leg-band stamped with the following inscription: "Write box 48, Kingsville, Ontario."

These four ducks' names were Polly, Delilah, Susan and Helen. On or about December 5th they left, and on the following day Dr. Rutherford, Chatham, Ontario, shot Helen at Mitchell Bay, Lake St. Clair, Ontario.

Well, I looked to hear from the other three, all winter. But to my delight, on March 10th, 1913, Polly came home, and on the 18th, Delilah came; and although badly crippled in the wing and leg, Susan came squawking down out of the heavens on March 30th. I caught each one and examined their tags; and for the next three months I did all I could to induce people to ask me how I knew that birds returned to their same homes, for I had double proof: First, these ducks were mulattoes; they had a black duck's breast, and a grey duck's wings. But the climax was the tags that I put on their legs.

That summer, 1913, Polly and Delilah each raised a family, but Susan remained in the hospital nearly all summer. That fall they all three migrated again, and Noah Smith of Paris, Kentucky, shot Susan, February 27th, 1914.

On March 14th, Polly came home. On March 21st Delilah came; she was accompanied by a Yankee sweetheart and this spot seemed too good to be real for him. When Delilah would come to me, he would scour the heavens above, but finally he believed what she said and he, too, came to me for food.

That summer Delilah raised her family, but Polly came home May 20th without any, and both ducks migrated again that fall.

On March 13th, 1915, Delilah came home, and on the 16th Polly came, but Polly had had a narrow escape, as part of her beak was shot off. The sight was pitiful. With a fragment of her beak hanging down she could hardly eat, so I mixed up some corn-meal and put it in piles for her. Finally I reached out and grabbed the opportunity, then with the scissors in the other hand I clipped the dead fragment of her beak off, and in a few days she appeared to eat quite naturally. Later on I caught the two sisters, put them in a twine sack, took them to town, stood them on a table and stroked them until they became quite contented; then I stepped back and the photographer took the photograph which is shown.

POLLY AND DELILAH

Wild ducks spending their third spring at my home. Notice where the piece has been shot off Polly's beak.

My boy said Polly got her beak a little too far ahead. At any rate she appeared to think that was a close enough call for her, and the next winter she did not migrate, but stayed here with our domestic fowls, and she was shot by a wild goose hunter in April, 1916. But Delilah continued to migrate and returned for the sixth time on March 25th, 1918. That summer she raised a family of twelve, which is, by the way, the largest family of mallards I have ever known to grow to maturity. The last I have any positive proof of seeing her was in September, 1918. During the six years she brought to my home five families, two eights, two nines, and a twelve. In 1917 she came home without a family.

Providing all of her descendents multiply as she did, how many ducks have you got in six years? Surely this is worth thinking over, and when we see that it runs up into the thousands we cannot help but be encouraged, and our confidence increased in His lovable, truthful promise to us, His children; for He says "Let the mother go that it may be well with thee, and that thou mayest prolong thy days." Who could ask for a plainer fulfilment of His promises?

Now in case the reader might think that possibly I am mistaken in the ducks, and this was not the same bird, I will say that outside of other proofs of her being the same duck (such as coming when we would call her, and now and then eating from our hands, her peculiar marking, and so forth), we caught her each year and examined the tag. In the spring of 1917, after she had returned the fifth time, Mrs. Miner and I caught her and gave her a new tag, as the old one was so badly worn.

Now before I go farther I want you to stop and think. Remember, these are just wild ducks that we are apt to think know so little. Yet the fact is, these birds have shied out around thousands of hunters who are hidden in the ambush with all kinds of decoys to assist them. Yet these ducks have outwitted them all, year after year. Then when they return they will almost eat from my hand the first day they arrive, when if they had allowed themselves to have ventured within two hundred feet of the hunters' decoys it would have been almost sure death to them. Can you blame me for enjoying nature study? Do you wonder that I have hung up the gun and am trying in my A, B, C fashion to tell you these unpolished facts? Yet I doubt if the best writers on earth could give you a taste of this grateful feeling in having your pets return to you year after year for food and protection; really it almost makes you feel you were personally present when He said, "How often would I have gathered thee as a hen doth gather her brood under her wings."

Another thing that interests me: These ducks always leave here in flocks, and return singly, except those that have doubled by bringing mates. I have never seen two with tags on return together. In 1914 I tagged twelve. One was shot at Gueydan, Louisiana and one at Cooksville, Tennessee. In the spring of 1915, day after day added to the number until on March 28th there were six sitting on the brick wall surrounding the pond with bright aluminum tags on their legs. In the fall of 1915 I tagged fifty-three, and in the spring of 1916 nearly half of them returned. In the fall of 1916 I caught and tagged fifty-four, and in catching these fifty-four I caught twenty-three that had been tagged previously.

CHAPTER XVII.

Birds as Missionary Messengers.

SINCE 1915 I have more than doubled the interest of my bird-tracing system by stamping a selected verse of Scripture on what previously was the blank side of the tag. Now whoever is lucky enough to get a bird with my tag on it also gets a personal verse of Scripture, whether he needs it or not. Safety first! No harm done. I said "personal," but of course there are exceptions. In case you are bald-headed and when out shooting you bring down a good fat goose wearing a tag, and on investigation you find that the message reads: "The very hairs of your head are all numbered. Matthew 10: 30," if you don't think this goose was intended for you just place the tag back on its leg and hand it to the other fellow.

However, I do not feel that I should pass on without first giving you an explanation of how this great advantage was handed to me.

One Saturday afternoon in the fall of 1914 I was standing in a shoe store in the town of Kingsville, conversing with two gentlemen, when a plainly dressed Salvation Army lassie approached us and holding out a small roll remarked, "Buy a calendar, gentlemen; buy a calendar?" I happened to be the last one to refuse, but as I shook my head I glanced at the situation. We three men all wearing good warm overcoats, and this girl, dressed in what I would call a summer suit. I spoke just as she was turning away. She at once whirled, her face beaming with smiles as she held out the paper roll towards me, while I dropped a quarter in her other extended hand and carelessly pushed what she had sold me down into my outside overcoat pocket. I have never seen her since to my knowledge.

A few days later I noticed a beautiful picture hanging on our dining-room wall; its outer cover appealed to me very much, so I got up and walked to it and began asking a volume of questions, Where did you get that? Who brought it here? Where did it come from? and so forth. Mrs. Miner turned and said, "Why you brought it home. We found it in your overcoat pocket."

By this time I had lifted the outer cover and found it contained a selected verse for me to consider each day in the year. This was the first one I read: "From this day I will bless you."

I then studied one after another of them until I had read and reread dozens and dozens of these encouraging promises that seemed to fill the whole room with heavenly bread right from God's own oven of love.

The overflow of my heart was: How can I pass it on? I decided to select a few of these verses that had hit me square in my living room, and have them put in booklet form, then pass them on to friends as my Christmas greetings.

That week we were burning our last kiln of drain-tile for the season. It had been our custom that I start work at one o'clock, a.m., my eldest son taking the first part of the night. I am on duty, firing, every half hour, which takes me from ten to fifteen minutes; then I withdraw from the heat and roar of the fires, and lean back in our old chair with my feet upon a wheel-barrow. The clock is hung where the glare of the light will shine on its face and I take things quite comfortable for fifteen minutes at a time. I pull the blanket up over my shoulders and lie right back.

It is a beautiful warm morning for the time of the year; in fact the park pond is not frozen over, and the ducks and geese are still here. The silence is broken now and then by the crowing of the roosters, which is Nature's introduction to the new day. The sky above my face looks bluish-black, illuminated with thousands of twinkling stars, and each is staring me right in the eyes. There I am—*alone*. I pick out a space between four bright stars and try to count the dimmer ones in that small area, until the whole heavens seem to burst open with wireless messages, and my heart is the central station.

I have said I am alone. Yes, I am alone in company with Him who has been the foundation of all my success; alone with Him who, time and again while in the northern wilderness, has heard my earnest, awkwardly-worded request and has guided me to my lost companions when my strength and ability had failed; yes, when the night has been as black as ink, and the stormy gale was causing the trees to fall all around us, He has guided me safely back to our tent that is pitched in the second-growth timber beside some little stream or lake. Yes, I am alone with the same great, loving Power who has made millions of bare-foot boys into real men, even after fathers' and mothers' kind teachings had failed.

Just then I heard the swish of a flock of ducks' wings and their low quacking as they dropped into the pond about two hundred feet away. At that moment one corner of my mind's eye had apparently drifted over to the three hundred and sixty-five blessings I had bought of the Salvation Army lassie for twenty-five cents, and like a star shooting across the heavens God's radio said: "Stamp these verses on what is now the blank side of your duck and goose tags."

I threw the blanket off my shoulders and jumped to my feet, for I now had my tagging system completed!

In less than a week I had the fowls of the air carrying the word of God, and in six months they were delivering it from the sunny side of the Atlantic to the far-off Indians and Esquimaux of Hudson Bay. And to-day I do not hesitate in saying that I have the most accurate and most fascinating bird-tagging system of any man, or combination of men, standing on the American continent, as the verse of Scripture has more than doubled the interest.

SHOWING BOTH SIDES OF ALUMINUM
TAGS AS I NOW STAMP THEM

This brought Rev. J. W. Walton to my home, here. Mr. Walton has been an Anglican missionary on the east coast of Hudson Bay for over thirty years And when he and I grasped hands in my dooryard we were compelled to believe that we were introduced by the fowls of the air, for his letter of introduction was several goose-tags which I had sent out in previous years. The geese were killed by the Esquimaux, who took the tags to the reverend gentleman for an interpretation.

This system also brought to me another letter from the far North, which is of unusual interest. It reads as follows:

"I have to admit that I have delayed the sending of this tag to you, longer than I should. Hope I have caused you no inconvenience.

"The passage of Scripture on this tag is one which had I fully realized God's power, and the full extent of its meaning in the past, how often would I have said 'Get thee behind me, Satan,' and would have come out of it 'more than conqueror;' but, sorry to say, in most cases the opposite has been the result. Rest assured your message has done some good."

One duck, killed in Louisiana, brought to my home thirty-nine interesting letters of inquiry. Among them was a letter from the Arkansas State Prison, reading as follows:

"My name is ——. My room-mate's name is ——. I am in here for overdraft on a bank; my room-mate, who is sitting at my elbow, is in here for murder. We have a paper here giving an account of a duck killed in Louisiana with a tag on its leg marked 'Have faith in God.' We have looked this up in our Bible; we find that the reference given is correct. We would be pleased to hear from you, to know more about your interesting life with the birds. However, if you do not see fit to write us, we trust you will not be offended at getting a letter from here. We remain,

Yours,

Arkansas State Prison

Little did I think when I stamped this verse on the tag that the duck carried away, that the message would ever find its way into a prison cell, and lodge in the heart of a murderer.

CHAPTER XVIII.

How Wild Ducks Conceal Their Nests.

POSSIBLY there is none of our birds that can conceal its nest better than the wild duck. This may be due to the fact that she has to be father and mother both.

In the first place she selects a spot where the foliage, dry sticks or weeds, are exactly the same color as herself. I once found a black duck's nest right beside an oak stump that was charred black by being partly burned away, and really if you weren't careful you might look at her all day and not see her, as she was exactly the same color.

Yes, I know there are a lot of people who will say "Oh, that just happened that way." I tell you right here it did not happen that way. This is a gift to help these creatures out, and there is no man on earth can conceal anything better than a wild duck can her nest. An intelligent man once asked me how I hid when I hunted wild geese. I told him I covered myself with a blanket, and in a few weeks I saw him returning from a hunt carrying a red horse blanket.

After the duck has the spot selected she gathers a few twigs and so forth, but she lays the eggs right on the bare ground, going to her nest late at night and leaving long before the stars disappear in the morning. As soon as the crows start scouring the country, she flies back to the vicinity of her nest. I have seen a duck give a crow an aerial battle three or four times a day. But of course two crows are one too many for her.

From the time she starts laying, she covers the eggs very carefully with grass and sticks before she leaves the nest, therefore they are absolutely out of sight and protected from a slight frost, such as we sometimes have after the wild ducks have started laying. When the eight to twelve eggs are laid she pulls down off her breast and covers them. Now comes the question, how can she pack these eggs in that down, and cover them with sticks and grass, and not leave a sign of down to indicate that there is a duck's nest within a mile?. This is certainly a piece of shrewd work.

Wild ducks seldom ever leave their nests in the daytime after they start to set. I often go back to the north pond and watch them come home to feed, just at dusk, and they are usually there at twilight in the morning. This compels me to believe they some-

CHAPTER XIX.

My Last Distinguished Family of Pet Ducks.

AT THE present time I have only one grey duck of my own. She is pinioned and lives in the park. In the spring of 1919 she paired off with one of the wild drakes that came here, built a nest and laid eleven eggs.

I have a pair of Egyptian geese in the park, and of all the web-footed devils I know of on earth, these Egyptian geese are the worst. I knew full well I must not let this duck hatch her young there, so a few days previous to their hatching I stole the eggs and put them under a domestic fowl. She hatched the whole eleven and in about twenty-four hours I moved them all to the north pond, shutting the eleven pets in a playground about two feet square which I made in front of their own stepmother. The third day I gave them their liberty by quietly removing the three boards, but of course left the hen in the permanent coop. I sat for a few minutes and watched them as they saw water for the first time. Finally all apparently lined up along the sloping bank of the pond, looking and peering sidewise as they slowly advanced to the edge of the water, where all stood still for a few seconds, then as suddenly as anything could possibly be, they dove into the water, just like eleven frogs, and equally as quick, some of them coming up fully ten feet from shore.

The first week I fed them a little custard, then gradually tapered off to oatmeal, throwing the feed in the shallow water so they would have to tip up to get it.

They grew quite rapidly, but the thirteenth was their unlucky day for a snapping turtle took one. Fortunately three other wild ducks were raising their families there, and these old ducks gave the alarm and I arrived just in time to see this little duck's finish; but the other ten got along O.K., for that was the last meal that old mossback ever required.

In about a week I heard these old ducks' alarming cries again. I hustled back and shortened the career of another snapping turtle, but this time my nerve was not very steady and I missed his head, but the ball split the roof of his house, causing it to leak, letting in the water that gradually pushed his life out, leaving him just strength enough to walk to shore.

About a week later I again heard these old ducks' call of distress, saying "Help, help! Help, help!" and this cry continued until I arrived with the glittering rifle in my hand; then it ceased. All were standing on the shore, and, best of all, my ten had learned the alarm and had also come out of the water; the forty or fifty ducks, young and old, were on their tiptoes, each with one eye directed towards the middle of the pond. So I hid myself in the growing rye surrounding the pond. Finally the three old birds ventured in the water about twenty feet in front of me, and just as I was about to give up watching they all three raised their heads and said "Quack! Quack! Quack!" and they swam quickly towards me and their young who

THE MULBERRY FAMILY

were preening their baby feathers on the bank. I could not see a thing. Yet they continued the alarm, as much as to say, "There he is!" Now what could it be? Finally I saw a little speck not much larger than an ordinary bean projecting above the calm surface of the water. I watched it closely and it still grew larger until I was sure it was the periscope of one of these old four-legged submarines. The ducks having my nerves keyed up to the highest tension, I wanted to make a sure shot. When this speck was as large as my two thumbs above the water I slowly cocked the high-powered rifle, took a steady aim and pressed the button, and I have never seen that turtle's head since.

But here is what is interesting: Of these three old ducks two were tagged in 1916, and have migrated and returned three times to my personal knowledge, and have undoubtedly been shot at, time and again; one has part of her foot shot away. Yet when this rifle cracked, right above the three, not one attempted to fly, but all rushed right up to the muzzle of the gun. This was only a starter of them exposing their knowledge; for ten minutes later each took her family right out into the water. Whether they knew I had killed the turtle, or if it was the calmness and safety brought about by the crack of the rifle the two previous times that gave them confidence to go out into the water, I do not know; only this, that they did go out with the appearance of perfect safety. Moreover I had no proof that I had killed the turtle. But time told that tale; the weather was very hot and on the second day and about the eleventh hour he arose, but minus a head.

Well, to return to the ten little ducks, I was trying to make them grow as fast as the old ducks did their broods. In other words I was racing with the old duck, but I was like Dad's fast horse, just fast enough to lose. Fortunately one day mine followed me towards the house and found the mulberries. These trees were only five years old and therefore hadn't much fruit, but the ducks ate every berry almost before it touched the ground. Now I had the old ducks a-going some, for these Mulberry ducks outgrew theirs. For three weeks they ignored me, but as the weather was dry and hot the bulk of this fruit gave out and the Mulberry family, as we called them, were glad to come back to their old stepfather.

They were hatched on May 25th. The day they were eight weeks old they arose and flew the full length of the pond, two hundred and forty feet. At nine weeks old they were going over the top of the whole premises including the seventy-five foot chimney at the drain-tile factory. On July 14th we caught, tagged and named each one. I put two tags on each duck so I could see how many returned in the spring without catching them, the one being the usual tag that I put on any duck; the other was a little narrower and contained just the initials of the duck's name. Their names were as follows:

Agnes Mulberry   Joseph Mulberry ⌉
Ruth Mulberry   Woodrow Mulberry
Mabel Mulberry   John Mulberry
Flossie Mulberry   Theodore Mulberry
Nellie Mulberry   Peter Mulberry.

In August the pond dried up and most all of my ducks went away. Mr. William Scratch, Kingsville, Ontario, shot Theodore Mulberry

on September 1st, at Cedar Creek.   Later on, in October, seven
of them were home again, and all migrated on December 2nd.   On
December 13th, Joseph Mulberry was shot by Mr. August Holstein
of Columbus, Ohio.   Mr. Holstein shot the drake near that city,
and on January 3rd, 1920, Mr. H. C. Leiding of Charlestown, South
Carolina, killed Mabel Mulberry near that city.   In the spring at
least three of them returned, but strangely I haven't any proof of
what happened to any of the rest; possibly some may be alive yet.

It may seem strange to you that I enjoy keeping a history of
different families of birds, but if you were to do the same I am sure
you would enjoy it far better than tracing your own family history,
for in tracing the history of the birds we are not so apt to find out
things we wish we had never known.

CHAPTER XX

Ducks' Love Soon Ceases.

DURING the last few years I have received letters from different men in America questioning about wild ducks' ways, and I have promised to answer in this book.

Yes, wild ducks, as well as geese, all go through an annual moult, their wing feathers all dropping out within a few days, leaving them unable to fly for from four to six weeks, according to the healthy condition they are in to produce new wing feathers.

The drakes have nothing else to do for the summer months, and they moult the latter part of June. Their wing feathers shoot out so fast they usually are flying again in about a month. But the ducks, as I have previously stated, are the most faithful mothers on earth, and neglect themselves for their families, not moulting before the young are full grown and have been flying at least two weeks. Then her wing feathers drop out, and because she cannot fly with her family they all desert her, and she sneaks away in the rushes and is seldom seen until she is able to fly again. By this time her family have completely forgotten all about her. I have never seen them pay any particular attention to her afterwards; in fact they pay just as much attention to a drake who possibly might have been their father, and by the first of October the whole family may be scattered and become comparative strangers to each other, seldom two of them ever being together. This is pointed out plainly by the ducks with tags on being dotted here and there among a flock of hundreds. Further proof of this is that only two or three sportsmen throughout America have ever reported killing over one; yet they will often say, "a flock of ducks came into our decoys; we killed so many; among them was this one with the tag on," and so forth. And as I have previously stated, we have never noticed two tagged ducks return together.

We often hear sportsmen speak of seeing floppers in the marsh on the first of September, apparently believing these are young ducks. I have never seen a young duck in my life that could not fly on that date. They usually all fly by July 20th. Sometimes an old duck will lay a second setting if the first nest is destroyed; this will put her back five or six weeks. The floppers that are seen in September are old ducks. We had a duck we called "Old Lamey;" she had part of her foot shot away. After raising her family she did not moult until August, and it was October 5th before I saw her flying.

One gentleman writes me, "If a duck loses her mate will she pair off again that summer?"

This all depends on the variety of duck. Wood ducks pair off and if one is killed the other is a failure for at least that season, but black and grey ducks will pair off the very next day. I have known a black duck to hatch some black and some half-grey ducks, all from the one setting of her own eggs.

During the spring months one often sees three ducks flying here and there all over the marsh. This is a pair of ducks and a strange drake interfering. Now I have never seen a case of this rough and ready Brighamy where the duck was the least bit to blame. The drakes are all the same, like barn rats. The less said the better.

CHAPTER XXI.

The Migration of Ducks.

EVER since I started tagging birds, my desire for this never-tiring sport has been constantly increasing, and to-day I have carloads of unsatisfied ambition flying all over America just because I cannot get my tag on them all. Altogether, I have tagged four hundred and fifty-two ducks since starting, and I am well pleased with the amount of interest the sportsmen have displayed in writing me from different shooting grounds of America where these tagged birds have fallen.

It is remarkable how these letters differ in tone, how men will expose who they are by their hand-writing, stating how they captured the bird, or how it got caught in a muskrat trap; this, of course, is their Latin way of saying "I shot the duck out of season." But about the limit was when a gentleman wrote as follows: "I am an officer of the law, and the other night while on duty I was in pursuit of two whiskey smugglers crossing our river. I ordered them to stop, but they did not heed, so I fired my revolver in the air, and down came a wild duck with a tag on."

I would like to match this "officer of the law" against a "detective" we have in our town. This man had been duck hunting and next day when asked "What luck?" replied, "Well, just middling; good and bad both. You know I had the old muzzle-loader, and I got up at Cedar Creek just daybreak; looked, and saw the largest flock of ducks on earth coming right towards me. So I squatted in the rushes, and when they came over I rose up, taking steady aim where they were the thickest, pressed the trigger, and both barrels snapped, but down came twenty-seven ducks. Really if the gun had gone off I know I would have killed a thousand!"

Another letter states, "I wish I could get more of the ducks. I was out all morning and got only twenty-four. The one with the tag on was amongst them. How is the shooting down your way?"

Worst of all was a well-educated man who never wrote at all, but the duck was seen by a friend of mine who reported it; then I wrote the doctor the second time, enclosing a self-addressed postal card before I got a short acknowledgment.

But like all other things in my life, the good that has been blown my way has completely drifted the undesirable under. I have received some of the most beautiful letters that ever were written by God-fearing and loving hands.

One man explains, "I received the message you put on the duck's leg, and it is so personal it makes me love you for sending it. Will you please let me keep it?" His request was cheerfully granted, for the message read: "He careth for you. Peter 5: 7."

A lady writes, "My boy shot the duck. Thank you for the message; it makes us friends."

A soldier boy writes, "Uncle Sam has called me to the colors and I must respond. Should I live to return I will be pleased to come and see you. You will find enclosed the tag I took from the duck's leg. Good-bye." On looking at the tag which this duck had carried for over a year and finally delivered to this young soldier, out for his last day's recreation before leaving for the battle-field, already soaked with human blood, I found that the message read: "For me to live is Christ, and to die is gain. Philippians 1: 21."

The following is a letter from Dr. Axby in reply to my printed pamphlet requesting him to return the tag. I know the Doctor will pardon my reproducing his letter, as I have dozens similar to it, but his was the first I came to.

January 1st, 1919.

Mr. Jack Miner,

I am in receipt of your interesting letter, and assure you we are glad there are such men as you in the world, and shall endeavor to remember your interest in game life and govern ourselves in accord with your wishes.

Here wishing you a Happy, Prosperous, Peaceful 1920, and more to come.

Enclosed find your tag.

Yours truly,
(Dr.) J. L. Axby.

The following letter would cause one to believe that there are States that have not yet been visited by Billy Sunday, particularly as the entire Bible verse was stamped on the tag:

May 3, 1920.

Box 48,
    Kingsville, Ont.
Dear Unseen Friend,—

On the aluminum plate bent around a wild duck's leg bore these words: Jude 1-21. I can't make out the meaning.

Wishing to hear from you,

Yours truly,
C............H.

HOLLY GROVE, ARK.,
Feby. 28th, 1920.

Box 48,

Kingsville, Ontario.

The mallard drake on which you placed the aluminum tag bearing the following inscription on one side, "Write Box 48, Kingsville, Ontario," and on the other side, "With God all things are possible, Mark 10: 27," was killed near this place a few days ago. We had notice put in the Arks. *Democrat*, published in Little Rock, Arks.

About the 1st of October of each year these ducks begin to come into this country, and they feed on rice and acorns and other seeds. Some years they are very numerous. We also have a few geese. They begin to go away from now on to the latter part of March. None remains except those which have been wounded too badly to make the long flight.

Will you please write me when you put the tag on this duck, and how old was he when you put it on? Do they stay in your country during the summer months? Write me any information concerning them.

Several years ago what we called the Sandhill Cranes came over here in large flocks, passing further south. I never saw but one light. It was about six feet tall, and was a brownish color. They have not flown over for several years. Do they belong to your country; if so, what has become of them?

Very truly,
T. G. TRICE.

Then a lady from the South gives a laughable account of what happened down there over one of the colored preachers getting a message in this most unexpected way:

Dear Mr. Miner,—

I think you will be interested in knowing about some of your geese and ducks. While I was in Mississippi last winter I visited in Louisiana and Arkansas. Along the last of November some of the negroes on the plantation went over on the sandbar to hunt for wild geese, and they got several ducks and two big grey geese, and on one of the legs was a tin tag with a Bible inscription on it. The old darky that happened to get it was a great preacher; could not read a word, but was gifted with lots of gab and exhorted quite a lot. He thought the message came down from heaven and they had quite a revival over it. I heard him one night and he said: "This am the message of the Lord. I saw Him descending with this fowl in His arms, and it flew right at me. And now am the Judgment coming, and we are the elected, and am going straight to His arms."

I don't remember just what verse it was, but I remember it was your address and think perhaps this will interest you.

Yours truly,

. . . .

The following are the names and post office addresses given me of each person who has killed or reported the ducks. And fully seventy-five per cent. of the tags reported have been returned and are in my possession.

IN CANADA

Alberta.—Arch. S. Coutts, Earlie.
F. A. Rispler, Lac la Biche.
Sam M. Englehart, Shorter

Manitoba.—T. H. P. Lamb, Moose Lake.
Theodore Dupus, Moose Creek.

Ontario.—W. S. Falls, Amherstburg.
F. C. Clarkson, Toronto.
A. Chaphus, Windsor.
Henry Smith, Walpole Island.
Thomas Moore, Amherstburg.
Alexander Moore, Amherstburg.
Mrs. Alfred Bratt, North Malden.
Harry Whitsell, Erieau.

Dr. Rutherford, Chatham.
John Harris, Kingsville.
E. O. Scratch, Kingsville.
William Scratch, Kingsville.
Franklin L. Warner, Fort Francis

Quebec.— Dr. L. P. Legendre, Ste. Croix.

Saskatchewan.—H. J. Koep, Englefeld.
S. W. Brooks, Humboldt.
Peter Sandstrom, Dubuc.

IN UNITED STATES

Alabama.—Henry Grayson, Ararat.
Edward J. Bangle, Mobile.
J. N. Wi nn, Florence.
Dr. S. C. Frederic, Mobile.
Hennan Schnur, Decatur.
Herman Putman, Point Rock.
Mose Harris, Madison.
Ottis Denson, Cullman.
J. H. Clerkler, Clanton.
J. E. Duskin, Montgomery.

Arkansas.—W. O. Sims, Manila.
Robert White, Holly Grove.
J. C. Cox, McGehee.
T. G. Trice, Holly Grove.

Delaware.—Ira Brittingham, Texas.
J. H. Griffith, Helena.
Irvin Clautte, Ulm.
A. E. Nuckolls, Higginson

Florida.—Walter Huff.

Georgia.—T. H. Clark, Milledgeville.
Miles A. Dolphus, Oconee.
R. C. Balfour, Thomasville.

Illinois.—E. G. Baxton, Pleasant, Pike Co.
R. R. Banta, Oquawka.
Jerry M. Lashbrook, Beardstown.
Edward Sholm, Peru.
Rev. Chas. Vandettum, Bushell.

James Walls, Elizabethtown.
Catharine Hobbs, Golconda.
Richard Hess, Elizabethtown.
Charles Johnson, Shawmetown.
M. E. Caire, Streaton.
Frank O. Ekard, Puttman.

Indiana.—Dr. J. L. Axby, Lawrenceburg.
Clarence Carter, Memphis.
Percy R. Gordon, Shelbyville.
Mrs. Andrew Brauman, Leconia
Roy Wellman, Michigan City.
E. R. Kemp, Evansville.
James Trautween, Evansville.
Charlie Frederick, Jeffersonville
James Walls, Evansville.
Clyde Likens, Garrett.

Iowa.—James Jarvis, Redding.

Louisiana.—R. C. Boisseau, Shevelport
D. P. Hysnel, New Orleans.
Eli Guidry, Gueydan.
R. J. Leblans, Baton Rouge.
Fred Frontenot, Washington
Mrs. L. DeJean, Opelousas.
Herman Hall, New Orleans.
H. W. Kofman, New Orleans
Jack Sims, New Orleans.
Abras Sonnier, Holmwood.
Jos. Zaunbrecher, Branch.

Kansas—Peter Miller, Halstead

Kentucky.—Mary Smoot, Owentown.
　　Edward J. Volz, Louisville.
　　Clyde Spencer, Frankfort.
　　Noah Smith, Paris.
　　Leonard Carson, Lebanon.
　　Neal T. Brisin, Westport.
　　H. B. Ogden, Sanders.
　　Miss Ohal M. Jennings, Louisville.
　　J. J. Oerther, Frankfort.
　　Floyd Standfield, Cowan.
　　Harry Porter Hightown, Beneco.
　　Floid Standfield, Paris.
　　J. M. Grubbs, Danville.
　　Hollie Peavler, Harrodsburg.
　　H. M. Wood, Louisville.
　　Lewis Davis, Hardinsburg.
　　J. C. Waite, Simerset.
　　Wm. Gatewood, Jr., Stamping
　　　Ground.
　　J. R. Francis, Providence.
　　Omar D. Arvin, Pembroke.
　　Al. Smith, Halstead.
　　James Chipman, Elliston.

Maryland.—John L. Bradshaw, Tylerton.
　　George B. Fowler, Lower Martboro.
　　Henry B. Price, Betterton.

Michigan.—Emory L. Ford, Detroit.
　　Geo. E. Bartlo, Detroit.
　　Charles LaPoint, Detroit.
　　Box 342, Grandy Ave., Detroit.
　　Vandes Gildersleeve, Rockwood.
　　D. M. Cummings, Rockwood.
　　James H. Quick, Rockwood.
　　J. C. Adams, Munich.
　　N. Rugee White, Grand Rapids.
　　Geo. W. Francisco, Newport.
　　Mr. Blank, Sault Ste. Marie.
　　James B. O'Donnell, St. James.
　　A. T. Story, Rockwood.

Minnesota.—William Gibson, Breckenridge.
　　Mrs. B. E. Kocher, Brainerd.
　　M. H. Carstens, Glencoe.
　　E. J. Houle, Hugo.
　　H. T. Wadtke, Zimmerman

Mississippi.—J. C. Miller, Smithsville.
　　Chas. Dunlap, Rosedac.
　　Tom Galliday, Bew Springs.
　　Homer J. Williams, Jackson.
　　H. H. Peason, Cedar Bluff.
　　R. E. Ramsey, Ellisville.
　　Dr. W. Sumrall, Balzoni.
　　J. P. Jones, Tar Lake.
　　Levi Marrow, Natchey.

Missouri.—D. B. Ashbrook, Carrollton.
　　G. E. Adcock, Boekerton.
　　Dorin F. Winters, Bragg City.
　　John W. Sawyer, Caruthersville.

Montana.—J. L. Dellart, Helena.

New Jersey.—Fred W. Meerbolt, Secaucus.
　　Willis T. Johnson, Lakewood.

New York.—F. A. Haughey, Watkins.
　　W. de F. Hayes, Long Island.
　　Clyde Koonee, Trenton.

North Carolina.—A. B. Wallace, Belhmen.
　　W. M. Webb, Morehead.
　　J. C. Parker, Vernora.
　　Clyde Koomer, Trenton.
　　W. H. Carter, Mocksville.
　　W. C. Wozelka, Smithville.
　　James Factor, Lidgewood.

North Dakota.—Walter Shield, Carrington
　　John B. Schneider, Fredonia.
　　E. G. Erbe, Bismarck.
　　Arthur Larson, St. Thomas.
　　James W. Factor, Sidgewood.

Ohio.—August Holstein, Columbus.
　　J. O. H. Denny, Fremont.
　　Lewis B. Erwin, Erwin.
　　Chas. Gibbs, Genoa.
　　Miss Flora Lambert, Orient.
　　Bill Pompard, Point Place (2 ducks)
　　R. I. Cox, Portsmouth.
　　E. H. Mack, Sandusky.
　　W. A. Beverley, Celina.
　　David Stout, Circleville.
　　Earle Moore, Seckiton.
　　Harry Smith, Greenville.
　　John H. Wright, Port Clinton.
　　K. B. Brown, Amanda.

Pennsylvania.—Marleah Moulton, Frankhannock.
　　Clarence Hibber, Richie.

South Carolina.—L. A. Beckman, Santee.
　　W. E. Bray, Anderson.
　　H. G. Leiding, Charleston.
　　W. F. Gaylord, Fountain Inn.
　　Bernard M. Baruch, Georgetown.
　　Eugene DuPont, Georgetown.
　　S. S. Owens, Hawthorne.

South Dakota.—Ben Hilderbrant, Crandall.
　　Olaf Jargenson, Hurley.

Tennessee.—John V. Thomas, Chattanooga
　　R. E. Lewis, Sale Creek.
　　Lance McAllie, Birchwood.
　　Harry Stamps, Cooksville.
　　W. P. Ray, Cooksville.
　　G. H. Elrod, Shelbyville.
　　Mack Stewart, Martha.
　　John Fite Robertson, Lebanon.
　　Johnson Little, Gates.
　　Forest M. Bell, La Vergue.

Texas.—J. Lewis Thompson, Houston.

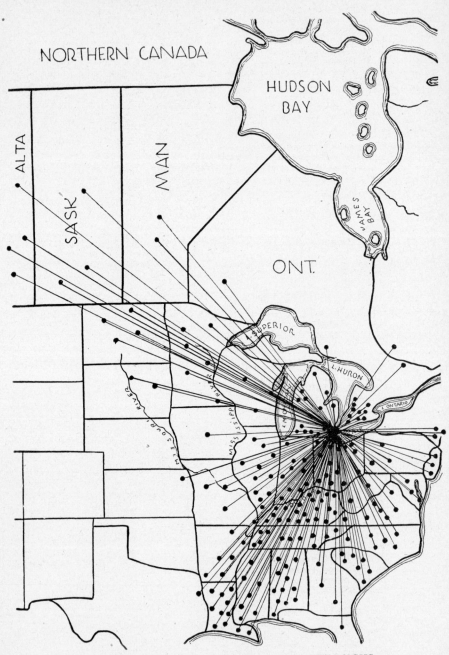

MAP SHOWING THE MIGRATION OF THE DUCKS

Virginia.—Rev. Albert P. Dixon, Williams-
ville.
C. S. Lawson, Saluda.
C. W. Waller, Martinsville.
Robt. J. Dunn, Sweet Hall.
Mrs. Sarah Burgess, South Norfolk.
Nelson Stokes, Fort Royal.
Will Ritter, Berryville, Winchester.

West Virginia.—Corporal John I. Smith,
Ravenswood.
Howard Haddox, Mahone

Wisconsin.—E. P. Gallaway, Fond-du-Lac.
Miss Hedwig Hener, Larson.
Geo. F. Bishop, Elk Mound.

The foregoing names are written as correctly as I can give them, as some of the signatures were quite a puzzle. However, the map will explain to you the migration of these ducks, as the round dots on the map, indicating where each duck was killed, will help you out.

The straight line leading from Kingsville to each of these dots does not prove that the duck followed that course For illustration, the two ducks that were killed in Alberta and Saskatchewan in the fall of 1917 left here with a flock of other ducks in the fall of 1916, and some of the bunch were killed in Georgia, Alabama and Louisiana. The lines are drawn simply to help you out; also to prove to your entire satisfaction that Kingsville, Ontario, is the hub of America.

I have only one request to make of the reader. That is: In case you call one of these men up, or write him, and get no reply, do not give up, but get after the other fellow, until you find out for yourself that the above are all facts.

CHAPTER XXII.

Can Birds Smell?

THIS is a thought that all bird lovers will come face to face with, sooner or later, and though we may not be able to steal bases like Ty Cobb, yet if we study the *game* and watch the *fowls*, *balls* of interest are sure to *fly* our way. There are very few people living in the country that haven't seen crows make some queer manœuvres when they are hunting food.

One hot July day, many years ago, as brother and I were nearing the house for dinner, one of these old black murderers went quietly flying across the road about two hundred feet east of my house. When about three rods in the field he gave a very sudden right-about-face curve, and hovered for about a second, then started stroking the air back to the fence. Dropping on the top rail he did not even take time to look around, but instantly jumped down among the thick growth of goldenrod, which was nearly as high as the fence. That instant my bare feet started throwing dust, and in less time than it is taking me to write it I had the gun and was pushing two loads of number six in the barrels as I ran to meet him. I got there just in time to draw one long breath, and as he came flapping up up out of the weeds he uttered a gurgling "Caw!" at my red face which was smiling all along the gun barrels, and his body dropped beside the road, but a great portion of his feathers floated away on the air. As we picked him up, four unhatched song sparrows spewed out of his mouth.

On investigation we found an old stump lying on its side in the fence corner; two projecting roots and its top held the middle about six inches off the ground; and right under there, nestled away in the dry, and perfectly out of sight, was this empty song sparrow's nest.

As the old birds were chirping around near us a real loud argument took place between brother and me as to how the crow located this nest. Brother's first question was, "Jack, didn't you know that birds could smell?" As I laughed he said, "What did you think their nostrils were made for?"

He insisted that this old ground-bird, as we call them, had been setting close all morning, and now, just at the heat of the day, the eggs had become too warm and sweaty; the mother had just gotten off to air them as Mr. Crow came flying over, and that the crow did smell the eggs.

I put up such an argument it apparently got on brother's nerves. He said, "Just you wait a minute," and he stepped out into the field and picked up a flat stone about eight inches in diameter, putting it on the stump just above the nest. Then he took a small handful of punk and placed it firmly on the stone. As the day was extremely hot it only required the least touch of a match and he had a smudge started; and sure enough, as the smoke rose in the air it floated to the exact spot where the crow was when he turned so suddenly. "Now," said brother, "are you satisfied?" and he took the stone, with the punk on it, away from the fence and put the fire out. But still we have no proof that the crow smelled the eggs. Yet we were absolutely sure that he could not, and did not, see them until after he dropped off the fence into the weeds.

Since that I have time and again noticed crows and bronze grackles locate birds' eggs where I know they cannot see them.

But I think the turkey buzzard furnishes us the most convincing proof of birds using their nostrils to locate their food, for we actually know that they will come for miles and miles, not to carrion, but to freshly killed beef.

Now here is a fact for you to analyze: One Sunday morning last June I got up at the week-day hour and took a stroll back to the north pond. For some unaccountable reason I forgot to take feed to the family of young pet ducks that were about four weeks old. When I arrived they all came scudding over the water to me. I had no feed so I picked up a little coarse earth and threw it out into the pond, and all went after it; as they rushed out I ran away and came, by a roundabout way, back to the house, first coming about four hundred feet across newly-cultivated earth where I had trees set out six feet apart; then I came out on the ball-ground and made a crooked path for fully three hundred feet in the dewy grass. As I neared the house I stopped for a few minutes looking at the climbing roses and listening to the birds, when I heard young ducks peeping. Looking up, behold you! here were the little pets following the same trail across the ball park. The sun was just high enough for me to see the path very plainly in the dew, and these toddlers did not vary a foot, but came, in single file, right up within twenty feet before they saw me. I then got some food and they followed me back to their old stepmother who was waiting in her coop for them. I then went and found that these little hungry pets had knocked dust in my tracks all though the cultivated grove. In other words, they had followed every step of my trail to where they overtook me.

On another occasion I had two young pet silver pheasants, and in

March, 1909, I went into the little park and forgot to shut the gate; then, instead of coming back through it I jumped over the brick wall to the north and went right on to my work which was at that time laying drain tile at the extreme north side of the farm, fully three-quarters of a mile from the park. In going there I had to pass through thirty acres of woods, where I visited three weasel traps; therefore I did not go in a straight course. I left home about seven o'clock. At nine, as I was working with my head down, I heard familiar sounds; looking up, here were my two pet silver pheasants pecking the earth beside me. They stayed there until eleven thirty, then both followed me back home just like two puppies, for their wings were pinioned and they could not fly four feet, and never could, as this was done when they were very small. They were about ten months old. There was not a bit of snow on the ground and the weather was quite warm.

Now these are only a few of the hundreds of convincing facts I have personally observed which compel me to believe that birds can smell. I have no positive proof that they can. But I know they can smell, just as much as I know they can hear.

I will tell you how to prove it to your own satisfaction. When it is snowing, take a piece of fresh meat that is cold, and lay it down in the centre of a field. Let it snow under, and if there are crows around see how quickly they will find it! Or if you are in the northern country, throw a piece of meat into the snow and let it drift under; the next morning watch the jay locate it. I refer to the snow because it is the best natural cover on earth and will give the fairest test, but if you are where there is no snow to try it out, just take some chaff, straw, or sawdust and cover your bait with that.

Now I will not say that a crow or blackbird will smell cold birds'-eggs, but if the eggs are warm and sweaty I know that these cannibal birds will locate the nest by the use of their nostrils. "Well," you say, "that cannot be; there was a crow came right up to the barn while I was in there." Yes, but remember he was accustomed to you being around there. Go to the woods where this same crow has been shot at, and see how close you will get to him if the wind is in his favor. The great trouble with the majority of us human beings is that we are too slow to observe.

I once saw a man run bang into a stone wall; his excuse was that he did not see it. When I was a boy in Ohio I went with an Englishman to dig out a rabbit. When we got near the end of the hole Old Jack, as we called him, dropped on his side and ran his arm right in, clear up to his shoulder. I was of course peeking very closely, to see the rabbit, but the instant I saw him pulling out black and white fur I retreated backwards over a pile of loose sand, looking back just in time to see Old Jack get it right in the eyes. And say! he came bounding out of that cavity without being urged, snorting, sneezing and coughing, and with his long hair thoroughly powdered with yellow sand—and something worse. He went here and there and all over at the same moment, trying to gather all the snow in the country in each hand to wash his eyes out with. I was of course all alone and had to conceal my joy. My joy however did not last long, for this poor fellow nearly strangled to death and it was fully fifteen minutes before he could speak; but finally, looking up at me with his eyes and face all apparently washed into one red blister he chokingly said, "Jack, Hi didn't smell the beggar till hafter Hi 'ad 'im by the toyle."

CHAPTER XXIII.

The Canada Goose.

NOW I have told you that by protecting the one swallow's nest at our tile shed there were twenty-five nests the fifth year; and how the sweet bluebird became so well acquainted with the members of our family as to permit us to remove the roof of her house while she would sit there within eight inches of our eyebrows, with her beautiful head turned sidewise looking us square in the eyes, and then permit us to put the cover back on, and she would not fly out. I have explained how the robins fairly swarmed around our home when there was neither shrubbery nor fruit to attract them there, and how the purple martins folded their wings and came down out of the heavens, warbling their songs as they descended, the very first day we had their home erected. But these truths are simple compared with the facts contained in this chapter.

Some one has said "the silly old goose." This, to my mind, is one of the many demonstrations of how a man's mouth can go off empty. For the facts are that our Canada goose has a great amount of knowledge, and many qualifications that the human race could well afford to profit by; and although I was born under the protection of the American eagle's wings, and respect him in every way, never shooting one in my life (though I scared one to death!) yet when you speak of our Canada goose, this bird is one of the most intelligent, self-sacrificing creatures on earth, and as for purity of character he has gotten the human race backed right off the boulevard into the slums, and no person on earth can study him without profiting by it. Personally, there has been many a time during the last ten years of my life when I have felt like raising my hat to the clean, gentlemanly principles exposed by one of these old ganders.

Now the question is, how did I become so well acquainted with them?

Well, about thirty years ago a few wild geese (as we call them) were alighting on a sort of prairie then known as Cottar. _ _ains, which is about four miles due north of my home. As I was a noted hunter several persons spoke to me about going out to shoot these geese, as no one had apparently been able to kill one. At length one hunter came to me in dead earnest. "Jack," he said, "you want to

THE CANADA GOOSE

To get the effect of this picture, hold the book above your head, as the Goose was, above mine, when I took the photograph

get out there and try them.   They come nearly every day.   They are old lunkers; I believe the old ganders will weigh twenty-five pounds." I enquired how many there were and he said, "Fifteen; seven in one flock and eight in another." As I stood, thinking it over, I said to this man, "If one flock is there, will the other bunch go and alight with them?" "Yes," he replied in a loud voice; "every time."

Well that day I went home, took the axe and chopped out the bodies of three wooden wild geese decoys; then I used a drawing-knife for the rest of the work; finally I had three geese standing on one leg in our back yard—one leg each of course.   And I had everybody who saw them laughing at me.   What color should I paint them, was the puzzle.   I had never been close enough to a wild goose to know anything about his color; I couldn't tell from hearing their faint "Honk!"   I finally decided to paint their breasts light and the rest a slate color.   The neighbors still kept laughing.   Then when there were no persons around I would practise the "Honk!" till the echoes from the buildings sounded something like it.

One morning, about two o'clock, my brother-in-law and I hooked up the Old Reliable and, believe me, we had some load in that old phaeton buggy, the three blocks of wood, a spade, blanket and lantern.   Away we went.   Fortunately when we got there the soft ground was frozen just enough to hold us up, so we took the lantern and scoured the fields for tracks.   Finally we found goose-prints in an old, partly drowned-out corn field which was adjoined by a field of fall wheat, no fence in sight.   It was evident that the geese lit on the wheat and then walked into the corn stubbles.   Here we selected our site.   Standing these three decoys on the wheat, I dug myself in on the edge of the corn field.   I say dug myself in, but not much, as the water was close to the surface; so I dug a coffin-like cavity about six inches deep and covered myself with a blanket which was, of course, the exact color of the ground.   Three corners of the blanket were staked and tied fast, arranged to cover this muddy coffin.   Then I gathered weeds and so forth and lined this grave to keep me out of the mud.

At the faintest sign of day the other fellow took the old horse and all the rest of our junk and drove fully half a mile away.   At last, just before sunrise my eyes caught a dark streak in the sky, away to the south.   So I examined the old gun, which was loaded with swanshot, lay down on my back in this bog hole, covering myself with the blanket and holding it firmly with my left hand with the gun in my right.   There I lay with just my eyes out, my heart almost beating the ground into a pulp.   It seemed so long I thought I must have been mistaken; they couldn't have been wild geese.   I quietly called, twice, "A-honk! A-honk!" Just then I heard a low reply to the east of me. Rolling my eye in that direction, here were the eight geese going quartering by. So I gave another low "A-honk!" and to my delight they turned and saw the decoys, answering as they bowed their wings to alight with them.

But the keen eyes of this old gander detected that they were false. Fortunately for me when he shied from the decoys he swung my way, and just when they got in the right place I threw the blanket off with my left hand; raising the gun and my body at the same time I fired, sitting down. At the first shot the leader crumpled up with fourteen swanshot driven almost through him, and his mate started to follow long before he struck the frozen earth, leaving two distinct puffs of feathers floating away on the frosty air, the six young screaming, and darting in all directions for their lives away from their fallen parents. They went screaming back in the direction from which they came.

As soon as my chum arrived we had a good laugh when we looked at the decoys and the real geese. We soon loaded all up and could hardly get home quick enough to repaint those blocks of wood. Then they looked O.K., and fooled many a goose after that. But the weight of these geese was far from twenty-five pounds, the gander weighing exactly ten pounds and his mate one pound less.

I hunted geese every spring from then on, but they soon got wise and moved their stopping place about eight miles west to what was then called Walker's Marsh. I even followed them up there and secured an odd one now and then. I never killed over six in one season. This will give you an idea of how scarce they were in this part.

But it wasn't until 1903 that I really tumbled to see the depth of the Canada goose. In March I saw a family of six passing my house. I felt sure they were feeding on Cottam Plains, so the next morning found me out there with a lantern searching for their tracks, and long before the last stars had closed their eyes I had five decoys out and the blanket staked down, ready for action. But it seemed they weren't coming.

The sun is just high enough to be making golden windows in the distant houses to the west of me when I look to the south and a short, dark line appears in the sky. It is geese, sure; and they are coming straight this way.

Just as I am crawling under I see, to my disgust, two men coming out to ditch, right on the next farm; my heart sinks, as they will scare them away. But on and on come the geese. I can now see them plainly, and begin to hear their long-drawn-out safety notes, "A-h-k! A-h-k!" Imagine my delight when I see them come right on past these men, heading straight for me.

As they come over the field that I am in, a call comes from under the blanket, "A-honk!" and the old leader replies, turning my way. Seeing the decoys, they all bow their wings and drop their black feet to come down.   But just before they get in range of my deadly aim, this cunning old father's voice suddenly rings out on the morning air, "Khonk! Khonk! Khonk! Khonk!" These sharp, alarming danger-cries are given in rapid succession, and every goose darts for his life.   Their terrified cries can hardly be described.   They finally fall in line again and fly back towards the lake.

That morning I was all alone and as I urged the driver along I was doing some tall thinking.   And really I felt like a one-cent piece coming home from Klondyke!   Here were my thoughts: Why did he pass right over, within shooting range of these two men, and then shy before he got that close to me?   Moreover, why were they so dreadfully frightened?   Possibly because he saw one red hair of my topknot projecting from under that blanket and, to his sorrow, he had seen that fellow before. "That's our deadly enemy!   Everybody get, for your lives!" were the cries he uttered.

Well, these thoughts presented themselves to me in this way: He does know me.   And these are some of the same geese that come around here every spring, for they frequent the same places.   To be frank, I studied wild geese until I felt like flying.   Surely they must be the same geese.   They do know me as their enemy.   No man on earth knows their cunningness and depth.   If they know me as their enemy, surely they would know a friend if they had one. But what can I do?   I own only ten acres of land, and it is very much disfigured by taking about three feet of the surface off for making drain-tile and brick.   But I will try.

So I called the neighbors (mostly boys) together and told them if they would not shoot at a wild goose around here I would bring some right to that place and we would shoot a limited number when the opportunity was right.   This seemed too good to be true, as only one of them had ever shot a wild goose, and all jumped at the scheme.

I graded up a bank at the far side of this sore-eye ten acres, making, not a pond, but a mud-hole.   Then I bought seven wing-clipped Canada geese from an old gentleman who had trapped them unlawfully, put them back in this cavity and fed them there.   They soon became quite tame and interesting.   This was in the spring of 1904.   The seven geese got so they roamed all over the ten acres, making this mud-hole their home; but no wild ones ever came.   In 1905 none came; 1906 brought the same result; and even 1907 came, but no geese.   And really I was the mark of the neighborhood;

the questions I was asked would surely jar the cherries on Aunt Sarah's Sunday bonnet.

But April the second, 1908, was my innings, for the whole neighborhood was aroused long before breakfast. "The geese have come! the geese have come! Jack said they would come!" and everybody had a gun.

Now I was face to face with another serious problem, but all listened to me as I explained that if we did not shoot at them until they got settled down and made this their spring home, the ones we did not kill would return next spring and surely bring more with them. Every hunter was very reasonable, and, after having a quiet chat, each took his gun back home. In about three weeks I hoisted the signal and every one was on deck. I believe I was the biggest boy of the bunch. All of us went over to the tile factory and watched these eleven geese from the upstair window until the goose fever got a few notches higher than our nerves. Then we all came down and marched up behind the embankment. "Now," I said, "don't shoot at them sitting, or you will hit my tame ones." Then I said, "Cock your guns," and I gave an alarming "Honk!" and that instant every one of the eleven geese was in the air, and "Bang! Bangety! Bang!" went the eight guns into them. When the soft coal smoke had finally cleared away, five geese lay dead on the muddy water. The other six, screaming with fright, flew away to the lake.

Now how fortunate this was for me: The eight guns came from five homes, and thus each home had a good fat goose for the oven. And all was going well so far.

I did not expect to see these geese come back until another spring, but to my surprise in about two hours they were circling high in the air and honking for their lost companions. Finally they went away again, but the next morning they were back, bright and early, and to my great satisfaction they lit and fed with mine, and it was surprising how soon they quieted down. I asked the neighbors not to shoot at them again that spring, and all kindly agreed.

Then came a whole lot more fun for the public. "Jack Miner is not going to shoot those six geese; he says they will come back next spring!" Really this furnished fun for a great percentage of the community. One old gentleman told me how his great-uncle Dave killed 'steen wild geese before breakfast; and this dear old gentleman's white hair just shook as he explained the points, how to clean right up on this six, and not one could get away if his plans were carried out. Why, bless your life, they had gotten so tame I honestly believe I could have killed them with a fishing pole. Yet of course

I respected his grey hairs enough not to interfere with his trembling thoughts.

One morning about May 1st, they rose up and circled higher and higher, and started straight north.

It was not until the next spring that the flood of sneering questions poured in upon me! "Jack, when do you expect the six geese to return?" And another smart fellow said, "Jack, which direction will they come from?" But feeling confident I would be able to laugh last I just gritted my teeth inwardly, and smiled from the outside, and answered as kindly as I possibly could. I only remember answering one fellow short. He said, "Jack, when are the geese coming." I said, "Likely they will come when they get ready."

Sunday morning, March 18th, 1909, the ground was frozen as hard as Pharaoh's heart. I was out watering our self-starter. While she was drinking out of the trough I was putting in the time talking to my pet geese which were not over thirty yards away. All at once they all started honking at the very top of their voices and acting extremely strange; but in spite of their chatter, when I pricked up my ears I could hear strange geese honking, and looking over my right shoulder I saw something that caused my heart to fairly jump. Here was a string of Canada geese, with wings bowed, coming right towards me. Finally they dropped their black feet and lit on the ground, some of them not over twenty-five yards from where I was standing, and I had the great pleasure of seeing these wild geese dance and flap their wings with joy as they honked aloud to each other, apparently introducing their families and friends. I fully expected to see them fly away at any instant, but no. As they saw me, the leader spoke quite sharply, and all was as still as night in a graveyard, with their eyes rivetted right on me. But they were quiet for only a few seconds; then they honked louder than ever, and our geese flapped their wings and shouted, apparently for joy.

Well I finally withdrew, coming away as slowly as a pall-bearer waiting to cross on the Detroit-Windsor bridge. I put the old nag in the shafts and we went to church; but for all the good that sermon did me, I might as well have stayed home. He evidently preached from somewhere between "Generations and Revolutions" but you could not prove it by me. All I could think about were these twenty-six Canada geese that the six had brought back with them, thirty-two all told. Best of all, it was my turn to laugh, and I wanted to get back home to give vent to my feelings, and as soon as the benediction was pronounced I was the first one out the door, got into our machine, and, believe me, we went home in high.

On or about April 12th I had the photographer out and the accompanying photograph taken.

THIS PHOTOGRAPH SHOWS THE TOTAL FLOCK OF GEESE IN 1909, INCLUDING TWELVE OR SIXTEEN OF OUR OWN, ALSO, A FEW DUCKS

THE FLOCK OF WILD GEESE, 1910

This photograph was taken after we had shot the twenty-six.

A day or so later I gave the signal and the gunners all came. We shot ten and let twenty-two go. And on May 1st they all circled high and took the airline Hudson Bay Limited.

That year did not bring me quite so many inquiries. One interested man asked how many I thought would come next spring; I said, "Possibly sixty or seventy-five." He said, "Is that so?" I replied, "I don't know." But on March 4th, 1910, they started coming again, and for two weeks the flock kept getting larger until there were over four hundred. We shot twenty-six and allowed the rest to go north, although we could just as easily have shot two hundred. But before they left I was fortunate in getting this picture, which gives you a glimpse of what game protection will do. Do not kill all you can but "Let the mother go, that it may be well with thee, and that thou mayest prolong thy days."

The last contingent left April 27th. By the way, this is the earliest we ever knew the last of them to leave.

Right here I wish to make an explanation, that although we shot twenty-six, they were not all eaten by us shooters, but were given around to our nearest neighbors.

On February 20th, 1911, they started coming from the South again, and in less than three weeks there was a small cloud of them. Really I did not know there were so many Canada geese on earth.

As I have previously stated, my home is three miles north of Lake Erie, and these geese most always go to the lake for the night; and at times when the first bunch would be alighting in and around the ponds at my home, you could not see the south end of the string of them, coming.

Now I faced another problem: Where was the feed coming from? Very true, I have made a little park just west of my house and have graded out a pond one hundred and ten feet in diameter; yet this does not furnish them with feed. So I quit feeding them in what we now call the north pond, and just fed in the park, thinking the wilder ones would go on and that only the old acquaintances would come to the house. But that did not work out very satisfactorily; they were bound to make my home their home.

One morning we neighbors were shooting a few at the north pond. We shot into a family of five. I shouted "Don't shoot, boys, they are too far off," but the words were too late. The bangs of the guns were the only reply I heard, and two geese fell dead; one extremely large gander fell with a broken pinion; the other two flew away to the lake. At my request the boys gave me the big gander. I took him to the house and performed a surgical operation on him, myself. I first tied the severed arteries with strong linen thread, then cut the end of the wing right off and let him go in the park. In

SPRING, 1911

The earth, the water and the heavens were literally alive with geese the fourth year. The photograph, of course, shows only part of the flock of geese. Drain tile and brick manufacturing plant is in the rear.

about an hour the other two geese came back, circling very high. By this time there were fully one thousand geese around the premises; all seemed to be honking to bring them down. Finally they circled over the park and this big, broken-pinioned fellow gave a honk, and instantly they answered and started to lower, making the air fairly hum as they descended. They lit near the house, with their wounded brother. To be brief, on May 2nd, the goose migrated with the big flock, but the big gander never left his broken-pinioned brother. Really it was one of the most self-sacrificing sights of my life to see this big gander give up all his liberties of this North American continent, and voluntarily live in captivity with his brother. We named them David and Jonathan.

DAVID AND JONATHAN

Dear old Jonathan! How he would get David to back clear across the pond, then run against the wind and try to fly! Yes I have seen this happen fully twenty times a day; Jonathan would fly across the pond, but when he saw his brother David was not coming he would alight and swim back to him. This sight took the desire to shoot out of most of my neighbors, and there has not been a goose shot on my premises since.

When fall came we thought possibly Jonathan might go South, but no; neither our cold zero winters, nor the extremely hot summers could drive him from his brother.

Jonathan's noble ways soon won the admiration of every visitor that came on our premises. While David was one of the heaviest wild geese I have ever seen, Jonathan stood a little taller, but not quite so heavy-set. He was very powerful and active; more so than any goose we have on the premises. Having both wings to defend himself with he always faced an approaching enemy. They lived together in the park for seven years, but sad to say, in January, 1918, one morning when I looked out the window, here was dear old Jonathan lying dead on the snow near the centre of the pond where they aways roosted. The hand-writing on the snow told the story. A great horned owl had attacked them in the night. The other eight or ten wing-clipped geese, including David, had run under the evergreens and shrubs. Jonathan, having both wings, gave the enemy battle, but being handicapped in the darkness, the owl sunk his grappling-hooks into Jonathan's head and put his eyes

THE DEATH OF JONATHAN

out, killed him and ate his neck off right at the breast bone, drew some of his entrails and ate them. Useless to say we all felt sad, and the telephone rang time and again that day, "Is it true an owl killed old Jonathan?" "Yes." And with a sigh they would hang the receiver up.

But I was determined to avenge his death. The other geese did not come out that day. When night came I concealed a trap in dead Jonathan's feathers, as I knew this murderer would come back. And the next morning this bird-eating devil was fast. Really I could have burned that owl at the stake with a good heart.

In 1912, owing to the weather being very cold and snowy, the geese did not come until March 16th.

In 1913 they came on March 10th. On Good Friday of the last-mentioned year the wind blew a perfect gale, and there was a five-acre field full of geese here, as thick as in any picture shown with the exception of the one where the ladies have driven them into a huddle. A piece of sheet iron blew off the engine room at the tile factory and rolled end over end until it struck the wire fence that enclosed the goose field. Every bird screamed and took flight, going with the wind. When they were about a half mile away they turned to come back, but this iron was bright on one side and they could see it. There they stood, floating in the air. Only we older people that have seen the clouds of passenger pigeons, back in the seventies, have any idea of what this skyfull of geese looked like. I stood and looked at them for a few minutes. Then I went and took the tin and rolled it up. This took me two or three minutes, as the tin and the wind were both stubborn. All at once I heard "Honk!" and behold, here were these thousands of geese alighting in the field again, some within one hundred feet of me. I finally took the roll of tin or sheet iron back to the buildings. Stopping on my way to rest and glancing back at the wild geese I was fully convinced that they knew me from a piece of sheet iron, for by this time they were all on the ground again, lying down facing the wind, and were equally as thick over all that five-acre field as they are shown in any one of the accompanying photographs.

Another advantage comes with the wild birds: There is always something new cropping up.

In the winter of 1909-10 I had eleven of my own, pinioned, wild geese. And as we youngsters wanted the ice good and clean in the park for skating, I turned the geese out and they were living over the fence, to the north. One stormy, cold day, as they were sitting in the lee of the tile factory buildings, two big American eagles attacked them. I ran in the house and grabbed my high-powered rifle in one hand and three or four cartridges in the other; out and down the road I went, just as fast as my moccasined feet would carry me. Soon I had gotten into the south end of the shed without being observed by the eagles. I at once ran upstairs, and went quickly but quietly, and fortunately to help muffle the sound of my moccasins, a little snow had drifted in on the shed floor. Soon I was at the north end.

Peeping through a crack in the side, I saw a sight that to me was beautiful, and I only wish I could give you the picture. For here, upon the crusty snow, were these two big, bald eagles, one about ten feet in front of the geese, the other fully four rods away. But where was the old gander that we called Tom Johnson, and his opponent, whom I have seen fight for fully half an hour for supremacy

GEESE RISING FROM THE POND
Photograph taken from the public highway

of the premises? Had they run under the shed, or flunked in any way? No, no. The nine weaker geese had huddled together and could have been covered with an ordinary wagon-box; but Tom Johnson and this other powerful gander were standing shoulder to shoulder, right in the face of this monstrous eagle. As the eagle would walk a little, sidewise, on the crusty snow, the geese, with eyes rivetted upon him, were doing likewise. There wasn't a sound uttered, but it was a great sight to see these faithful, self-sacrificing old ganders at the head of their little bunch with their wings up, ready to strike, saying by their actions, "You must cut us down before you can have one of our loved ones."

There I stood for fully five minutes, with my nerves just tingling, at the highest tension. Finally I couldn't stand it any longer, and I slid the three cartridges into the magazine of the rifle and quietly worked the lever which threw one cartridge into the barrel. As the north slide door was about one inch open, I sneaked over there. If those eagles had touched a goose I would have knocked a hole in one big enough for a dog to jump through.

But good things always come to those who wait, and eventually the eagle farthest away turned her head sidewise and began to show signs of moving, which she did, but not towards the geese. She just simply squatted, opened up her broad, powerful wings, and with a few strokes she started straight west. In a few seconds the other turned half around, rose up against the wind, and followed. But the geese kept their eyes continually fixed on them as far as they could be seen.

Yes, they apparently settled by arbitration. When I saw how it turned out my heart bubbled over with more love than ever for these two beautiful birds, and as I started for the house I couldn't held but thank Almighty God for the Canada goose and the American eagle, and ask Him to hasten the day when this whole world mass of humanity will settle their differences as these lovely birds did on this occasion. As I took the cartridges out of the rifle and hung it on the gun rack, I caught myself singing the chorus of an old song my mother used to sing:

> "If I were Queen of France,
>   Much more the Pope of Rome,
> I would have no fighting men abroad
>   Nor weeping maids at home;
> All this world would be at peace,
>   Every king should have his rights,
> For I'd have them that make the quarrels
>   Be the only ones to fight."

Yes, such good lessons as this are continually darting at one who is on speaking terms with the Canada goose.

Some time ago I purchased a pair of Egyptian geese from a breeder in Illinois. As they have such beautiful plumage I thought they would add to the attractions around my home, but they turned out to be meaner and far more treacherous than stagnant ditch-water, continually hunting trouble with any creature whom they can dominate. November 14th, as I was out feeding the birds, they caught a wild duck and both piled in, and would have killed her in less than a minute only that a big wild Canada gander heard her squawk. He left his family, who were feeding, flew across the pond and with one blow from his powerful wings he knocked that Egyptian goose all but cold; the other Egyptian took the hint, just in time, giving the duck her liberty. And that Canada gentleman was back at his post in less than twenty seconds.

CHAPTER XXIV.

Nesting Canada Geese.

IN 1907, the third year I had my clipped Canadas, one pair nested, and every season since I have had one to three pairs raise young. This is the very time these old ganders especially expose their incomparable, clean, noble ways which even we human beings might well envy them.

One spring I had a painter from town out here brightening things up a little, so one day I told him to paint the cornice of the bird house, which is about seven feet high. I paid no more attention to him, but went on with my work at the tile factory, about three hundred feet away. All at once I heard a scream that was joined with language too loud to look well in print. I got out just in time to see this scared man come rolling over the brick wall, his legs and arms sticking up like odd sections in a Ferris-wheel. To see and hear him wrinkled my red face into a broader position; he came towards me with both torn shirt-sleeves fluttering in the wind and white paint dabbled on one leg of his trousers, without either hat, paint, pail or pipe. He began to reel it off. Then it all came to me in a flash that I had forgotten to tell him about the goose-nest that was concealed in the weeds near that spot. And now it was too late to give him any explanation, for really he did not know whether he was bitten or stung. While he was not hurt a particle, he was nearly frightened into fits, and he could not, or would not, believe there were only two geese there. I finally went and found his pipe, Christy hat and paint pail, but he never would go back in that enclosure, and worse still, I doubt if he has ever forgiven me as he thought I put up a job on him.

One picture would do for all the pairs of Canada geese I ever saw nesting. While the gander takes no part in building the nest nor setting, turn about, on the eggs, as some birds do, yet he is always guarding her and is never over two rods away, seeing all enemies before they do him. He will usually lie flat on the ground, his black neck and snake-like head straight out, and if any creature goes right on by, all is well; but should one note him and stop then he will suddenly jump on it from an unexpected quarter. His looks and hissing honks will almost frighten any other creature into decline, and while frightening is his chief defence, yet I know from personal experience how he can bite and hang on like a bull pup while he deals unbelievably heavy blows with the first joint of his powerful wings. The worst blow I ever got in my life was from an old gander that I caught to tag; he struck me on the jaw with the first joint of his doubled-up wings and believe me, I had the mumps for weeks.

While I have seen the goose run at a domestic fowl or so, yet she does not pretend to do much fighting. She usually leaves that

ON GUARD

This photograph shows a faithful gander guarding his sweetheart while nesting. He is telling me in plain goose language: "I don't care if you are Jack Miner. Don't you come one foot nearer or I will break your camera." And past experience caused me to take his word for it.

strenuous exercise for him, and depends on his protection; and well she may, for he never fails her. He will even leave his family and fight for her.

A pair once nested near the tile kiln and a collie dog attached this gander. The goose won out, but the dog bit the end of his backbone right off. I saw the blood running down his legs and in a few days I noticed he was always in the one place, lying down by his sweetheart. I went over and found he was sick and so weak he let me pick him up. I saw what was wrong, so I went and got the turpentine bottle and poured some in this decaying cavity and fully a spoonful of maggots rolled out. I then brought the dear old fellow water and food, but it was fully a week before he could stand up. He finally got well, and I still have him, but he was dying at his post. His name is Tom Johnson.

A GALLANT VETERAN

This photograph shows Tom Johnson guarding his mate as she turns the eggs. Note the disfigured tail feathers, which never grew in properly after his fight with the collie dog.

I never saw the wild geese go near where one of these pairs was nesting. So one spring I took fully ten bushels of corn and scattered it around near a nest. And the thousands of geese that came here would not combine their forces and go near, after the corn, or interfere with his preserve, but would prefer flying all over the country to feed where some of them are continually getting shot. This will explain to you how they respect each others' rights.

WITH THE LITTLE ONES BETWEEN

As soon as the young are hatched, the gander always guards them from the opposite side. In other words, if the young are west of her he will be west of them again, keeping the young between the parents. Note the roll of Tom Johnson's eye

CHAPTER XXV.

Our Model Canada Goose.

WHILE I am writing as plainly as I dare, yet I want you to keep an eye between the lines.

For two springs in succession, two pairs of my geese nested on the bank of the north pond, just one hundred and twenty feet apart, each gander always guarding and never going thirty feet away. An old goose I had in my flock apparently couldn't control nature and she went and built a nest on the bank right between these two pairs of geese, or about sixty feet from each nest. These ganders did not interfere with her in any way, shape, manner or form; but if an enemy approached her, both these ganders would leave home and would attack him with fury, while if you went near either of their nests, only the one would fight you; the other would stay at home. Both years every egg in their nests hatched, and the young were hearty and strong. This odd, or single, goose set for five weeks on four eggs the first year, and I let her set seven weeks on five eggs the second year. I broke every egg, and not one showed any sign of fertility. Remember, this is not almanac history; these are the facts, as I know them.

Do these geese inbreed? This is a question that apparently bothers a great percentage of us smart human beings, and often in the spring of the year when the geese are sitting around by the hundreds I hear this question asked by all sorts of visitors; I think this is chiefly because of the extreme uniformity of these birds both in size as well as in color.

I have tested this out sufficiently to satisfy all my curiosity. I went so far as to keep four full brothers and sisters in an inclosure by themselves for nearly three years, and they lived together as brothers and sisters only. But March the third year I heard the two geese giving love-sick cries and they kept fighting the wire towards where some wing-clipped ganders were. So I opened the gate and let them together, and inside of two weeks they paired off with these strange ganders.

A young goose will lay four eggs the first year, and usually five the second. After that I have had them lay as high as seven, but in their wild state I know they must lay as high as eight for I quite often see an unbroken family here with ten in it, eight young and the parents; but six is the average brood of young.

During my life I have often crept upon a deer or peeped over the top of a hill at a moose, and with the frosty air in my favor I have watched them fully three-quarters of an hour, or until I got froze out, just drinking in pure nature. Time and again I have taken a little twig in my fingers and cracked it, and I am sure the deer's hearing is at least three times as sharp as ours, or what I might hear at twenty feet the deer would hear at sixty feet; but the hearing of the moose is not as sharp as that of the deer, nor their eyes as quick to locate one. Of all the creatures that carry the latest electric equipment with them I know of none to compare with the Canada goose. One bright, frosty day in January, when the snow was about six inches deep, my wing-tipped geese were out of the wind with their feet pulled up. There they sat on the crusty snow like so many fireless cookers. I called them to dinner, but they replied "Bring it to us." When I would toss three kernels of wheat in the air all would honk, but when I went through the same motion, empty-handed, they would not answer. I stepped the distance and it was over three hundred feet. I am sure these birds saw the three grains of wheat that distance.

But there is no branch in my nature study that has caused me to sit up and take a more bubbling-over, sympathetic interest than to see these poor maimed birds come to me for protection when they really need it. I have seen as high as six lying in front of my dining-room window at once; in fact, I have picked up as high as seven in one spring that came here and died of their wounds. What touches my heartstrings more than ever is that the wounded ones always come to the park pond and usually sit on the side nearest our house. Possibly while we are eating dinner one will stand with his breast toward us and dress the wound made by a buckshot in his breast; then to get him closer we put the field-glasses on him, which show the details; and here the feathers are all fallen out for fully a half inch around the deadly, dark little hole that is causing him so much inward pain and leaving his life hanging in the balance. I tell you any humane being having a heart and actually knowing the facts about these poor creatures needn't be surprised to find his eyeballs sweating.

And to see how they heal their broken legs is still more interesting. On April 2nd, 1915, a leader of a family of eight came home with one leg hanging down which was undoubtedly broken by a large buck-shot. He had no more control over it than he would have of a stick tied to him. When he lit I noticed he hovered until he got the right spot, then he lowered away and came straight down into the water. There he stayed with head up and watched until his family went and fed. Then, while they watched, he rose straight up and hovered until he located the ear of corn preferred; he then carefully lowered, and turning the ends of his wings sidewise for crutches, he let his body carefully down, leaving his broken leg straight out beside his tail. Then reaching out with his long neck he pulled the ear of corn under his breast and piggled the kernels off until he had sufficient. He then put his wings out again, making crutches of them, and with a peculiar spring he was in the air and came down in the pond as before. On the third day he was standing on the bank with his broken leg straightened around in place, and from a distance he looked to be standing perfectly still, but a close investigation showed there was a constant twitching in the broken limb. We timed him, and this dear old father stood exactly in the one spot and in this same position for over six hours at a time. In less than three weeks it was evident that the bones had knit together, for when he would alight on the ground he would just throw himself a little to one side and let his weight down on the one leg; as he walked he would put his game leg through the motion, just touching the toes to the earth, taking the weight off with a short, quick stroke of the wings. The fourth week he ceased to use his wings for assistance, but would put his foot down and go limping across the lawn. During all this time of his untold suffering and agony, this admirable creature never ceased his duty, but kept a constant watch over his loved ones and if the least thing happened out of the ordinary around the premises he would speak quietly to them about it. Exactly one month from the day he came here, wounded, he led his family very high and they all floated away on the air, headed for the North.

The above is only one out of dozens of cases that have come to my observation. Out of the thousands of Canada geese I have closely examined, I have never seen one with a leg or foot healed crosswise, and there are always odd ones, here with broken legs. We have seen one or two with one leg a little shorter than the other. In that case the other leg is always a little the longer.

I know of no bird or animal that can equal them for getting well after being wounded. It is said that a cat has nine lives; if that be true, the Canada goose has at least eighteen, nine on each side of the border.

In March, 1912, a wounded goose came to our park, rested a while in the water, then walked quietly towards the house and finally lay down, its feathers touching the park fence, just exactly thirty feet from our dining room window. I went out to it. She would not let me pick her up, but would allow me within four feet of her.

That night it snowed fully six inches, and she drifted nearly all under but her head.   I looked and thought she was dead, so I went up to her, upon the opposite side of the fence, and she did not move. I opened the gate and approached, but before I got within ten feet of her she awakened and would have flown but that I withdrew. (Notice how she knew I was now inside the inclosure.)   Well, that goose did not move ten feet for three days, eating a little snow now and then that had drifted there.   I threw shelled corn beside her and she ate a few kernels.   As the bank of snow had all melted on the fourth day, she walked to the water and drank, but came right back and lay down.   But in about three weeks she was going over the top again.   This goose had no limbs broken, but was shot through the body.

One of the most encouraging facts that have been demonstrated by my experiments with these most intelligent creatures is how readily and gladly they will come to man for his protection, or how easily this promise of our heritage is confirmed: "Let man have dominion over all."

Previous to 1919 our Canadian Government ignored all the requests my friends and I made to help me feed these birds, which belong to the people of America; and as I am not a man with means, I just feed them enough to tickle their palates and give them a desire to come back.   The result is they scour the country for miles around, getting the ears of corn that are mostly knocked off by the corn-binders.   This of course gives the shooter an opportunity, and one day in April a neighbor who was ploughing near by saw a single goose.   He noticed it was going very slowly and showed signs of weakness, so he stopped and watched it.   Instead of rising over the trees and dropping in the pond, it went under the boughs and came to the ground near the house.   Little Jasper, who was then three years old, was outside playing.   Running in the house he said to his mother, "Mamma, goose out here; goose out here, mamma." His mother saw by his looks and actions there was something out of the ordinary, so she went out with the little tot and he pointed under a spruce tree, the boughs of which touched the house.   And there the goose, with her wings spread, lay dying.   They called me from the factory, but when I arrived it was stone dead.   On examination I found a buckshot hole under the wing, and it was evident that her "powerhouse" was punctured.   The clotted blood on one foot proved to my satisfaction that she had been shot fully five minutes previous to dropping.   Then I traced the blood back from where I picked her up and found that she lit within ten feet of our back door, for there, on the brick walk, was a big splash of her blood.   In a few hours I found that this goose was shot over five miles away.

Do you wonder at me loving them? Can you blame me for feeding them beyond my means, when this is only a faint, roughly-written picture of their trust and confidence in me?

The real home of love is the heart, but the brain is apparently given power to educate the heart to either love or hate. But any man who does not love those who first love him, I don't think has either heart or brains, and to say he even has a gizzard would be a disgrace to these birds.

CHAPTER XXVI.

Do Birds Have a Language?

THIS is a question I have to answer, and I am fully prepared to say "Yes; yes, I know they do." As proof of this statement, one could shut me in and blindfold me, and if I can hear the wild geese I will tell you a certain portion of their actions, while if I were to hear a Chinaman talking I wouldn't know whether it was cleaned windows, dirty laundry, or ham and eggs he wanted me to have.

One evening last spring, after the wild geese had gone to the lake, I strolled back to the north pond to visit a pair of my own geese, but could not find them, nor would they answer my call. I came to the conclusion they had gotten out, and as I have had this pair thirteen years I became quite anxious. Daylight the next morning found me over half a mile north of the pond, watching and listening, to find trace of them. I finally saw hundreds of them coming from the lake and alighting all around the premises, mostly in the pond mentioned, and the air was continually echoing with their honks. Then I heard the voice of the gander I was looking for. I knew the tone, for I went straight to it, and found him guarding a nest with one egg in it. This explained to me why he did not answer the night before. Yes, I was over half a mile away when I heard and knew his voice from the thousands of others. And before you doubt my word, I want to ask you: If you were in a city of millions of people and on going to the telephone a voice you had been acquainted with for thirteen years or the voice of one of your own household came tingling into your ear, would you not know this voice? This question is just as reasonable.

On October 10th, 1917, as we were eating breakfast, six geese dropped on the pond. I left my porridge and went to the door and called "Chuckie! Chuckie! Chuckie!" The old gander raised his head and answered loudly. So I went to the barn and got twelve ears of corn, came back and went into the park where they were. When within about fifty feet I stopped and had a good look at them. Then, just to see what they would do, I threw an ear of corn at the old gander. The four young at once jumped in the air, but he just said "A-a-h! A-a-h!" and all dropped down again. So I threw another ear, and they again jumped, and he spoke again in exactly the same tone, "A-a-h! A-a-h!" (All is well!) and they immediately dropped on the ground as before. This was repeated several times. He may have told them that that fellow was strong in the back and weak in the mind and didn't care to eat us wild geese; at any rate when I threw the last few ears they took his word for it and did not attempt to fly. My reason for throwing the corn at him was to prove to my own satisfaction that he had seen me throw it before, as, when taking a bag of corn out, I sometimes stand still and throw it amongst them. This old fellow's confidence in the safety of this place will be fully explained to you when I say that he actually dodged some of these ears. Yet it took him fully fifteen minutes to convince his family that there was no danger. The goose, his mate needed no introduction to an ear of corn; she started eating the very first opportunity, but the four young were dreadfully shy of those golden ears of corn, and it did amuse me to see him introducing them to it. With one eye focused on me he would reach down and pick up the ear in his beak, shake it until he got that grain loose, then reach out and drop this kernel at the feet of one of these big babies. But when he did get them started they cleaned off nearly every cob before it came his turn to start in. Yes, as hungry as he evidently was, he stood guard until the other five ravenous appetites were re-lieved, then he willingly took the leavings. To prove they had come over the top for a long way, these six geese ate every kernel of these twelve small ears, at the one meal. Then after going in the pond for a few minutes they came out on the green sod to rest and did not fly around for a day or two.

In about ten days they were as tame as ours and I concluded we could drive them under the net. So one day when all was quiet and no strangers about, I asked my mother-in-law's daughter to help me and she cheerfully consented. We unrolled enough binding-twine to go clear across the pond; then as she held one end and I the other, stretching it about two feet above the water, we drove them quietly towards the net. Finally ours, which are educated to that purpose, led the way, the six followed them in and the trap-door fell. I, being so confident of getting them, had six tags already stamped, and they were in my pocket. So I opened the door and let our geese walk out. The six others huddled together in the corner of the pen, but as I approached the gander opened his wings and faced me. I at once overpowered him and clamped a tag on his hind leg, then took him to the door and let him go. Did he fly away to the lake? No! He did not fly two rods, but lit about twenty-five feet from the door, and his beautiful breast just heaved as he called aloud for his loved ones, "A-honk! A-honk! A-honk!" The interpretation is, "Come on! Come on! Come on!" As I was catching number two I heard a commotion at the door; I looked around, and this lady who was holding it preferred being on the inside looking out, for this old gander had come back and was fighting the wire to get in at me. To be brief, he never left the door until every one of his family was liberated.

Now remember, I am telling you about the same species of bird that I once crawled all the buttons off my wishbone wishing to get a shot at him with a high-powered rifle, fully three fields away; and, like thousands of other men who have tried the same plan, I seldom succeeded. But now he was trying to get where he could strike me with his wings. Well, for his faithfulness I recaught him and put a tag on each of his legs, making seven tags for the six geese. On each of these seven tags we stamped the following verse of Scripture: "No good thing will He withold from them that walk uprightly. Psalms 84: 11." We named this gander Sir John Moore, after a noted, self-sacrificing General I have often heard father speak of.

They all migrated in December, and the first week in March I received the following letter:

To whom it may concern:

Outside of tag "Write Box 48, Kingsville, Ontario." Inside of tag, "No good thing will he withhold from them that walk uprightly."

These words were found on a band on a wild male goose's leg. The gander was captured March 1st, 1918, and I am doing as the words on the band requested.

He was certainly a nice one, weighing twelve pounds and as fat as butter.

I certainly would be pleased to hear from you telling me how, when, where and why the band was put on his leg, and I wish you would please tell me all you can tell me about the habits of the wild fowl up in your country.

They come down here in December, but the winter was so cold this year that they went farther south; but they came back in February and are still here. They feed in the rivers and creeks at night, and at sunrise they fly out in the wheat fields for green wheat until sundown, and then go back to the rivers. They leave here for the far north about the middle of March.

I remain waiting for your reply,

LINDEN ARCHIBALD,
Kennedyville, Kent Co.,
Maryland, U.S.A.

I at once wrote Mr. Archibald and he kindly returned the tag.

On March 19th as we were eating dinner one of my boys spoke up quickly and pointing out the window exclaimed, "Look, father!

Look!" And sure enough, here was Sir John Moore and four out of five of his family standing in front of the window eating corn, the two bright tags glittering on his legs.

This Moore family stayed together nearly all the time they were here, the five of them going to the lake at night and returning early next morn'ng. Fortunately it was one of the young that got killed, hence the family was not broken up.

Now and then during the month of April the Johnson and Smith youngsters, yes, and sometimes the McDonalds and Jones' and other young Canadians too numerous to mention, would call on these three young Moores and all would go about the premises together, apparently playing "Pussy wants a corner," "Drop the handkerchief," "Coward, coward, can't catch me," and so forth. But I never knew these, or any other young Canada geese, to be gone from their parents over an hour at a time during their stay here in March and April, and I am confident these families do not break up until they reach the nesting ground.

Well, about the 25th of April, 1918, Sir John Moore and his family disappeared, and in August I received the following letter:

> Fort George, Hudson Bay,
> June 26th, 1918.

Dear Mr. Miner,—

Enclosed find four tags which I received this morning from an Indian; and as our boat is just leaving for the South, I am sending them to you at once. He tells me an interesting thing about these tags, as he says there was a flock of seven geese came to their decoys, and this Indian and another got four of them, each of which had a tag on it. One of the others killed by another hunter had two tags on.

There was a good flight of geese this spring, but not very many were killed.

The wavies, or snow geese, were very numerous this spring. The Indians say that they have not seen so many for a long time.

Hoping the tags reach you safe, I remain,

> Yours sincerely,
> L. G. Maver,
> Fort George, Hudson Bay,

The reader can scarcely imagine my feelings when I read the message that each one of these tags contained: "No good thing will he withhold from them that walk uprightly." This was proof that Sir John Moore's family was exterminated. It was not that I am opposed to the Indians getting the geese; no, no. It was only the thought of my special pets all being killed. As for the Indians and

Esquimaux getting these birds, I believe all honest, conscientious, thinking men will agree with me that there are no people in America who are more justified in shooting them than these natives up at Icicle Junction with their backs to the wall trying to exist. Personally I feel that the best missionary work I have ever done in my life is the thousands of geese I have fattened up and permitted to go back to that isolated country where they were hatched.

Although these tags were mailed from Fort George, Hudson Bay, these Indians may have brought them for three or even five hundred miles, Fort George being their trading post.

Now I have given you quite a collection of rough, unadulterated and unpolished facts about the ways of our lovely Canada geese. And when I call them lovely remember I do not mean because they are so uniform in color; nor is it because they are mostly all Canadian born. Not at all. It is on account of their winning ways and I really want to say Godly principles that in many respects could point the finger of shame at us human beings. This is why I call him "our beautiful Canada goose;" and if five per cent. of us Canadians really knew him, the other ninety-five per cent. could not, or would not try to, keep him off one corner of our Union Jack.

CHAPTER XXVII.

The Career of Jack Johnson.

IN THE spring of 1907, after I had had these seven wing-tipped geese three years, this old gander and his sweetheart started housekeeping near the west bank of the north pond, about two hundred feet north of the north door in our factory. The nest was built on the bare ground near the remnant of an old rail fence, giving me a good, clear view of it from the door of the factory at an elevation of about seven feet. It was evident she was an old goose, for she laid six eggs. And many an interesting hour I put in watching this pair of birds, as I could keep one eye on the machinery at the same time.

As this old gander would scrap any approaching enemy we called him Jack Johnson. He would stand about a rod from her, with his long, black, snake-like neck and head straight up for hours at a time; one would hardly notice a move; he looked more like a fixture than a living object. If a hawk or a crow was sighted, he would walk up, right to her nest; but if a dog went galloping over the fields, he would be lying flat, and any creature would almost touch him before it would see what it was up against.

Remember, he sees everything before it sees him; and only those who have seen one do it will believe how they can draw themselves down on the ground without being detected. When in the water it can bury its body under, leaving just the head and neck out and a few of the feathers along the back, and with the neck slightly curved one couldn't believe it anything but a long, wicked-looking snake. I never knew a creature that could put on a wickeder or more poisonous look than these Canada geese can.

One day as I was standing in the factory door with an eye turned towards the goose nest, I saw the old cart-horse, Charley, grazing closer and closer to the nest, and a shudder came over me, fearing he might put a clumsy foot in it. But where is Jack Johnson, the fellow who is always watching; now an enemy is approaching and he is gone! The goose is lying flat on the nest and I can see plainly her black neck stretched out on the ground, and her head curved towards this big horse that weighs over sixteen hundred pounds, and feet on him like pancake griddles. All at once the sight grows doubly interesting, for here is Jack Johnson stretched out flat, and pushing himself along with both hind feet until he is within four feet of Charley's heels. Charley is apparently unconscious of having an enemy on earth as he is quietly grazing closer and closer to the nest, his big knees bending forward for fully a second before he makes steps.

Finally when he gets within three feet of Mrs. Goose she slowly rises up, spreading her wings at him. His big ears go forward at once, and he gives a slight flinch backwards, with both eyes rivetted on the goose. That instant Jack Johnson grabs him on the heels with his beak, and strikes him with both wings at once, while both geese seem to honk at the same time. Really I never saw a horse so nearly scared into fits as he was. His tail went into the air as he uttered a combination of loud snorts, and, with his four feet almost jarring the earth, he ran because he could not fly. Judging from his actions he did not know which end he got bit from, for he first jumped sidewise away from the nest. When he got about a hundred and fifty feet away he halted, and with his head erect and his tail bowed up, it added fully one hundred dollars to his appearance. But when he saw the geese flapping and rejoicing over their victory he started again, and if it had not been for the barn-yard fence possibly he would have been going yet.

As the nest had no protection, the old goose of course had to set in the sun, and she finally took sick and left the eggs. I believe she was sunstruck. At any rate she nearly died. So one day we men went and fought old Jack away and took the six eggs. I put them in warm water and found each contained life, so I made a nest in an old washtub and a Plymouth Rock hen volunteered to act as stepmother. In four or five days all six of the eggs hatched, and I removed the cover and let the light in, and the hen showed no signs of pecking them, but on the contrary started to teach them some chicken language. The next day we removed them in a pen near our back door where there was a nice growth of young clover and so forth. We fed them just a little custard as a coaxer, and these goslings were really tamer than their stepmother. And how they did grow! The rapid way in which young Canada goslings grow is almost beyond human belief. At three days of age I have seen them run through two-inch-mesh poultry netting, and at six or seven weeks they are full grown and only experienced eyes will detect the young from the old at one hundred feet distance.

Now this family of goslings never went five rods from our back door, but were continually gorging themselves on this clover. And of all the big babies I ever saw, young wild geese are the limit. After they were larger than their stepmother, I have often seen them huddle around her, putting their heads under her wings, each raising her a little higher until she would be completely off the ground making herself into a portable home for the heads of these six goslings.

But the sad thing was to see this old gander, and to hear him continually giving those three searching, sad honks. We put blocks of wood and pieces of fence-rail in the nest, but this broken-hearted old fellow rolled them away. The sick goose stayed in the pond near by the nest, but he strayed all about the premises, constantly hunting for the six eggs or the goslings that he evidently knew were in them, returning every few minutes to his sick sweetheart. He would bow and talk to her and nip a few blades of grass; then off again on the same beat, honking, east, west, north and south. I never saw anything to equal it. If his honking was heard by the six goslings it was of course all Latin to them, as they knew no other parent but this old hen.

Well, the novelty of having these pets near the back door soon grew a little unsanitary; and we found they were a week bigger every seven days; and my brother-in-law's oldest sister gave me to kindly understand, in as pleasant a manner as the English language can possibly be rubbed in, that our back doorstep was not a wild goose roost, and that these geese had to be removed immediately if not a little sooner. So I concluded to take her word for it. But at that time I had only the one big field away from the house. So one bright morning in June, as the sun was just high enough to be sparkling on the dewdrops that were apparently hanging on every blade of grass, I started from the house as usual to build a fire under the boiler at the factory. I called to the goose family, and all followed me through the gate, really quieter than domestic fowls. As I passed through the barnyard I kept on dropping a little feed, and they kept right after me until they came to nice, clean, dewy grass. There I left them and started on. But I hadn't got five rods away before my whole body and nerves were all shaking at seeing and hearing old Jack Johnson coming from the north pond, flapping and honking like a creature that had gone completely mad.

I turned and ran back, fearing he would kill every one. But he beat me there, and thank God he did. For instead of killing them as I feared he might, when he got within about six feet of them he stopped, and with his head and neck straight in the air, his beautiful chest just heaved, and I am not exaggerating in the least when I say that his honks could easily have been heard for a mile and a half. What he said I don't know, but each gosling lay flat on the ground and he put his head on each, apparently caressing and loving them. In turn each got up and flapped its baby wings.

Just then I cast one eye to the north and here was the old, sick mother coming, falling down with weakness every rod she came.

This was the first time I had seen her over the bank of the pond since she left the nest, and the young were now over five weeks old. Old Jack looked and saw her, and ran up and apparently told her all, for she tried in her weak way to come faster. But this dear old father really made several trips back and forth to the young before she got there.

Now comes something worth while for me, and I don't want any reader to ask how it was that this old pair of beauties knew their young. I only know they did know them; that is all. There I stood, bare-headed and bare-footed at the most beautiful time of the day. The whole earth seemed to be transformed into a rainbow of God's pure love, with both ends pouring out upon this one spot; for to see this dear old, broken-hearted father and their sick mother united and knowing their six loved ones which they had never seen, or, in other words, standing and witnessing the reunion of this broken family, caused my brain to fairly whirl in thought, until I melted down, like a little child.

Finally the eight of them all started for the north pond. But Jack looked and saw the hen following; so he just stepped back and gave her one blow with his stub wing which sent her moulting and screaming with terror towards the chicken house. But in about fifteen minutes when I returned from the factory the goslings came back after their step-mother, Jack following them. I succeeded in coaxing her out and he saw her family salute and caress her, as they uttered volumes of baby talk, apparently expressing their sympathy. This old gander never touched her afterwards, and the hen lived out at the pond with the eight geese until the snow drove her in. No other fowl on the premises dared venture near her, for the gander guarded her as one of his family from then on.

The old mother goose got a little better towards fall, but when winter set in she took a change for the worse and one day in January I went back and picked her up and decided to bring her to the house and doctor her up. When I got to the cow-stable I turned the cow out, leaving the goose there while I went to the house for dope. When the cow passed out the door, old Jack Johnson, who was right on my heels ever since I picked up his mate, flew into the cow like a bull-dog and gave her a real trimming. On returning from the house I found he had driven her around the corner, but was still fighting and honking at this innocent old beast.

When I opened the cow-stable door I found the old goose's struggle was over. She was dead. And while her faithful old mate was around out of sight, still busily engaged with the cow, I took the goose out and buried her; therefore he never saw her afterwards.

To be brief, he fought the cow, on and off, for two or three weeks

Then he seemed to content himself by watching her. And for two and a half years he kept constant guard over her, and never was seen to be over three rods away from her head. On several occasions she broke out, but he followed and was seen over a mile from home. In fact she needed no bell to be located, as his honking answered the purpose. During the summer months he slept at her

FAITHFUL AFTER DEATH

Photograph showing "Jack Johnson" standing at the cow-stable door watching the cow, two years and three months after the death of his sweetheart.

head in the pasture field, but when winter came and the cow was stabled, he always slept on the doorstep. One morning in March I snapped him there.

He apparently blamed her for his trouble, and paid no attention whatever to any other goose, not even his own family. His sad honking, however, became so dreadfully mournful to one and all that I finally got rid of him.

On another occasion I kept a widowed goose for four years and she still honked for her old love. Now, if anything happens to one of a pair around here, I will give you the other, as I cannot stand to hear their deep, mournful cries, that to me make the whole place gloomy.

I have heard good honest men say that their wild ganders when turned with a flock of tame geese will mate with more than one goose. But here at my home everything is as near the natural state as I can possibly make it, and I haven't seen these geese show any inclination toward acting that way.

Here is a fact hard for you to believe, for it is beyond the human power's control. These wild geese come here from the south-east Atlantic coast, arriving about March the first; if fed and protected they will not leave here for Hudson Bay, where they nest, before April the twentieth to May the first, living here under exactly the same conditions as our wing-clipped or pinioned ones do. And ours usually lay the last week in March.

This year six young were hatched on April the 27th, and it takes twenty-eight or twenty-nine days for incubation alone.

Or to give you a better explanation I will say, take a pair of these wild geese, clip their wings and keep them here. In about three years they will nest, but will do so fully a month earlier than if they had their wings and could go to their natural breeding ground. Possibly their reason for nesting earlier when they are compelled to stay here is to get their young well developed before the extremely hot weather sets in, as I have had them die in dry, hot weather. On the other hand, when they are three days old they will toddle around among the white frost on the clover leaves and enjoy their meal as if it were sugar-coated.

Now I am aware that I have been altogether too lengthy; but I have so many of these interesting facts that I can't, apparently, ring off.

I know you educated people call it nature, or instinct; and really I have heard such a variety of names for this goose-knowledge that I don't try to look up the meaning of these artificial words; for I am sure if all their meanings were boiled down, and all the man-made, artificial names were skimmed off, the real interpretation would be—

"G O D."

Last summer, about the first of July, as I went from the factory to the house, Mrs. Miner said to me, "What is the matter with your geese? This old pair and the four young ones have come to the house and honked two or three times. We have driven them back to the north pond, time and again." I said at once, "Were there only four young that came up?" She assured me that was all. But the looks and actions of the geese were enough; I knew there was something wrong, for when the old pair saw me they honked aloud.

I hustled through the shrubbery and these geese followed me. On my arrival at the water's edge the meaning of their mysterious actions was revealed, for I saw the gosling lying dead upon the east shore. I hurried along and picked it up. On examination I found a small head of rye in its wind-pipe. The noise of the machinery where I was working had prevented my hearing the alarmed cries of the parent birds, or I would have gotten there in time to save its life. However, it was then too late; the gosling had been dead at least an hour.

So I took it by one foot and carried it in my hand; and the parents and the four remaining young followed at my heels right back to the house. I buried the gosling beside the rose-path, with the broken family of geese standing within fifteen feet of me. We had to drive them back several times before they would stay and it was fully a week before they would content themselves back at their home where they had lived all summer.

WILD GEESE AT MY HOME

These birds belong to you as much as they do to me. They winter on the South-East Coast, and nest on Hudson Bay. In fact the only bird in this bunch that belongs to me is the lady to the left of the two in the lower photograph.

CHAPTER XXVIII.

The Migration of Our Canada Geese.

AS TO the regularity of the migration of our Canada goose which is pointed out on this map, I must say I am greatly indebted to the kind assistance of the Hudson's Bay Company.'s agents and those of the Revillon Fur Company, and I have a great ambition to lay aside all home cares and enjoyments and in the near future treat myself to a three months' trip to the nesting grounds of our Canada geese, where I will have the great pleasure of grasping the hands of all classes of these men whom the geese have let me know are on earth.

As proof that these men are genuine I am reproducing some of their letters.   The following is the first one I received:

Hudson's Bay Company,
MOOSE FACTORY, ONT.,
August 19th, 1915.
via Cochrane.

Box 48,
    Kingsville, Ontario.
Dear Sir,—

I have an aluminum ring with the above address stamped on the outside and number 15 on the inside.   This was taken off the leg of a Canada Grey Goose shot by an Indian last spring about the 15th April a few miles south of the H.B. Post of Eastmain on James Bay. The Indian who shot it said that it was in a band of about fifteen and this particular goose appeared larger than the others and of a lighter colored plumage.   It was probably bound for the breeding grounds, north, from the fact of its being in a flock.   A good many geese hatch all around the bay but these are generally seen flying around in pairs before nesting.   These birds are very easily tamed and I have seen some here taken very young which, after they have grown up, would continue staying around the place after being turned loose.   I would be interested to hear from you the particulars of this goose and hope I have given you all the information you require about it. I am,

Yours faithfully,

W. E. CAMSELL.

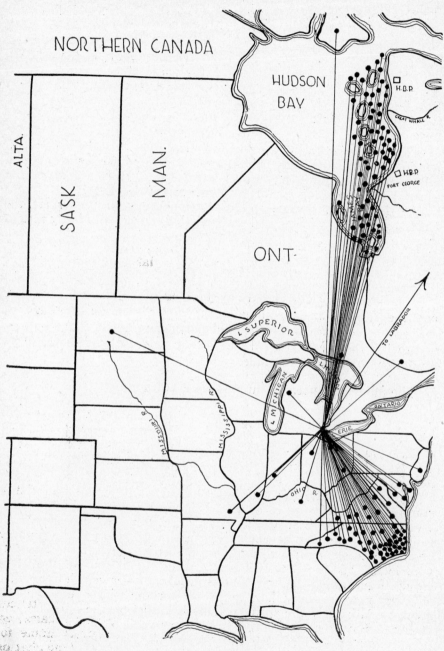

MAP SHOWING IMGRATION OF THE CANADA GOOSE

Later, in January, 1916, I received another letter, as follows:

> Hudson's Bay Company,
> FORT GEORGE, JAMES BAY,
> via Cochrane.
> 27th January, 1916.

Box 48,
　Kingsville, Ont.
Dear Sir,—

This is to inform you that an Indian last week brought me a band, bearing the above address, which was taken from the leg of a goose, killed about the middle of October last at Comb Hills, a point on the coast of James Bay about forty miles south of this Post.

As the Indian seemed to expect something for giving me the band, I paid him a dollar and shall be glad if you will kindly refund same to me.

> Yours truly,
> OWEN GRIFFITH.

I at once sent a few dollars to these agents requesting that they pay the Indians and Esquimaux one dollar each for the tags. I also requested them to give me all particulars about that country, as to what the geese feed on, where they nest; in fact, that any information would be acceptable.

The following letters of interest were written me:

> Hudson's Bay Company,
> MOOSE FACTORY,
> via Cochrane, Ont.
> 14th Nov., 1916.

My dear Jack,—

I was very glad to get your letter of August 30th, and must thank you for your enclosure of $5.00. I am sure you will think I have been a long while in answering your letter, but I have been over in England this summer and only returned to this part of the country about two weeks ago; it was only on my arrival here that I received your letter, and as there will be a packet out as soon as the ice is strong, I am taking the first opportunity to answer your letter.

I am now stationed here at Moose for the winter and shall be going to Albany in the spring. This is a post on the opposite side of James Bay to Fort George, but a very good place for game, especially for those birds we call "wavies." The correct name for these birds, I believe, is "snow goose." It is a strange thing that on the west coast of James Bay we get almost nothing but white "wavies," with an occasional blue one in the flock, while on the east coast it is just the opposite with almost nothing but blue (grey) with a few white ones in the flock, while a short distance farther north (on the east coast) at Whale River the white reappear again in large numbers, so that they evidently cross the bay on their annual migrations.

There are lots of geese both on the east and west sides of the bay, but I believe that more pass on the east (Fort George side) than the other, as the coast is rocky with lots of islands where they can breed. We have some islands out in the bay called the "Tioms," which are great breeding places.

The Indians who killed those tagged geese said that they seemed to be tamer than the others and came out of large flocks and down to the decoys when the rest of the band would not turn.

About three miles north of Fort George Post there is a big bay (salt water) with lots of mud and grass at low tide, and in the spring almost every flock of wavies and some geese feed in this bay on their way north. The Indians never hunt them on their arrival in this bay, but gather on a long hill on the other side and then shoot at the birds as they are going off. They generally get up in small flocks; as they have to rise considerably to clear the hill, they can be seen getting up some time before they get to the hill, and then every one runs along a path and tries to get right under where the flock is going to pass. Of course if three or four flocks get up at the same time there is shooting on different parts of the hill and the hunters are apt to spoil one another's sport. The Indians say that once these birds leave this bay that they do not feed again till they get far north (Hudson Straits or Baffin Land). In fact a wavies' nest is a great rarity. Strange to say they do not feed in this bay in the fall.

We have no wild rice in the bay and the birds seem to feed mostly on grass in the salt water, and in the fall they go out to the islands to feed on berries; they fly out to the islands in the mornings and back into the small bays for the nights.

I am staying with Mr. Camsell just now and he tells me to be sure and remember him to you. He is going to walk out to the line in March and will perhaps try to look you up.

I am enclosing you some photos which I think may interest you. I have written on the backs what they represent.

The Indians get lots of fish in their nets but not much in winter except with hooks.

Mr. Camsell showed me the photo of yourself. Please send me one.

Well, I will write you again, and in the meantime remain,

Your sincere friend,

OWEN GRIFFITH.

The following four letters all explain themselves.

The Hudson's Bay Company,
JAMES' BAY DISTRICT OFFICE,
MOOSE FACTORY,
June 15th, 1918.

Dear Mr. Miner,—

The enclosed metal band, No. 18 S, was brought here to-day by an Indian, by name Andrew Butterfly, who killed the goose carrying the band, while hunting in Hannah Bay, south-east of James' Bay.

Andrew informs me that the goose was killed on April 28th, 1918.

We are all very much interested in your experiments down here, and make a point of returning the bands we receive. If you require any further particulars about the geese killed, please let me know, and I will try to give you as much information as possible.

Yours faithfully,
GEO. WATSON.

Mr. Jack Miner,
Box 48,
Kingsville, Ont.

The Hudson's Bay Compan··,
Great Whale River Post,
via   Cochrane, Ontario.

Dear Mr. Miner,—

I have delayed answering your letter of Sept. 4, until I saw some of my hunters from the north, so as to get as much information as I could about the nesting place of the geese, etc.

The Esquimaux tell me that a good many birds nest at some large islands, about north-west of this Post. The islands are called the north and south Belchers, and some of them are fairly large. One of them has a large lake extending nearly the whole length of the island and this is the place where a good many of the geese nest. I have received two tags from the natives who stay on these islands, and I enclose them herewith.

The hunters from the far north told me that quite a number of geese nest about 300 miles north of this place; and I have let them know that if they kill any geese with tags on, to bring them in to the Post, so very likely I will be able to send you some next spring when the natives again visit the Post.

I don't know what has happened to the birds and animals this season; I have never seen it so poor for all kinds of game since I have been up in this direction, and I am hoping that we have an early spring so that perhaps we may be able to get some of your geese or other game.

I have been showing your pictures of the geese in the pond to some of my hunters, and they tell me that they wish they were only eating some of them; and of course I have to tell them that the spring will soon be here and that they may kill some of the geese they have been looking at in the pictures.

Well, I see the war is now over, and every one up at this place was very glad about it. The natives have some very funny ideas about what the war was really about, and as each man held that his idea was the correct one, there have been some lively discussions about the matter, and this controversy has helped to pass the time at this isolated place.

Well, trusting things are going all right with you and that your geese are well and fat, I remain,

Yours sincerely,

L. G. MAVER.

The Hudson's Bay Company,
James Bay District,
MOOSE FACTORY, May 8th, 1919.
Refer to No. 303.
Subject: Two goose bands returned.

Jack Miner, Esq.,
    Kingsville, Ont.
Dear Sir,—

Whilst making a trip last winter up the east coast of James' Bay as far as Great Whale River on Hudson Bay, two of your goose-bands came into my possession, and I beg to return them herewith.

The band marked 17 was on a goose that was killed in October, 1918, about thirty miles north of Eastmain by Charles Shashawaskum, a Cree Indian.

The goose that was carrying the band marked 18 was killed last fall near Cape Jones by Richard Fleming, an Esquimaux.

One dollar has been forwarded to each of these men out of your fund, held by Mr. Nicolson of Rupert's House.

Yours faithfully,

WM. C. RACKHAM,
District Manager.

Address: C|o The Hudson's Bay Company,
              Moose Factory,
              Clute Post Office, Ontario.

RUPERT'S HOUSE, CLUTE P.O., ONTARIO,
20th June, 1918.

Mr. J. Miner,
    Box 48, Kingsville, Ontario.
Dear Sir,—
    The enclosed tag No. 18 S was handed to me the other day by an Indian who killed the goose to which it was attached about thirty miles north of this Post. I believe two or three other tags were procured by some Indians who do not deal with me, but no doubt they will be forwarded by the trader to whom they were delivered. As far as I can ascertain your interests seem to be pretty well looked after around the bay generally.

                              Yours sincerely,
                                        A. NICOLSON.

THE INDIAN ACHIMAYA, who in the spring
of 1915 shot a goose tagged the same year

During my correspondence with the Hudson's Bay Company I have received from them several interesting snapshots. This fellow with the smiling face, I understand is the man who shot the first wild goose I ever tagged.

The old lady whose photograph is shown with this is the grandmother, and was reported as the oldest woman around Hudson Bay, but she actually did not know how old she was, and I think one glance at the photograph will convince you that both statements are apt to be true.

INDIAN WOMAN, FORT GEORGE

Reverend J. W. Walton, the missionary from that quarter who visited me last winter, smiled all over his face when I showed him her picture. "Why," said he, "she was the dearest old lady you ever met, always wanting to help others carry their load; but she died about eighteen months ago."

Now it is a fact that thirty-six of my returned goose tags have come from Hudson Bay. Yet it would be well for us to remember that over eighty per cent. of these birds were tagged in the spring, and they went direct from this tame spot to James Bay, thus giving the Indians and Esquimaux the tamest opportunity. We are quite certain that two or three were killed by them within three days after they left here. One goose, tagged and liberated here on April 24th, was killed at the Belcher Islands on the 28th; another, liberated on April the 22nd, was killed at James Bay on the 25th.

On two different occasions when the geese were leaving here at five p.m., I telegraphed the C.P.R. agent at Stralak, Ontario. Stralak is about sixty miles north-west of Sudbury, Ontario, or about four hundred and fifty miles north of my home. On both occasions I got returns before nine o'clock the next morning. My first reply was "Geese are crossing at Metagama." The next year, under similar conditions, the reply read, "Geese are passing at Spanish Forks and at Pogmasing." These three stations are on the main line of the C.P.R., about seventy to ninety miles north-west of Sudbury. At these three particular points the railroad is running nearly straight north, and I doubt very much if the geese would be over four miles out of their east-and-west lines on their northern trip the two different years.

During the same period of time I have a lot reported from their winter home along what I called the south-east Atlantic Coast.

The following are the names and addresses of the gentlemen who have reported the wild geese.

IN CANADA

Hudson's Bay.—Simon Alisaibi, Sr., Moose River, James Bay (4).
Peter Henlisty, James Bay.
James Ouchigan, Moose River, James Bay.
E. Renouf, Fort George (10).
George Cheechoo, Hannah Bay.
William Solomon, Albany River.
S. Archibald, Salt Water Lake.
Sidney Archevall, Charlton Island.
Unnamed Eskimo, Belcher Island.
David Roberts, Hannah Bay.
Peter Hemlitz, Moose River, James Bay.
George Cheechoo, James Bay.
Henry Goodwin, between Moose and Albany.
A. S. Ward, James Bay.
George Napach, Cape Jones.

John Napach, Cape Jones.
John Kipusen, Fort George (2).
John Kenauteewat, Comb Hill.
Young Benjamin (a youth), Fort George.
Thomas Sealhunta, Pipestone.
Thomas Sealhunta, Jr., Pipestone.
Johnish Sealhunta, Fort George.
Eskimo Bill's son, Little Cape Jones.
Unknown Eskimo, Belcher Island (9).
Simon Alisaylee, James Bay (2).
James Oachigan, James Bay.
Hudson's Bay Agent, Great Whate River (2).

Labrador.—Arch. Pardy, Hamilton Inlet.
Chas. Michelin, Northwest River.

IN UNITED STATES

Delaware.—Shedest McMurray, Frankford.

Illinois.—Joseph Cepak, Bumbguard, Bar.

Indiana.—Gust F. Stunhs, Lacrosse.

Kentucky.—John Dulworth, La Centre.

Maryland.—Ben Nuth, Baltimore.
Linden Archibald, Kennedy.
Marshall I. Bradshaw, Tylerton.

Michigan.—Harry P. Smith, Holland.

Missouri—Elton Richard, New Madrid.

New Jersey.—Oliver T. Crammer, West Creek, Ocean County.

North Carolina.—C. H. Ulmer and party, Rose Bay (2).
Sandford Barnes, Currituck Shooting Club.

North Carolina.—Continued.

L. G. Jenkins, Littleton.
Cossil B. Forbes, Poplar Branch.
Wm. Twoford, Waterlily.
C. E. Jones, Knotts Island.
Paul Montague, Pamell's Point.
Stanley Armstrong, Fairfield.
Tom Green, Corner Island.
Lewis L. Lewark, Nag Head.
Ivan Smith, Littleton.
C. S. Boomer, Swan Quarter.
L. T. Johnson, Mamis.
Dr. H. C. Baum, Pine Island.
E. W. Brumley, Woodlight.
E. C. Toppins, Jr., Swan Quarter.
W. F. Fherkildson, New Holland.
Francis Clark, Pine Island.
L. O. Turford, Powell's Point.
M. C. Britt, Elizabeth City.
C. A. Ulmer, Rose Bay (2).
M. M. Hayward, Corner Island, Currituck.
J. H. Mayo, Habusken.
Dr. H. Fayetteville, Carrituck Sd.
W. R. Williams, Bethoven.
Carl White, Poplar Branch.
R. E. Flora, Shawboro.
John E. Thayer, Poplar Branch.
J. M. Cox, Middleton.

O. G. Edwards, Springhope.
J. G. Gaskill, Habusken.
W. D. Bowden, Waterlily.
L. D. Twoford, Powell's Point.
J. C. O'Neil, Poplar Branch.
George Syme, Raleigh.
W. N. Mason, Bath.
T. O. Twoford, Powell's Point.
Pattie L. Robertson, Bertha.
W. R. Robertson, Springhope.
J. B. Flora, Elizabeth City.
H. C. Wozelka, Edenton.

North Dakota.—Marshall Bradshaw, Tylerton.

Ohio.—William Sherman, Montezuma.
Martin T. Boss, Curtice.
Charles Dorstin, Celuia.

Virginia.—J. B. Frazier, Hampton Roads.
H. E. Bonney, Norfolk.
Emmett Cooke, Gritua.
H. M. DeJaruette, Fredericksburg.
John E. Thayer, Cape Henry.
P. Q. Gillian, Norfolk.
J. C. Bristo, Richmond.
E. C. Hallman, Tangier.
Haywood Whitehead, Townsend (2).

I am here reproducing one letter from the South which gives us a fair explanation as to when the geese come to, and leave, their winter home.

SWAN QUARTER, N.C.
Nov. 15th, 1917.

Dear Sir,—

I killed a goose yesterday, the 14th of Nov., on the Lake of Matmostuate, Hyde Co., N.C., with a band on his left leg with your address on it. It said "Write to Box 48, Kingsville, Ont." So at your request I am taking pleasure in doing so. Inside of metal band was a Bible verse; it said: "Keep yourselves in the love of God. Jude 1: 21." You will please write me and tell me how you caught the goose, and when you put same on him and all about the geese in Canada, and their raising there. They come on our lakes about Oct. 15th, and stay here until March 15th. Then they all leave and go north to places unknown to us. Lake Matamoskeete is a great place for hunting geese. There were about three hundred killed the day that I killed this one. Will close. Write me soon and a long letter, and tell me all you know about them.

With best wishes for you and yours, I am,

Yours very truly,
C. S. BOOMER.

One of the most recent and interesting of the letters I have received is the following:

> Hudson's Bay Service,
> James Bay District, Canada,
> FORT GEORGE POST,
> July 25th, 1923.
> via Mattice, Ontario.

Dear Mr. Miner,—

I am enclosing herewith five tags taken off geese killed by my hunters in the vicinity of this post this year.

Should you ever desire further information I shall ever be glad to assist you in the excellent work which you are doing, to the best of my ability.

I am, however, rather afraid that some of the birds which recourse to your sanctuary are lulled there into a greater trust in mankind than is well for their continued well-being, as undoubtedly some of these birds, on leaving the sanctuary you afford them, fall very easy victims to gunners.

With great appreciation, I beg to remain,

> Sincerely yours,
> E. RENOUF.

In 1919, Mr. Sainsbury of Toronto, one of our Canadian explorers, was in Baffin Land. There he ran across some Esquimaux with a goose that had my tag on it. They were superstitious about the goose, but when Mr. Sainsbury explained it to them, they tore its skin off, and ate the goose, raw. This is away north of timber line, where the Esquimaux eat their meat raw. The dot on the map showing the migration of the geese, away to the north of Hudson Bay, is where Mr. Sainsbury pointed out the place to me on his map

RETURNED DUCK AND GOOSE TAGS

The rolled tags appear exactly as when taken from the legs of the geese.

CHAPTER XXIX.

Catching and Tagging the Wild Goose.

THIS was a proposition that tested my staying qualities to a standstill, although it is true I had tagged lots of smaller birds, including the wild ducks; but that was like coaxing candy from a baby, too easy to be interesting.

Yes, some one has said, "the silly old goose!" But bear in mind that it is through this silly old goose's ability to outwit the human race that there is one living; we would have killed and eaten them all, long ago, but they outwitted us and went over the top. So if they are silly, what is our number, if you please?

Well, silly or not, it took my little, single-cylinder brain over seven years to outwit them. Actually I studied them more than I did my financial obligations, and that's saying a whole lot. Very true, they will allow me to walk among them, and odd, wounded ones have eaten from my hand. But don't hold him, or interfere with his liberties, as one note from his beak will alarm all the geese within a mile.

In November, 1919, there were fifty-five ducks feeding here and when I pulled the trip-wire I caught fifty of them; but the "silly old goose" would walk by and say "A-h-h! A-h-h!" and my family would say "Ha! Ha!" The variety of contrivances I made during these seven years! And the blisters there were on my hands during that time, caused from cutting and fitting gas-pipe frames and trap-doors and stretching poultry netting over the same, are blisters I will long remember. Then to see the geese come, glance at it and walk away, would make any human being feel small enough to pass a ferret in a gun-barrel. In fact this got to be a family joke. Little Jasper said, "Papa, how many goose nets are you going to make this summer?" Yes, I am a firm believer in the words, "Let man have dominion over all," but in this case I have surely been a poor actor.

At last a thought germinated that proved a success. I dug a canal forty feet wide and sixty feet long between two ponds. This canal was made at the mouth of the drain tile that supplies the ponds with spring water, the last water to freeze and the first to thaw out. A high gas-pipe frame was built to cover the whole canal, with a trap-door at each end, This was neatly covered with two-inch-mesh poultry netting, stretched good and tight to prevent it bagging and

MY FIRST SUCCESSFUL CATCH OF WILD GEESE

flapping in the wind. The trapdoors were left constantly up, and our domesticated geese were educated to winter under this, in the open water at the mouth of this drain tile. This contrivance is at the north ponds, where the geese remain quite wild.

It was completed in December, 1921, and March, 1922, found me away from home on a lecturing tour. When I opened a letter from my boy saying, "Father, your goose-net is a success; we saw fully twenty-five follow ours under, this morning," can you really blame me for reading it twice?

In a week or so I arrived home, and was greeted with these cheering words, "Father, there were dozens of geese feeding under the net last night. We are feeding shelled corn and wheat under there, and the wild geese go under without ours leading the way." Early the next morning I was up and dressed, and quite excited, for I was up in the little "oblookatory" long before the geese arrived from the lake; but sure enough, when they came fully forty went under to feed. And they were just as good as caught, for my previous experiments have taught me how to make a trap-door that works to perfection. Just picture, if possible, the way I was stepping around! Here I had been seven years catching one hundred and nine geese, and no two bunches were caught alike; in other words, every catch was an experimental failure! But now I am going to catch them by the hundreds. Yet I must not pull the trap-doors while the big flock is here, to frighten them all.

On April 21st fully eighty per cent. of them had gone north. Sunday morning, April 22nd, only about three hundred were here, and it was now or never, for that spring.

I climbed up and watched them while Dr. Rob Sloan, of Leamington, who is one of my greatest helpers, stood below to pull the trip-wire. The opportunity arrived. I signalled the doctor, the trap-door dropped in the twinkling of an eye—and sixty-one missionaries were in captivity!

In catching the sixty-one we found a pair tagged in 1917; two others had had their legs broken but were healed straight.

Well, now the big flock is gone, and they know nothing of this disturbance, so now I will enlarge on this successful plan, I thought. So in the summer of 1922 I completed my big net having over 5,000 feet of area in it. One trap-door is one hundred and twenty feet long, one eighty feet, and another forty feet; all three are dropped by the one trip-wire.

That fall, 1922, about 300 geese came back, but there was not much water as the spring was very low. Yet on December 5th I caught fifty-three, and on Saturday, April 21st, 1923, I caught two hundred and seven. Some catch! "Let man have dominion over all." Now I have caught three hundred and twenty-one in one year.

A BIG CATCH IN THE BIG NET

Photograph shows the west wing of the big net. Note that the trap-doors are down on each side and we are driving a bunch into the catching-pen, which is a little corner at the end, only twelve feet square, with a trap-door to keep them in there. The trap-door can be seen hanging above, ready to fall.

While watching these last two hundred and seven gradually working their way under the net, my field-glasses showed eleven standing on the bank with bright aluminum tags on, but not a goose in the two hundred and seven had been tagged before. In other words, I have never caught a goose twice in the same net. "Silly old goose!"

It will be plainly seen that we haven't had time to hear from many of the three hundred and twenty-one that were caught during the last year or so; but out of the one hundred and nine that I caught between 1915 and 1921, seventy have been reported killed, and fifty-seven of the tags are back in my possession, but altogether up to the present date, January, 1925, I have tags of 139 of the geese reported killed, as follows:

Sixty-nine from Hudson's Bay; forty-five from North Carolina; ten from Virginia; three from Maryland; three from Ohio; one from Ontario; one from Delaware; one from North Dakota; one from Illinois; one from Missouri; one from Michigan; one from New Jersey; one from Kentucky; one from Hamilton Inlet, Labrador; one from Indiana; one from Ottawa River, thirty miles north of Quebec.

Now the fact that seventy out of the first 109 geese I tagged have been killed gives us a good deal to think about, possibly the key to such a remarkable success in this tagging system. But even this would be perfectly useless without the brotherly co-operation of all classes of real men I have located right across the continent. It all compels me to believe that the Gospel message stamped on each tag has really rendered great assistance. A few weeks ago Rev. J. W. Walton, the missionary in the Hudson's Bay district, sent me a box containing twenty goose tags. The natives of that territory carried these tags to Mr. Walton for an interpretation. Now only two out of these twenty tags had been put on previous to 1922. One tag was marked 1917. The goose bearing this one was killed by an Esquimaux in May, 1924. Brother sportsmen, notice that of the first 109 geese I labelled, to my knowledge only one has lived to carry the tag seven years.

Mr. Walton writes me stating that he carries one of these tags in his pocket. He says it often helps him to open up a helpful conversation with strangers.

Now while the ducks do not in any way compare with the geese, since they are much easier captured and shot, still the tagging of the ducks has also brought me some worth-while information. Out of the 452 ducks I have tagged, 197 have been reported; but I have tagged very few ducks during the last three years. Three ducks have lived to carry the tags six years. Last Fall, 1924, I re-captured a duck tagged in 1918. If she lives to return next Spring, and I hope she will, she will break all duck records on this ranch.

CHAPTER XXX.

Game Protection.

THIS, a sportsmen's problem, may appear to you as being entirely out of place in a book like this; yet I want you to read, for I feel fully qualified to discuss this matter in a conscientious, fair and square, look-you-in-the-face manner, as I have the itching of my own trigger-finger fairly well harnessed, and have no desire to shoot any bird other than the cannibals; but on the other hand my boy, Ted, who is twenty-three years of age, and for whom I would willingly lie down and give up the ghost if it were actually necessary, likes to shoot, and I sometimes think he is as crazy for a gun as I once was, but that seems impossible.

Nearly twenty years ago I organized the South Essex County Game Protective Association, which, by the way, now has advanced into the hands of some of the best and most self-sacrificing sportsmee this earth can produce. And let me say right here that they havn stood, and are still standing, right behind me, backing me up in every just undertaking. If every county had an association of the same material the question would all be solved, for when these men asked our Dominion Government to proclaim a bird sanctuary around Jack Miner's home, in less than three months no shooting was allowed within a mile of my house, and the game warden came and declared it a Crown Lands' Bird Sanctuary.

To be sure, I have tasted the insults one experiences when he changes from a pull-down to a builder. An insulting doctor once said to me, as he stood in the safety zone and shook his fists at my red face, "Jack, you are just like old Uncle Joe; when he used to dance he wanted everybody to dance, but when he got religion he wanted everybody to pray."

Now the first thing to consider is that over ninety per cent. of the people in America don't want to shoot. They want to see the birds alive. They take nothing from the shooter, but the shooter takes all from them. Which should control, the ninety per cent. or the ten? I say there can be pleasure for both, if properly managed; but the shooter must be considered last, for the fall of one bird out of the air from his deadly aim gives pleasure to one only, while thousands are deprived of the thrilling enjoyment of seeing that bird alive. God says, "In any wise let the mother go and take the young to thee;" yet some of our people want to shoot the mother before she lays the eggs to hatch the young that He says we can have. Yes, a man may be a good, shrewd business fellow, but when he gets a gun in his hands he appears to lose all self-control and does not expose enough brains to give him a headache.

Government game wardens are usually a bunch of men appointed by pull and favor, and don't know a bit more about game protection than I know about the price of pork grease in Jerusalem. If called by its right name it would be "political protection," and I don't have to lie to tell the truth about it. However the less said the better, and it is of no use to us to look back at the past. We must remember Lot's wife stopped and looked back, and she turned into a pillar of salt; Pat's wife stopped and looked back, first over one shoulder and then over the other, and she turned into a beer saloon.

Personally I don't like to hear any one complain unless he has a carefully thought out suggestion for improvements. Therefore I will proceed to give you my plan, which is based on twenty years' intense interest and careful study.

First of all, every county in America should organize a real live, wild-life conserving association.

Delegates from each county should meet in annual State or Provincial convention with our Parliament members present to hear the discussion.

Appoint our game keepers by right, and not by favor.

Compel them to give an itemized account of every day's proceedings.

During the spring and early fall months let them go to the schools and give half-hour talks to the rising generation on the value and enjoyments of our out-of-door life. During the winter months this same game keeper could often take a bunch of school boys with him as he goes on his visits, carrying feed, and building shelters for the birds in time of need. This would prevent a game keeper from having to make an eagle out of a gnat fly in order to hold his job. Yes, the fellow who dissected the baby hawk's crop and found it contained crickets and grasshoppers, he could attend such a convention and demand the privilege of airing his views; but hawks and owls that live in Canada during the months of December, January and February do not live on grasshoppers during those months, therefore such questions might open up something higher than a grasshopper discussion.

Every gun should be licensed high enough to pay all expenditures, but no State or Province in America should be allowed over one month's open season on migratory birds until they are more plentiful

No person or persons should be allowed to feed artificial grain to birds for the sole purpose of slaughtering them. This would encourage the replanting of more natural duck and goose foods, and make our marshes more productive.

The bag limit should be kept down. Not that this bag limit law is easily enforced, but for the steady education that it is wrong and unsportsmanlike to slaughter. Any man who wants to shoot more than five ducks in a day, or twenty-five in a season, is not considerate of the other fellow's North American rights and privileges.

But the whole proposition is hinged on better education, and when the people of this continent wake up and find out that good, sensible game protection pays two hundred per cent. annual dividends, then we won't lie back and yawn and say it is no use trying.

As proof that I know what I am writing about, I call your attention to my own success, that you are compelled to believe. Now if one man, with limited means and no natural advantages, but backed up by good neighbors, can do what has been done here, what can the wealth and effort of one hundred and twenty-five millions of people do with our natural advantages?

Yes, I have demonstrated that the sanctuary plan is a sure preventive of extermination. With plenty of such places where neither rich nor poor dare molest them, bird lovers can have first choice and the shooters the overflow. We can have more tagging stations to enable us to trace the birds of different localities, as I have done here. We can organize an international bird-lovers' association. In fact, we can have anything that will lead to deeper interest and more education as to the value and enjoyment of our birds. Personally I have more confidence in a thimbleful of education than I have in a barrelful of bayonet-point compulsion.

Two years ago a gentleman in Peterborough, Ontario, engaged me to come for two days; I went to each school and talked as best I could. The following spring this dear man gave bird-house prizes to the same children. The accompanying photograph shows the results.

Now to those who think it not worth while: You are depriving yourself of a pleasure that is knocking at every man's door. God left the wild life in our care, and it is not a question of what we can have, but the question is, Will we have?

Just close your eyes and ears and abandon all of nature's sights and sounds; what extra attractions would spring have for you? On the other hand, just multiply the present attractions tenfold. Can it be done? Yes; "come over into Macedonia and help us," is my message to you.

CHILDREN WITH BIRD-HOUSES, PETERBOROUGH, ONTARIO

CHAPTER XXXI.

Creating a Bird Sanctuary.

A BIRD sanctuary is a suitable area of ground set aside for the birds to congregate in for shelter, food and protection, where their natural enemies are destroyed, and where neither rich nor poor dare molest them, "nor thieves break through and steal."

Here the birds will congregate in countless numbers, especially during their migration, and hold their great annual picnic and vocal contest, which enables each to select the best sweetheart. As soon as she consents to fly in a double harness with him and he says "I will, so help me Sun, Moon and Stars," they are off together, some for life, others for one season only. Now as soon as God's wireless says to them "The weather is O.K. at your nesting grounds," they join in a sort of a God-be-with-you-till-we-meet-again chorus and rise high on the evening air, and before the stars close their eyes again, these winged creatures are one thousand miles farther on, and the rising sun finds them singing on the same old perch of last year, right near their nesting place. I said evening air, because most birds migrate during the night.

The non-migratory birds will winter in this same sanctuary. Last winter, the eighth winter my sanctuary was set out, I fed over one-half bushel of wheat daily to the Bob White quail that wintered in there. As soon as spring came, these quail all left, and are now scattered over at least a two-mile area of the very best farming country, breeding on nearly every farm. And best of all, I have wheat ready to feed a bigger flock next winter.

The sanctuary plan is the only way I know of to control the two-legged cannibal, he who apparently will not allow his heart nor brain to act at all, but simply lets his murderous trigger-finger control his whole carcass. It may sound strange to the reader that I speak so harshly of this class of being, but it is personal knowledge that causes it. Being in the woods so much through life, depending as a hunter does, largely on my hearing, my ear drums have been kept exceptionally active, and up until the last few years I could almost hear a gnatfly sneeze; the result is I have heard a whole lot of things that would have sounded better had I been totally deaf.

One day a man came here with two or three younger fellows.

The pictures above of geese in flight are taken at the North Pond. Notice the evergreens in the distance which run around the pond, forming a windbreak and a shelter during storms.

The pictures above show the birds at the South Pond, with houses and tile plant in the background. These four prints give a fair idea of the kind of pictures presented in the 1,500 feet of motion picture films of geese which have been taken on the property.

including one of his own boys.   After showing them around, I came to the park and called the pheasants, and three beautiful Golden Pheasants came out and just spread their gorgeous plumage.   As they strutted across the green lawn, all fairly held their breath at such an eye-feast.   I turned to go to the house, made a few steps and changed my mind.   The boy said, "Oh father, just wouldn't they look nice in our woods?" The father switched his cud over and said, "I'd like to see them in the woods when I had my old No. 10 shotgun."

Years ago I stocked this township with Ringnecked pheasants, and all the power I had was "Please don't shoot the pheasants." A hunter got on the street car three miles north of my house, and as he quieted down he slapped his hand on his gamesack and remarked, "I've got five of them in here the red-headed blank-blank will never see again!" Now this man is hardly acquainted with me and I know he has nothing particular against me; only he just wanted to curse the man that had given him such a good day's sport.

There is another man in this township that apparently sent word to me in a roundabout way that he had three duck-tags, and if I would give him a dollar each for them, as I did the Esquimaux, I could have the tags.   Now these tags were put on young ducks that I raised here, and owing to the water drying up in the north pond that summer, they left early in September and went to this nearby water.   But if this man lives until I give him a dollar each for the three tags off these hand-raised pets, he will sure hold the world's record for longevity.

One of the common questions asked around my home is: "How do you understand the birds so well?" Really, the birds are an open book.   The question is how to understand humanity.   Seventy-five per cent. of the hunters that shoot the overflow of birds from my bird sanctuary can easily be called my enemies, while the fact remains they would never see a goose, let alone shoot one, if I did not feed, pet and harbor them here.   But I have this consolation: If I met with their approval—Well, 'nuff said!

This makes me think of Ikie and Jakie.   Jakie had apparently been imposed upon.   Ikie, trying to console him, said, "Jakie, don't worry.   Our Saviour had enemies." "Yes," replied Jakie, "but my Got, look vat they done to him!"

A sanctuary where one expects to entertain water fowl should, of course, be quite a large area of land and water; the reader can plainly see this point; and a natural marsh is, of course, the proper place.   But a sanctuary for the non-water birds can be made anywhere in the country or suburbs of a town; possibly a ravine with a small stream running through it would be preferable.   A great many sites can be chosen where the trees and shrubbery are already grown. Personally, I prefer growing my own trees, it is such a pleasure. Five acres makes a nice sanctuary. I would sooner have two five-acre sanctuaries, a mile or a mile and a half apart, on three thousand acres, than one fifteen-acre sanctuary, for the same area of land. These sanctuaries should be on or near the public highway so that the game-keeper could drive to and from them, the same as the mail carrier to the country mail box. This would enable him to visit an almost unlimited number of them every three days. What an enjoyable occupation this certainly would be for him, knowing that during the severe storms every bird in the country was in there, safely under his care. "I had rather be a doorkeeper in the house of my God, than to dwell in the tents of wickedness." Or I would sooner be a gamekeeper, caring for the birds in these little sanctuaries, than I would dwell in the Waldorf Astoria, free of charge.

If you contemplate planting one, first summer-fallow the land for one year. Plant evergreen trees, seven feet apart, eight rods wide all around the outside, leaving twelve to fifteen rods square in the centre. Here you will build your feed-racks and feed-bungalows. Set this out with all kinds of fruit-bearing shrubs and vines. Now, with a dog-and-cat-proof fence around the outside, your eyes will be opened as to what you can do with the birds.

I got my trees from the Ontario Forestry Department, costing me less than one dollar per thousand; I cultivated them for five years. The eighth year my trees were so thick you couldn't see a box-car a rod from you.

The fifth year one pair of mourning doves came and built; the ninth year, doves nested by the hundreds, and their sweet, cooing voices continue from early daybreak until the stars appear again.

Of course, to grow a sanctuary from seedlings—trees that are no bigger than ordinary tomato-plants—takes time; but remember, the Great Provider, Himself, couldn't make a four-year-old jackass in ten minutes. All of these things take a little time, but time well spent. Every golf course in America should be a bird sanctuary; just a small clump of shrubs here and there does the trick and brings the songs that you golfers cannot afford to be without.

"Oh, but how can we get the birds to come?" is the great cry. Please leave this to the birds. Don't you worry about them, nor don't run all over America to take care of them. Just build the sanctuary and let them come to you to be taken care of. My experiments here have proven that they will come clear across the continent to be cared for, and that the sanctuary plan is a sure preventive of our birds becoming annihilated by their enemies. Just the other day as I walked through my jungle four beautiful woodcocks flushed

SCOTCH PINES, PLANTED MAY, 1914
Photograph taken July, 1922.

from under the boughs that I pressed back. After an absence of over forty years the dear old woodcock is back on the same soil!

Yes, the sanctuary plan will permit us to have Bob White quail all along southern Canada. Quail in such a place will stand almost any kind of winter. It is simply up to us to take more pleasure in doing such things. It is no longer a question of what can we have, but a question of what will we have.

Remember, you can sit in your parlor with the best piano in America, and if some one doesn't reach out and touch the keys, that instrument will remain dormant, and you will be deprived of the lovely music it is capable of producing.

CHAPTER XXXII.

Our Native Swans.

THE SWANS we usually see in our parks throughout America are not natives of this country, and a great many people are not acquainted with the fact that we still have hundreds of real, beautiful, wild swans at large in this country.

Now in North America there are only two varieties of native swans, the trumpeter and the whistling swans. They are both pure white. Often we hear of a flock of swans being seen with some dark ones among them; these are young birds; swans do not get pure white the first year. The trumpeter swan is by far the larger of the two varieties; this bird weighs between twenty-five and thirty-five pounds, and is well-proportioned, not waddle-y like these European swans that are in our parks. But unfortunately for this, the largest migratory bird in America, it nested in what is now the cultivated parts of our continent; the result is it is almost exterminated. But the whistling swan, which is about one-third smaller than the trumpeter, I am pleased to report is still here by the thousands.

Shortly after I got the geese educated to come here the swans started congregating along the shores of the lake, three miles south, where, as I have previously stated, the geese usually go to roost, and occasionally a flock will follow the geese here in the morning, but I have never been able to induce them to alight, possibly on account of the ponds being small and muddy. There seem to be more of these white beauties every year, and one evening last April when the geese went to the lake, the voices of the swans could be heard at my home, apparently welcoming the geese back to the calm bosom of Lake Erie. Before sunrise next morning I was out to the lake, and as I looked over the bank, about one mile west of Kingsville, here were over three hundred swans feeding in the shallow water, all within a stone's throw of shore; a little farther out was a line of two hundred more; and the sandbar, which is from one-quarter to one-half mile out, was simply white with them for fully half a mile. While it was impossible to count them away out there, yet I am sure there were over a thousand. Remember, I have a powerful pair of glasses, and these birds were not gulls, they were swans; and

THESE WERE "WILD" SWANS. THE WILDNESS SEEMS TO HAVE DISAPPEARED

really the bunch of five hundred which I counted in the water did not look one-half the size of the flock that was on the bar.

But the encouraging part of it all is that these birds nest still farther north than the wild geese, therefore there is no danger at that point.

The last few years I have become quite well acquainted with the bird proposition around Niagara Falls, and it is sad to think that so many of our choicest waterfowl are meeting death in this rolling foam. Now I haven't lived there, and there is a whole lot I don't understand about the situation, but it seems that early in the spring these swans come to the open water above the Falls before the rest of the lake is open. Night comes on and they put their heads on their backs and drift, like so many white pillows. At times a bunch ventures a little too far, its members are caught in the rapid water, cannot rise and over the falls they go. Fully seventy-five per cent. are either killed with the ice or are drowned; those that have life enough left crawl upon the icebridge that is formed just below the falls. Now with the iron bridge just below them, and the hundred feet of a foaming falls in front of them, they are apparently bewildered. Not having strength enough to rise straight up they sit there, and gradually grow weaker and weaker, and if the night is frosty, the spray from the Falls simply freezes them into a helpless condition.

Mr. Wm. Hill, of Niagara Falls, told me that one morning last spring there were over forty live swans on the icebridge. Mr. Hill is a man well acquainted with the whole situation, and he got five and expressed them to me, but they were so weak they could hardly stand. One was bruised with the ice and died. Later on two other gentlemen sent me two more. The photograph shows the six swans in my park a few months later. Notice what beauties they are, and they couldn't look worse if they were paid for it, as they have just moulted. The photo shows them on land as well as in the water. Note what neat, trim beauties they are!

Now I am going to put them in my north pond and try to breed them there.

WILD WING-TIPPED SWANS
Happily at home on one of our ponds

CHAPTER XXXIII.

The Line of Migration.

A GREAT many writers that come here report this place as being on the line of bird migration. That is a mistake, for this is no more the migrating line for the birds than Chicago, Detroit or Toronto.

Very true, I am only fifteen miles west of Point Pelee, the most extreme southern part of mainland in Canada, and where thousands of small birds come to cross Lake Erie. But what does a duck or a goose care about hunting a short water flight across Lake Erie, when the latter can rise up and go one thousand miles without alighting?

For thirty-five years o my bloodthirsty life it was my great ambition to shoot a swan to mount with my collection. Did I do it? No. Why? Because very seldom was one ever seen around here. I only know of two being shot in this township, one shot over forty years ago, and the other about twenty-five years ago. Yet last spring when I went up to the lake to see them I could have shot between five and ten at one volley. Not because this is in the line of migration. No; no. But because it is all in the line of education!

The geese have been educated to come here for food and protection, and the swans have educated themselves to know that where the geese alight spells safety for them. And although the wild swans have not lit in my pond yet, I have the satisfaction of knowing that hundreds come within three miles of me, and it has all been done through love and education; for when the wild geese convinced me that they knew me as their deadly enemy, and afterwards showed their love toward me by flying to me from all directions for food and protection, they conquered and won one of the most bloodthirsty and cruel, deadly enemies the birds of North America ever had. And it is not because of the line of migration, but because of that blessed peace, and education, whose doors stand continually open. And if ever this dear old earth is made free from devilish, revengeful fighting, it will be through this same dear love and education, man towards the fowls of the air and the beasts of the field, man towards man, family towards family, and nation towards nation, as compulsory, bayonet-point heathenism always leaves a crimson revenge in its wake.

CHAPTER XXXIV.

Inquiries and Answers.

A S I am a very poor writer and cannot afford a stenographer I am answering, right now, a storm of questions so that I trust I will prevent our female mail-sorters from overloading my mail box.

1. How can I get the wild geese to come to my pond?

If you can get them to alight within a mile, or any reasonable distance away, feed them there, scattering the food while they are absent. After they have been coming regularly for a week or so, go sidling near them with a team of horses as if you were working on the farm. Never drive straight at them, but go quartering past. After you have tried this on a few times during the week and haven't frightened them away, try the same stunt without the team, watching them very closely, and if they turn their breasts to the wind, withdraw, very carefully, not by turning back, but by going quartering away. Always wear the same clothes, and in two or three weeks your birds will get to know you.

Then as you approach anywhere near them, call them, in any way you see fit. They will learn to know your voice. Now you can dress up and wear a stove-pipe hat for aught the geese care. Your voice will quiet them, and by your actions they will know you.

Now gradually move your feed and attractions towards where you want your birds to come, and they will come and will compel you to believe they were glad of the opportunity.

2. Why do you put your full address on the goose and duck tags?

Because it has been a success, while a number is much harder to trace. I have had dozens of rings and tags of different kinds sent to me that were taken off pigeons and wild ducks, and the numbers could be easily read. I advertised them time and again, and up to date have not received one word of proof as to who put them on. Moreover when you have the stamp made, one stroke of the hammer on top of mother's flat-iron completes the trick, and your post office address is the only real way to do it right.

3. Where can I get a stamping outfit?

Almost any stencil manufacturer can fit you out. I have two

stamps, one for the small birds, making letters about the size of small newsprint, and for the ducks and geese the stamp is fully five times as large.   I also have a set of individual letters and figures for stamping the Scripture text and so forth.   I don't think my whole outfit cost me over twenty-five dollars.

4   I saw a bird the other day; it was about so big and from where I stood it looked to be ringed, streaked and striped.   What was it?

The woods and fields are full of such beauties, and I am acquainted with them all, but do not know them by their proper names. Dear mother taught me the names of our commonest birds.   That was the only way I had of knowing them.   I, of course, had a name for every one.   The Nuthatch I called the tree-creeper; the Wood-thrush was called the brown linnet; the Flicker I called a fiddler; and the buzz of a rattlesnake in the long grass automatically called my bare feet upon a log.

5. What bird lays first in the spring?

Here in southern Ontario, the great horned owl is the first I know of to nest in the trees, and the horned lark is the first to nest on the ground.   Of the latter, I have seen the young able to fly on April 3rd.

6. What birds breed the fastest?

Bob White quail are the fastest breeding birds I know of.   If not molested they will beat the English sparrows more than double. The quail raises two broods a year, and quite often three.   I know a pair of quail that reared thirty-eight young in their first two broods. These were in charge of the old male bird on October the 10th, while the female had a brood of tiny chicks that I could not count.

What handicaps this little potato-bug-destroyer has! She is exposed to all kinds of enemies the whole year round, especially during December, January and February, when nature is clothed in her white robe (Bob cannot change his color) while the English sparrow, or flying rat, has a hole prepared that he lines with feathers and only has to come out an hour or two during the day for food.

7. What are the best trees and shrubs to attract birds?

This depends largely on the trees and vines your soil will produce.   My soil is clay loam, first class corn ground.   I am planting mulberries and elderberries, wild grapes and red cedars, and some sumach which grows fairly well; but sumach will, of course, do better in sandy soil.

I know of nothing to equal the mulberries.   I have mulberry trees only five years old and it is hard to believe the amount of bird food one tree will yield, starting to ripen about June 15th and continuing all through the fruit season, or, in other words, from six to ten weeks.

The red cedar is another tree we must have, as it affords shelter as well as food, the berries, like the wild grapes, hanging all winter.

Where the climate will permit, by all means plant some mountain ash. The big, crimson clusters of fruit hanging on the mountain ash trees in northern Ontario are more beautiful to me than the great Woolworth, or the General Motors office building of Detroit; and what they look like to the hundreds of birds that feed on them during the fall and winter months can only be imagined when we are returning from a moose-hunt, late at night, cold, tired, and hungry.

But the two outstanding ones, to me, are mulberries and wild grapes, the berries for summer, and the grapes for the winter.

8. How can I get the birds to come to my window in the winter?

Make two movable self-servers and nail each to a top of a barrel. Feed cracked nuts, a little suet, etc.

Set your feed-racks a rod or two apart, back among your shrubbery. As soon as you have a nice bunch of birds coming keep moving your racks toward your house; this can be done by just moving the farther one around in front of the other, each time.

9. How long does it take our common birds to hatch and fly from the nest?

Robins set from thirteen to fourteen days, and fly in about two weeks. But wild birds are not like our domestic fowls. If the latter leaves the nest, or stays off one night, that brood is about sure to all die. But if a robin is disturbed, such as staying off the nest for six or eight hours at a time, the young are very apt to hatch. I have known cases of this kind when the eggs didn't hatch until the fifteenth day.

I once set a hen on nine wild duck eggs. She started out fine, and set steadily for two weeks. Then she changed her mind, so I changed hens; but number two was no better. I then took the eggs and put them under hen number three, who finished the job on the thirty-second day, when seven out of the nine hatched, but they were very weak. Yet I managed to raise five of them to mature ducks. Duck eggs should hatch in twenty-eight days.

Barn swallows fly in about thirty-five days from the time the first eggs are laid; yet it must be remembered that young swallows must be able to float in the air before they leave the nest.

The chipping sparrow is about the fastest bird I know. On June 16th a female started building in a little cedar tree one rod from her other four babies that were still in the nest under the care of her mate. At noon the 17th she had her nest completed and one egg in it; June 18th, at 9 a.m. there were two eggs in the nest; and at 7 a.m., June 20th, she was setting on four eggs. At 3 p.m., July 1st, all four eggs had hatched, and on July 11th the four baby birds flew out of the nest into the other trees.

The mourning doves only lay two eggs at a setting, but still they breed fast as they raise four or five pairs each year. I have never seen three eggs in a mourning dove's nest; we quite often see one egg, but this is a case where some nest-robbing bird stole the first egg. On July 23rd two young doves flew from a nest; on the 25th and 26th the mother laid two more eggs in the same nest; on August 9th the two young were hatched, and on the 22nd both flew out. This spring was very backward, but there were young doves larger than sparrows in a nest right near my house on April the 19th. And they keep on laying right into September. I have tagged the young doves, but have only heard from one; that was killed in Georgia. Last winter a few doves wintered here with us.

I might also say that I have tagged dozens of young robins but have only heard from one; that was killed in Missouri.

But you can just rest assured where birds get peaceable treatment and shelter, all that can return do so. This can be said of all species from the wren to the Canada goose.

10. What birds lay the largest eggs according to their size?

Killdeers and sand pipers lay the largest eggs according to their size of any bird I am acquainted with.

11. What is the most powerful bird for its size?

The screech owl. I have known a screech owl that evidently did not weigh over four ounces, to kill a domestic fowl that weighed over six pounds, the owl alighting on the hen's head at night, eating her eyes out, and eventually killing her.

12. What do you mean by pinioning birds?

Clipping means just simply clipping the wing feathers to prevent the bird from flying, but pinioning means to take the wing off, bone and all, at the first joint. This is usually done when birds are young, before the wings have developed. A sharp needle and thread is used for tying the two arteries. Then with the scissors the wing is snipped off. But remember, when this is once done, that bird can never fly again, as the wing cannot grow on any more than an amputated thumb upon your hand.

If a bird is slightly pinioned it may not be able to fly when it is fat and heavy, yet this same bird may get thin and on a windy day rise up and make fairly good headway in the air.

This operation may look cruel to some, yet while birds are young, before they can fly, their wings are apparently numb and they do not mind the operation at all. If birds are to be kept in captivity it is the proper thing to do.

But remember, one bird in the bush is worth ten in the hand; so do not let us figure on keeping them in captivity more than we can possibly help; for that is cruel.

13. How long do birds live?

This of course depends largely upon the variety of bird. Wild geese will undoubtedly live to be as old as a human being. I have two breeding pairs with their wings pinioned; three of these birds were originally wild, but Tom Johnson (Jack Johnson's son) was hatched here on May 17th, 1907. He paired off in 1911 with a goose that was wing-tipped in 1909, and old David and his sweetheart were both wing-tipped in 1911. So you see the youngest one of these four birds is at least thirteen, as they would be not less than a year old when they came here, but I have absolute proof that Tom Johnson is now over sixteen. And none of these pets shows any sign of old age. In fact, they play and frolic about the premises with their families as if they were the biggest boys and girls of the bunch.

Wild ducks will live to be over fifteen. Old Susan, the mother of the Mulberry family, was hatched here in May, 1909. I pinioned her. She raised a family every season until this year, but I have noticed that the last two winters affected her very much; in fact, now, when I go out to them, she acts as if she would like me to give her a cane to help herself up the bank. Another fact about her is that in 1921 she laid only seven eggs and raised six young, five of them drakes; the last year she dropped one lower and laid only six eggs; all hatched, but were very weak; one died in the nest but the other five lived to migrate. But all were drakes. Therefore, ten out of the last eleven ducks old Susan raised were drakes.

Another old black duck hatched in 1905 was killed by a great horned owl in January, 1918; she was fat and healthy when killed. I got the owl.

A greenhead drake came here in 1907. One wing was badly shot so I took it off. This drake died in 1917.

But in every case they show signs of weakness first during the winter; therefore it is plain to me that if they have the use of both wings and can migrate to a warm climate, wild ducks will live for fifteen and possibly twenty years.

However, this is a point that I don't think we hunters need worry a second about, as I am sure not one per cent. of our game birds die of old age. Out of the four hundred and forty ducks I have tagged, only three lived to carry the tag six years, to my knowledge, seventy-five per cent. of the tags being returned in less than three years.

14. How shall I build a martin house?

A martin house can be built almost any style desired, say on a miniature scale of your own house; supposing your house is thirty feet square, build your bird house on the inch scale, which will be thirty inches square; or if you want to build a smaller house, build it on the half-inch scale.

By all means have a system to build on. I once heard a colored man say he didn't fear the average human family near as much as he did a yellowjackets' nest, "'cos de hohnets am so doggone well ohganized."

The rooms in a martin house should be not less than six, and not over eight, inches square. The door should be level with the floor, same as our dwellings, the doorstep or verandah one-half inch lower than the floor or door. Door should be one and one-half inches wide, made in any style desired.

White is the best color to paint, trimmed to suit your own taste.

To set house up, first put in two ordinary fenceposts, about four to six inches apart, four feet in the ground and four out. Now put the martin house pole between the two posts, with pole about three inches from the ground. Bore half-inch holes right through all three, one hole about three inches from the top of fence-posts, another about six inches from the ground, and bolt all three together through these holes. This leaves the pole high and dry, and by taking out the top bolt and loosening the bottom one, it permits you to raise and lower the house very easily when you want to clean it out or paint it in the fall. If left up, stop the door to keep out the "flying rats."

Now don't think it a difficult job to build a martin house. It is a sunny pastime.

Some years ago I happened to be in Brantford, Ontario, when a telephone call requested me to come over to the School for the Blind and give them a talk on birds. A second thought caused me to answer, Yes, and the accompanying plate will prove that these dear children listened to me, and I can assure you I listened to them, as several of these smart lads told me how and where they had "seen" different things. At the close, a vote of thanks was moved; the seconder, a youth of about sixteen, used some words I shall never forget. He said, "It is a pleasure to me to second this motion, but coupled with it I just wish to say, dear Uncle Jack Miner, that although we have never seen the sun, we are not blind; we can plainly see all you have been telling us. People often speak of the night being dark. With us there is no darkness. It is all light "

In a few months the boys sent me the accompanying photograph of a martin house constructed by their own hands.

This last June I visited a few towns on the Canadian side of the St. Lawrence River. I took particular notice of the beautiful little parks, the neat way in which they were kept, etc. Really, fifty dollars put into a nice, neat martin house would add thousands of dollars to the attractiveness of these grounds, for I never saw more purple martins in my life where there were no bird houses than there were around those quaint, ancient Canadian towns, but not a bird house. The martins appeared to be building in the eavetroughs and the cornices of some of the old buildings.

MARTIN HOUSE BUILT BY THE BOYS STANDING BESIDE IT, BOTH OF WHOM ARE TOTALLY BLIND

15. How fast do birds fly?

This is a question hard to answer and prove, and one upon which we may differ. I have heard men say that geese migrate at the rate of one hundred and twenty miles an hour. While this may be true, I have no earthly reason to believe it.

My home is three miles north of the lake; these geese go to the lake to roost and in the morning they rise, high and as they reach the shore there is always some one with a high-power rifle to greet them; these volleys of shot on a still morning will tell you the very second the geese have reached shore and are coming our way; and in every case, it will be over three minutes before the geese get to my home.

Moreover, when they start for Hudson Bay I have time and again wired ahead of them, and on three different occasions I have got returns, and if they were the same geese I wired ahead of, they were travelling between fifty and sixty miles an hour.

Capt. Eddie Rickenbacker, the aviator, tells me that he has often overtaken geese in the air, and the only way they could travel one hundred miles an hour was by dropping, which they did to avoid him.

Because a goose was killed at Hudson Bay three days after we tagged it here, and because another one was killed at the Belcher Islands, Hudson Bay, four days after being tagged here, at my home, this does not prove anything, as we have no proof how long these birds lingered here after being tagged, nor how long they were there before being shot. But there is one thing I am quite certain of: That the great majority of them make the flight from my home to Hudson Bay without coming down, and I firmly believe they go about fifty miles an hour, and not two miles a minute as some report them to.

16. What became of the Passenger Pigeon?

This bird was about twice the size of the mourning dove, and so much the same in looks, ways and habits, that the mourning dove could be called a miniature pigeon.

In the early '70's these pigeons migrated through Ohio in countless numbers, I might say in clouds. We came to Canada in '78, and I am sure I have not seen five hundred pigeons since.

Some people advance the theory that a storm blew them all into the lake. Why, bless your life, there is no lake in America that would hold them all!

I am firm in my belief that they were exterminated by a contagious disease.

The last three pigeons I shot, I shot in the fall of 1884. I was then nineteen years of age, and have a distinct recollection of what they were like. These birds were all three diseased, and were not over two-thirds the actual size of the healthy passenger pigeon. I took them home, but mother said they were not fit for food.

In northern Canada the snowshoe hare, or native rabbit, becomes so numerous about every seven or eight years that a disease sets in and fully ninety-nine out of a hundred—yes, I might say nine hundred and ninety-nine out of a thousand—of them die off. I have seen the skeletons lie in the swamps by the dozens, and when the snow came I hunted, three weeks later, and only saw the tracks of two rabbits. This same exterminating disease system has controlled the native rabbit in Canada, and they have died off on an average of every seven or eight years, as far back as man has any knowledge of them.

Whether this is a correct explanation of the disappearance of the passenger pigeon, or not, I have heeded the warning, and have arranged my ponds on the bathtub system, and during the late summer months the water is all let out, and the ponds allowed to dry up; then I sow wheat and rye extremely thick in the bottom to purify the soil, as the sun, and the cropping of ground, will purify the soil the same as circulation will purify water. The overflow pipe is then closed, and when the fall rains come and raise the spring, the underland drain, which is laid from the pond to the spring, floods it over, and preserves the green food in the bottom of the pond for the birds when they arrive, as this green food in the bottom of the pond will not rot but will keep fresh so long as the water remains icy cold.

17. Whereabouts in Canada is your home? And what can you raise there?

My home is two miles north of Kingsville, Ontario. Kingsville is a neat little beauty spot nestled on the north shore of Lake Erie, due north of Sandusky, Ohio, and twenty-eight miles south-east of Detroit, Michigan. Its population is about two thousand, with three well-attended churches, and two first-class hotels.

By the way, Kingsville is the most southerly town in the Dominion of Canada.

Now we can raise almost anything here, from a flagpole to a boiling-hot political quarrel, but our chief crop is corn. We condense it into hogs, and ship them just as they run. Then we bank the money to buy more land to grow more corn to feed more hogs, and so forth, and so forth.

CHAPTER XXXV.

Sportsmanship.

MY BOOK would not be complete without giving you a handful of the material that built the foundation for my enjoyable life.

Now, as I see it, there is a great difference between a sport and a sportsman. As to the sport, I think the less said the better. But the word Sportsman spells a great many great words; first of all it spells *others* and *self-sacrifice*, for to be a real sportsman one cannot stand alone.

When I was a lad eight years of age and slept with my two brothers, I was awakened one morning by the touch of father's powerful hand, and he whispered, "Jack, do you want to go with me for a pigeon hunt?" and my bare feet were soon on the floor. About sunrise found father and me crouched in an old fencerow that bordered a wheat stubble, and the pigeons alighting, or trying to alight, on two dead-topped hickory trees that were in range of us. As they would hover, father would give them both barrels; and really, he made it rain pigeons for a while. Soon my little gamesack and father's hunting-coat pockets were filled to the limit and we were on our way back home, all smiles, and anxious to get there to tell how it all happened.

Father promised me when these pigeons were all eaten up he and I would go again. About the fourth day (or morning, I should say), we were off again; but to my disappointment father had invited another Englishman to go along, Mr. Thomas Perkins. Father called him Tommy. I was more disgusted than ever when we arrived at the shooting grounds, for what did father do but put Tommy in the same hiding and shooting place that we had occupied a few mornings previous, right between the two hickory trees, while he and I went across the field and watched by a big dead elm, where we had only seen a few flocks alight the previous morning. You see the pigeons would alight on these trees before flying down into the stubble.

The fun soon started. I say "fun" but to me it was a clear case of disgust, for every flock that came went to the two hickory trees, and father would almost lose control of himself, laughing and chuckling over the way Tommy was rolling them down. "There" he said, "I am sure he killed eight that lick!"

Finally a flock or two came our way, and out of the four shots father fired we got only twelve, and really the dear man did not seem to be watching our side of the field, but got all his enjoyment out of his friend's success.

Finally Tommy waved his hand to us to go over, and as these two met, each tried to talk the faster. But as for me, I was disgusted right from my bare feet to my red hair; I did not have my little game-sack half full! However, I helped pick up pigeons and soon we were off for home. But every fence we came to, the morning's shoot was rehearsed by these two old English sportsmen. When we came to the spot where each went his way, Tommy reached out his hand and gripped father's in a firm, heart-warming way, as he said, "John, I want to thank you from the bottom of my 'eart. That's been the nicest bit of pigeon shooting, John, I hever 'ad." Then as he turned to go he stopped very suddenly. "Oh, 'ere," he said; "I don't want more than a half dozen of these birds, and you have a big family; 'ere, Jack, put um in your bag." And really the dear man loaded me down with pigeons.

That morning's sport did not stop there, but for the next forty-five years I had the enjoyment of hearing father occasionally rehearse the pleasure of seeing Tommy roll the pigeons down. And thus I was raised to know that when one invites another on a hunt, he is your guest, and the more pleasure your guest has, the greater your accomplishment.

Now I am a man that stands five feet, ten inches, and weighs about one hundred and eighty-five pounds; but this I am certain of: Any sportsman would have to be a bigger man to hold a bigger and a better time than I have had.

On the other hand, this earth does not produce bigger and better men than it has been my privilege to hunt and sleep with in the wilds of America, and I do not think there is a better place in this world to find out who you are associating with than when on a hunting expedition.

After my brother and I were accidentally separated I thought very little of going to the wilds again; but a bunch of my friends came to me and insisted that I go with them. As a result, a small party was organized and I went along, as what I considered a guest, for I was allowed to do anything I saw fit; they even carried the water, did all the cooking and sawed the wood, allowing me to do the splitting of it, as I understood the axe maybe a little the best. To say the least, we had one of those enjoyable outings, a good desire to go, plenty of food and plenty of game, and a good desire to come home.

After we were home and settled down with our loved ones again, one evening a rap came to my door, and on turning the knob, who should be there but my dear old hunting party, not loaded down with moose-meat, but with oysters, and they surprised me by their presence. But my surprise was still greater when one of them rose up from the table, called me their leader, and read the following address:

"Our dear Gorilla Chief"

This, in all probability, will be the last meeting of the Quebec hunting party for 1901.   If we should be permitted, in another year, to go again to the wilds of Quebec, there will possibly be some changes in our company—new members added, and some of our present members unable to be with us.

We wish to express to you, our leader, the thanks which are your due, for the kindness shown us all on our hunting excursion and ask you to accept this present as a token of our appreciation. We know that we could not have had a leader more thoughtful of our comfort and pleasure.

It is with grateful hearts that we remember that each was the equal of the others in your estimation, that no rough language was allowed in camp, and that when Sunday came round, no guns were shot off and the hymns of "home, sweet home" were sung and enjoyed by all.

That you may be permitted to lead hunting parties into Quebec for many years to come is the sincere wish of

> LEONARD MALOTT,
> JAMES DOAN,
> WESLEY ULCH,
> ELIHU SCRATCH, Sec.

Actually, up till that minute I had had no thought of them looking upon me as their leader. The words contained in the address filled my living room, and I could hardly reply. But my thoughts drifted back to that September morning of 1873; and if this address were in its proper place, it would be engraved on the tombstones of those two dear old men who set me such a self-sacrificing example of good sportsmanship on that little pigeon hunt, so long ago.

BUT BEST OF ALL I LOVE BOYS, AND BOYS LOVE ME IN RETURN

This photograph is of my Sunday school class twenty years ago

CHAPTER XXXVI.

Conclusion.

IN CLOSING, I wish to say to my many friends that I have done as you requested: I have written the book. And have made many mistakes, often repeating myself when I had volumes of untouched material; yet I have done the best I could.

And to the purchaser, don't think your money is thrown away; for if I get a profit it will surely go towards helping our migratory birds over the top.

On going to the publisher I expect to order a few thousand copies. If I see that these are appreciated by the public I may write a booklet on Boys and Home, although I have nothing from which to write but practical experience, being just a grown-up boy myself; mother said I would never be of age. Yet I feel fully qualified to deal briefly with this most important subject, knowing that H-o-u-s-e does not spell Home.

I can sympathize with all classes, especially him who thinks himself down and out, for I have had black and blue proof that a good, swift kick in the right time and place will give a bare-foot boy a good lift in

After Ten Years

PUBLISHERS' NOTE: *It is now over ten years since we placed on the market this book, entitled* JACK MINER AND THE BIRDS. *It met with ready acceptance at the hands of the public, sold readily, and the demand for it has increased, season by season, ever since. In order to meet this demand we are now placing on the market the present enlarged edition at a popular price. In addition to the original material, this book has several new chapters written by Jack Miner ten years later, which bring the account of his activities at his bird sanctuary up to date in book form.*

THE REILLY & LEE CO.,
325 West Huron Street,
Chicago.

MIGRATORY BIRD SANCTUARIES—*Are They a Success?*

I have absolute proof that the most sought-after birds will change their migration route in order to come to sanctuaries for food and protection. This rightly and justly gives the bird-lovers first chance with their long-focus-lensed cameras to secure pictures which will live on and on, through generations. The flight-shooting between sanctuaries, that is still possible, allows the average shooter the privilege of securing all the game he should have, and helps him control the itching of his never-satisfied trigger-finger. Also it leaves him with a broader smile and, I believe, a clearer conscience than if he killed the box-car bloody limit that I understand is still allowed by the Migratory Bird Treaty.

Best of all, where the birds are properly fed and cared for in sanctuaries, this system prevents the wholesale slaughter that is carried on by market hunters or by thoughtless or self-centered men using baited fields. I use the word "thoughtless" because I am absolutely certain in my own mind that there are many, many good, honest-intending men who are shooting fully five times the ducks and geese to which they are entitled, and are doing it without any thought of the average North American citizen's just rights and fair, though limited, privileges.

I am ready to admit that there are shooters who are putting out hundreds of dollars' worth of feed for ducks and geese, and are not shooting any more than the average shooter should. But these men are about as scarce as angels on earth.

About the most interesting baited-field duck stories, to me, are told by some innocent officials or men in power. Time and again I have heard such a man say, "Oh, Mister Miner, these men feed thousands of bushels of grain. Really, they don't kill many ducks. Why, when they rowed us out to the blind, there were at least five thousand ducks there and they scared them all away and never allowed a single shot into them. But in about one-half

Geese now know the Jack Miner Bird Sanctuary is a place of safety and stay all winter. A winter scene of Canada Geese around Jack Miner's goose trap.

hour, the ducks started coming back in small bunches of three, five, seven, and so forth. Yet if fifteen or more came, we were not allowed a shot for fear we would kill too many."

Ha! Ha! Why, bless your life, this is systematic duck-shooting and hoodwinking. Yes, I say "hoodwinking." For the facts are that if those men had shot into the flock at long range, they would not have killed more than three or five ducks, but they would have scared the great flock away; as it was, none were frightened, and small bunches soon came back and were slaughtered as they came. Remember, professional duck and goose shooters never shoot to scare.

Not long since I received a letter, short but to the point, saying: "Express me two old, mated pairs of geese; price is an after consideration.'' Now here is what these old, mated pairs are used for: after the hunter has his live decoys stationed out, he ties the goose of one more mated pair out about twenty-five feet in front of the blind or hide. The goose is wearing a harness that is made invisible by her feathers and she is taught to stand tied. Her sweetheart, the gander, is taken into the hide. Then as soon as a family of five or eight or possibly ten geese is seen coming, the gander is let out at the opportune time. He at once starts honking, and, with open wings, rushes to his old sweetheart. Their loving honks start the whole flock of decoys to puncturing the air with loud, welcoming honks that echo and re-echo up and down and in all other directions. The deceived wild geese, hearing these, shut off the gas, put on their four-wheel brakes, and descend in front of possibly three automatic or pump-guns.

The above is just one crude flash of duck and goose shooting, using live decoys, especially on baited fields.

Please allow me to state further, in all kindness, that baited fields or the use of live decoys, is not sportsmanship. It is taking an unfair advantage. And the taking of an unfair advantage is not sport in any game, nor at any stage of the game.

It is true our forefathers did put out salt in the back fields, to bait the deer; but this was done in order to secure needed meat for a family. But to set a salt-lick to bait deer, is the most degrading thought a sportsman can entertain. To do so is to take a shamefully unfair advantage of the deer.

Now, to the sportsmen of America: please do not think I have any enmity against any person who shoots more game than he should. No, no. Far from it. For who am I? Why, fifty years ago I was a market-hunter, and left a trail of blood behind me.

About forty-five years ago a few wild geese started to alight and feed in this county and township; and of course I started after them to secure a few. I was so enthusiastic that I crawled nearly all the buttons off my wish-bone, wishing to get more of them. During the five or seven years I chased them I am sure I didn't kill twenty altogether. But, thank God, my ability as a hunter and shot eventually introduced me to the best class of high-principled sportsmen the world could produce, and my thoughts started to change. I found other ways to get warm clothes, without doing market-hunting. In 1892, one pair of wing-tipped bob-white quail that I saved from the previous fall's hunt and kept in a crude wire cage, supplied me with sixty-three fertile quail eggs to experiment with. And I have gradually cultivated the friendship of the birds until now they come to me from all points

of the compass, and the only ones I shoot any more are the enemies of the more lovable and cheerful and valuable birds.

Is the migratory bird sanctuary a success? Hunters, think of it:
on May the first, 1930, I had more than one hundred occupied

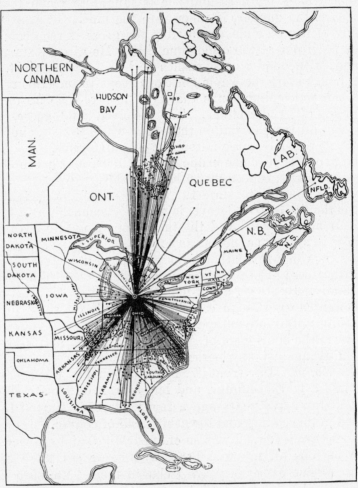

Migration map showing where the geese, that were tagged at
the Jack Miner Bird Sanctuary, were killed between
1915 and 1931.

mourning doves' nests on one acre of land, all within two hundred
yards of my back door!

While this may sound strange, right here I want to make a
public confession. It is this: all I know about humanity and birds,
God, my dear mother, men and birds themselves have taught me.
It was Mother who, in the first place, told me how beautiful they

were, and tried to teach me to distinguish the different birds by the sounds they made. About the first one of God's promises I read, He said I could "have dominion over the fowls of the air." When the birds began to come to me, and hunters started to annoy me, saying unreasonable things about me and my motives, then the dearest of men came forward and helped me control my crimson disposition. Day by day, both men and birds helped me. As the birds honked, quacked and sang, big men's smiles grew broader, and I studied the birds' ways and I finally started catching them. But it was slow work. I was seven years catching my first 109 wild geese. During the last seven years, on the contrary, I have caught over eleven thousand of these big fat old Canadian honkers, and there is no doubt in the world but that there are over five thousand, and possibly six thousand, of these geese still alive and carrying my private tag.

A few years ago a Mr. Jones started a bird sanctuary near St. Thomas, Ontario, about one hundred miles east of me. He sent me pictures of geese, there, with my tag on them. Yes, these geese were travelling back and forth. And you can depend on it, they will go from one sanctuary to another. This gives the average shooter all the opportunity he needs to secure all he should have, between sanctuaries.

Birds of North America migrate from one country to another. A large number nest and raise their young, and spend the spring and summer in Canada; but as fall approaches, they fly to the southern regions of the United States. Therefore, as the birds are natives of no one country, there exists a Migratory Bird Treaty between the United States and Canada, which arbitrates matters so that all game birds on the continent are afforded equal protection in migrating back and forth between the two countries.

It is now twenty-six years since I first noticed a decrease in various species of birds on the continent, both among the song and insectivorous birds and also among game birds. When I began my investigation of the causes of the decrease in numbers of ducks and geese, I found an answer in the increased numbers of hunters, and their use of the automatic pump-gun. Man appeared to be devoting too much time to the killing of game birds, and not enough to their welfare and protection. Thus I conceived the idea of starting a sanctuary — a place where birds would find shelter, food and protection from the guns of hunters.

Not possessing wealth, I was unable to build large ponds, but as I was engaged in the brick manufacturing business I turned one rather large clay-pit into a lake, fenced it off, and posted my invitation to the birds. I first purchased a pair of wild geese, clipped their wings, and placed them in the pond. Then I scattered corn around, and sat back to see others swoop down. This was in 1904. And I continued to scatter corn until 1908 before there were any additions to the two geese I had placed there. That is how scarce wild geese were at that time.

The first visit brought eleven geese, and these remained about eight weeks before they flew away. They returned the following year with twenty-two others, remaining eight weeks. In 1910, more than three hundred dropped in to see me: while in 1911, there were so many that it was impossible to make any sort of a

One corner of Jack Miner's Bird Sanctuary on a cold January morning. Jack Miner now winters approximately 5,000 Canada Geese. They go north in the spring to nest and bring their young back in the fall, the most of which go on south for all America to benefit from.

count. To present some idea of how many have come each year since that time, it requires a fund of $10,000 every year to purchase food for them. Thus the sanctuary idea and the idea of artificially feeding the waterfowl, have proved themselves. After twenty-six years of work, I am convinced of the success of the sanctuary as a measure for the protection of birds.

Many people have accused me of "protecting birds to die of

old age." This is far from the truth. My idea is simply to prevent the extermination of ducks and geese, and to provide for another generation the same enjoyment in these birds which this, and past generations, have had. I am not in any measure opposed to a man's shooting eight or ten ducks, or two or three geese, for food; but I am opposed to men going out and slaughtering game birds, just for the sake of killing.

A sanctuary does not take anything away from the hunter. It increases his chances, rather.

Fifteen years ago the beautiful white whistling swans were reduced to hundreds on this continent, and were in danger of be-

A close-up of native whistling swan on one of
Jack Miner's ponds.

coming extinct. I visited Niagara Falls and found that these birds were being caught by the hundreds in the death-trap which that river presented. It seems that the swans, on their northward migrating flight, used to make Lake Erie, fifteen miles above the Falls, their first stopping place. There they would drop down into open water, tuck their heads under their wings, and go to sleep, resting from their long flight. Many, doing so, would be trapped by the swift current of the river, and be carried over the Falls. Some which survived even that experience would succeed in getting out upon the ice-bridge below the Falls, only to become coated over with ice from the freezing spray of the Falls, slowly freezing to death.

I discussed this deplorable condition with William Hill, better known as "Red" Hill, a life-long student of the Niagara River and its currents. He informed me that geese and ducks had in other years fallen prey to the river, but that my sanctuary, up in Essex County, was now luring them away from this harm. "I haven't seen a wild goose around here, since you began drawing them to your ponds,'' he told me.

"Then, why can't I attract the swans away from it, Red?" I asked.

I secured several pairs of swans to serve as decoys. That was the beginning. Last summer, more than four thousand of these beautiful waterfowl spent from a month to six weeks along the lake shore at Kingsville, where the government details Royal Canadian Mounted Police to protect them, both day and night.

Not only do ducks and geese find shelter in my sanctuary, but around the ponds have been planted several rows of evergreen trees which, serving as a wind-break, attract hundreds of song and insectivorous birds.

The thing that pleases me most is that since my sanctuary has succeeded, hundreds of similar ones have been started by the provincial and dominion governments of Canada. Also in the United States countless hundreds have been established.

Our Diminishing Ducks and Geese

International readers, please consider these crudely written facts without being offended, as it is not my intention to give offense. I do, however, want all to understand plainly the situation.

My national relationship is the same as eighty-five per cent of our migratory birds, except that they are Canadians by birth and United States tourists during the winter, while I am a Buck-eye by birth and a Canadian by adoption. Therefore I am one hundred per cent North American, with the same love and high esteem for Dover Center, Ohio, and the American people, as my father displayed for his birthplace, Leicester, England, and the English people,

Now, as far as wild game is concerned, the settled parts of North America have long since gone through the stage of having something for nothing. If we are going to bring the game back — and this we can do, if we choose to — we have got to pay for it. The average shooter pays at least twenty-five dollars for a gun, and five dollars for ammunition. Surely he should be willing to pay another five dollars for something to shoot at, this five dollars to be divided between federal and state, and Dominion and provincial departments. If he is not willing to pay the five dollars, let him go without a license. Remember, kindness without firmness is a total failure. So that's that.

Now we can reclaim all the duck feeding, breeding and resting grounds America ever had, yet unless we abolish the use of live decoys, baited fields, and rented blinds, and all the other unfair advantages and commercialized means adopted for us, to say nothing of ever-increasing thousands of shooters using equally improved and advantageous shooting equipment, our ducks and geese have got to go with the sand-hill crane.

Yes, it is true our ancestors did put out a salt-lick and shot the deer which came, from ambush. But remember, that was done to get easy meat near the house. Moreover, a salt-lick was only a local advantage, while a baited field for our migratory birds is a continent-wide advantage. We can no longer blame our wealthy, alone, for carrying on this advantage. There are men here in our Canada that hardly own the controlling interest in their own farms, yet such farms are posted, and they have a flock of live decoys and a corn-stalk slaughter-house in their back fields. Gentlemen, this practice has got to be stopped.

One of our conservation leaders says, "Public shooting means no shooting at all." Please allow me to take exception to that statement, and say: private shooting of our North American migratory public birds, means no shooting at all for the public.

I should like to have it plainly understood that while I am the general ramrod of a successful migratory bird sanctuary, I am not opposed to a limited amount of shooting. I never was opposed to it. I am, however, absolutely opposed to ten per cent of us exterminating what rightly and justly belongs to all one hundred per cent of us.

Furthermore, I am personally opposed to a closed season, set in order to let the birds multiply, only to have them slaughtered by the present system.

Sportsmen of America, be fair, and before you throw this writing — and the writer! — in the wastebasket, do a little personal investigating and thinking. How many ducks and Canada geese are there left, east of the Mississippi River, compared to the number of shooters? Take this pointer, in starting your investigation: seventy-five per cent of the geese east of the Mississippi River, winter in southern Illinois, North Carolina, Virginia, Maryland, and Delaware.

Another fact well to be remembered is this: one hundred thousand geese can utter millions of honks, but millions of honks are not millions of geese.

Now, to all of our North American people, let me honestly say this. Since the spring shooting has rightly and justly been abolished, our Canadians do not have an average of over three weeks' worth-while duck shooting at our northern-bred ducks. These same ducks start concentrating on the shooting grounds of the South by November first, and stay for nearly four months. Therefore, let me offer this, what I consider a Golden Rule suggestion: Let all North America be allowed four weeks open season, instead of three and a half months, with the privilege of dividing this four weeks into two two-week periods. All open seasons to be closed on or before December 15. And let the season's total bag limit be six ducks and two geese. Yes, it is a small bag-limit, but it is every bird we can afford at present.

Please allow me to ask, in all kindness, why do we shooters want a longer open season or a larger bag-limit on our publicly owned, internationally migrating birds, than we do on our home — that is, provincial or state — raised upland birds? One pair of green-head mallards, wood ducks, pintails, baldpates or darting teal, migrating back and forth across our lovely North American continent, will bring thrilling sights to millions of our people, where dozens are privileged to see the upland birds that are usually in the back fields, hiding on the ground.

The fall of one of our migrating birds out of the air, from your — or my — deadly aim, can bring pleasure to one person only, while thousands are deprived of seeing it alive. Therefore let us discourage the taking of all unfair advantages, and substitute flight or pass, shooting. This gives the average shooter five times the shots for the kills he makes, and requires ten times the science, as there is no man living who can judge the speed correctly at all times. This method gives the proper lead to our great variety of swinging, curving, darting ducks at various distances.

Upland Game Shooting Reserves

Since I have been appointed a member of the Ontario Special Game Commission, and as I have travelled over North America, preaching conservation, justice to all and favor to none, I have met many wonderful men. Yet I have been astonished at the great variety of opinion as to what constitutes justice to all.

Some of these men own their own upland game shooting reserves and buy, raise and liberate non-migratory birds, and allow them to multiply in such reserves. These are birds such as quail, partridge, pheasants, and so forth. I say that such men have a perfect right to shoot every day during the open season, if they see fit to do so. And, in my opinion, these men are public benefactors.

For illustration: I have, during the past few years, visited such large estates as those of Mr. Henry Jewett and Mr. Arthur Buhl, of Michigan. These men own thousands of acres of land, and buy thousands of dollars' worth of upland-game birds, mostly pheasants and quail. In addition, they have their own hatcheries, where such birds are being bred and liberated upon these properties by the thousands. The minute they start hunting and shooting them, with their bird-dogs running here, there, and all over, I know the majority of the birds fly over the fence onto public grounds, and if allowed to, they will breed there. Thus, these wealthy men are keeping the whole county stocked with the same game they prefer. The birds are mighty glad to fly over the fence away from their owners' dogs. I do not hesitate to say that such men do not get twenty-five per cent of the birds they raise and liberate at their own expense, on their own property, for, bless your life! — one man I know has over thirty bird-dogs on the same property, and has a man hired permanently to take some of them over the estate daily, for exercise. I am here to tell the world there is nothing birds will fly farther from than a pursuing bird-dog. This same man told me he had liberated three thousand English pheasants, this past summer, and had only shot twelve.

Another prominent man I know in Michigan is liberating them on his reserve and neither shoots them, nor allows others there with guns. Yet he is condemned by some hunters. On the other hand, hundreds of hunters are rushing to that county to hunt pheasants on public property around the outside of such estates.

I can say the same thing about fishing reserves I have been privileged to visit. On one occasion I strolled away by myself and sat down on a bridge fully one-quarter of a mile above the border of the reserve. While taking a half-hour sun-bath and rest there, I saw more fish going on, up the stream, on public property, than the ten of us caught in three days on this half-million dollar reserve.

Readers, personal experience has taught me this fact: you cannot do anything for the public, nor have anything for the public, unless you are so situated that you can also control the public.

As far as raising pheasants on one's own property is concerned, it is no more difficult than to raise chickens, and they can be raised, I believe, more cheaply. I am speaking from experience. If anyone reading, doubts this, he may write to the Biological Survey, Washington, D.C., and he will find that up to 1903, 1904 or 1905, I exported more English ring-necked pheasants into the United States than all other Canadian breeders. Therefore I say again, that these birds that are raised on one's own property belong to that man just as much as did the ones I sold, by which means I made my hobby self-sustaining and was enabled to liberate hundreds which became public property when they flew over my fence. I had the great satisfaction, at that time, of knowing that I, at my own expense, stocked this county with them.

I say again that all sportsmen as well as government officials should encourage and commend such private enterprises, especially where they are raising quail and Hungarian partridge.

Remember, I am now referring to non-migratory birds only. The migratory birds constitute a different proposition entirely. In fact there is all North America's difference between the two. For illustration: the migratory bird is hatched in the northern part of North America, pays no attention to national or international boundaries, and winters in the extreme southern part of the continent. These birds belong to the public of both countries, and to no individual. Thus, no individual, because he has wealth, has any more right to them than the man who is carrying his dinner-pail to his daily toil. Moreover, if there are lakes or other inducements to migratory birds in an upland game shooting reserve, no man should be allowed to use artificial feed and live decoys for no other purpose than to attract them there to be shot. Because these migratory waterfowl belong to the public.

In short, any man has a right to shoot his own privately raised game on his own private property. But he has no right to feed, decoy and slaughter our migratory birds, which belong to rich and poor alike.

Is Dogging Deer Right?

As hunters and nature-lovers of Ontario, we all want to see the deer increase. Then the first thing to be considered is the deer, and not the hunter. Such being the case, is the dogging of deer right?

To begin with, I want to look all people in the face and say: I know it is not the dog that is keeping the deer down on ninety per cent of this province: for there is not over ten per cent of Ontario being hunted over for deer by sportsmen. It is because of the wolf. Still, I do say the use of dogs is a handicap to the deer and an assistance to the average hunter over that small portion in which we are hunting. As a rule, the men who are holding out the firmest for the dog are aged men, like myself. But the question is, is it right?

Being a lover of dogs — deer-dogs, coon-dogs, bird-dogs, and everything but fighting dogs — I feel justified in expressing my views as a citizen of Ontario. As a boy I would have had my deer-dog sleep on my bed if Mother had allowed it; but she, dear soul, in her humorous English accent said: "No. It is not 'ealthy for a dog to sleep in our 'ouse."

I know it is wrong to hunt deer with dogs, because it is taking an unfair advantage of the deer. Also I know there are many men who, like myself, feel a thrill when they hear the dogs coming. My own personal experience and its thrills, teach me this. But today the great majority of hunters are using the dog for just one purpose: to get the deer. I say, leave the dog at home, and let the deer increase, and we will all get our bucks the same as they do in other places, Pennsylvania, Nova Scotia and Michigan, where they do not allow dogs and have, as a consequence, deer in numbers.

Another question I want to ask is this: where have deer increased if dogs are allowed? The answer is: nowhere. Such being the case, and it being agreed that we all want to see deer increase, then why allow the dog?

I know the answer of many a reader will be, "We might as well have them as the wolves." That is the only reasonable excuse you can advance. But, remember, two wrongs will never make a right.

Every fair-thinking hunter will admit this: that at the fall season of the year, every mother deer should have the quietest month of her life if we expect her to bear young. At this season especially, she should not be run until she is terrorized, exhausted, finally be compelled to swim some ice-cold lake for safety. If this is not unhealthy for them, then why do we not see more doe swimming thus, voluntarily, at this time? You seldom see them go in, even to cross a river. In fact, they will walk a mile to reach rapids, where they can wade across. I will admit that a buck will cross a lake at this season of the year, but when he does you can depend on it that there is a doe on the other side.

In or about 1898 or 1899, deer became so scarce in Essex County, through this section being thickly settled and being closely hunted accordingly, that the Ontario government wisely prohibited the shooting of them for ten years. At that time I do not believe there were twenty-five deer left here; and I know, from first-hand observation, because I hunted foxes without dogs through this county. The result of that legislation was that the deer became quite numerous in the limited wild territory which remained for them.

Then, one year before the closed season expired, two or three camps of Indians, accompanied by the usual number of unnecessary dogs, moved into the heart of this deer range, and the deer were terrorized and driven to the ends of the earth. The odd one was killed nearly twenty miles away. The last one of which I have any personal knowledge was seen out in Lake Erie. Two honorable farmers took a rowboat and rope and went out and brought it ashore, and placed it in a box-stall; but it died that night.

In Newfoundland the dog question is quite a serious one; so much so that in some parts, no person is allowed to even keep one. The result is that the side-hills are grazed off by sheep and have become perfect sheep pastures. And, instead of the average settler keeping dogs, he has a small flock of branded sheep. How they winter them, I do not know; but I saw them by the thousand in the month of June. In other parts where dogs are allowed, that is all they have. There are thousands of farmers in Ontario today who would be raising sheep were it not for dogs. Which is more valuable to a needy people?

Why do I stand for the buck law? Because the last doe I shot was a sermon to me. And that, remember, was over twenty years ago.

I was tracking four of them — a buck, doe, and two fawns. Hearing the brush crack, my rifle went up, and I saw the big doe leaping, quartering, from me. I pressed the trigger. Down she went. The flash of the two fawns' tails waved among the evergreens in the distance. I advanced a few steps. The wounded doe, the mother of the family, rose to her feet, the blood dripping from her side and a look in her eyes that will always haunt me a little. It was as if she said, "What more could I have done? I have raised you two fawns. But now you have shot me and closed out all hope of my giving you two hundred per cent annual dividends for life."

Yes, I have, I admit, shot as many doe as you have. And possibly would, at that time, have been a little annoyed had you spoken to me reproachfully about it. But was it right for me to shoot the mother of the next year's hope? I leave the matter for you to judge. If we do not all see alike on this question, please do not let our differing views make us enemies. Some of the best lifts I have ever got in this world have been friendly, constructive criticism and explanation.

Remember, too, that I am well aware of what it is that is keeping the deer down in Ontario, and have been for the last twenty-five years. It is the wolf. But, as I have stated already, two wrongs will not make one right.

If you are a farmer in Ontario, and raising sheep, you are well aware that dogs are apt to get among the sheep and destroy numbers of them. Even in the face of this do you go out and kill the lambs and the mothers, and cut off the hope of your flock increasing whether dogs get among them or not? To me the same principle applies concerning our superior wild sheep, the deer.

My father always told me: never take advice from a failure, but watch success, and prevent having to do much experimenting. Therefore I want you to take a look, as I have been privileged to do, at our little Nova Scotia. In 1896 that province had no deer at all. They liberated nine that year, and five more in 1906. In 1916 they declared an open season on bucks, and in the fall of 1933 I understand from the best of authorities, they sold 11,000 deer licenses and have now got to declare an open season on bucks and doe alike in order to reduce the herd; for they have only 21,000 square miles of territory.

Look at Pennsylvania, a densely populated country with only 45,000 square miles and ten million people. It had no deer and scarcely any game in the early 90's. Yet now they are annually killing from five hundred to seven hundred bears, and as many as twenty-five thousand buck deer, and the deer have become such a problem that this year they have had to declare an open season on bucks and doe alike. According to the last government report they killed in December, 1933, over 97,000 deer.

There is also this point, which I believe you will agree with me is well worthy of consideration. If you will take time to look it up, I think you will find that in comparison to the number of hunters, there are far fewer fatal accidents to men, where the buck law is in force. Why? Because men have, in such districts, educated themselves to hold their trigger-finger until they see horns, the same as we have done in hunting moose. Remember, this last year over half a million residents took out hunting licenses in Pennsylvania alone.

Another argument advanced by hunters is that if the buck law is enacted, the doe will still be shot, but will be left in the woods to rot. My reply to that is: are the twenty or twenty-five thousand deer hunters of Ontario more dishonest than the mass of hunters in these other places, where the deer under the buck law have increased until their numbers have become a problem? In other words, if the doe are shot and left in the woods in other places, why have they had to declare an open season on the female deer also, in order to reduce their herds?

Let me repeat: take the wolves out of Ontario, stop the dogs running deer, and pass the buck law, and in ten years' time you will have no deer argument left. No one will want to take a dog, or shoot a doe, any more than they now do in Pennsylvania, Nova Scotia or Michigan.

In conclusion I wish to state: the buck law allows deer to increase. It educates the hunter to automatically think and look before he shoots, and thus saves lives. These being facts, why should we, old hunters who want to see deer increase for the benefit of our children's children, be opposed to it?

THRILLS OF AN UNDERPRIVILEGED SPORTSMAN'S LIFE

Yes, readers, and the thrills grow to be more thrilling as the years ripen the human mind to more and more appreciation; to value more truly the blessed body- and soul-building, powerful advantages God has given us in the study of His great, great out-of-doors.

Personally, I am compelled to believe that my handicaps have brought me favors that money cannot buy nor take away.

For illustration, as soon as I was big enough to toddle after Father on a pigeon-hunt and pull the top rail of a high fence down on me, I can remember Father shouting in his English accent, " 'Ere they come, Jack; 'urry up and 'ide.'' And soon I got the thrill of hearing the thunder of that old black powder, and the pigeons rained down all around and about me.

Later on came the thrill of moving to the much talked of Canada, and locating and catching my first den of sweet little, pretty little, hard-biting little red foxes.

Then, when fall came on and we were all meat-hungry, I slipped out one snowy Sunday morning and had the thrill of my life. For in less than an hour I had killed my first deer. I was then only thirteen years of age and could neither carry nor drag it; so I ran home for help.

Sportsmen, remember this: youth is the springtime of life, and age is the harvest. At the price the average sportsman is paying for his sporting thrills today, I have long since been a multi-millionaire.

Years and years before we had open season on moose in Ontario, I hunted them in Quebec; and time and again I have enjoyed the tingling thrill of having a small carload of moose at the mercy of my rifle. From 1903 till 1917, they were nearly as thick in Ontario. (Moose, I believe, is the largest antlered game on earth.)

I have flashed a light into a bear's den, and been thrilled by seeing three of these black clowns' pretty faces looking hopelessly and pitifully at me.

I have answered the howl of a wolf. And as proof that I fooled him, I soon saw him come, quartering, towards me. Without any exceptions, I had the sporting thrill of all my shooting career as I pressed the trigger and saw this monstrous timber-wolf leap high in the air as that high-powered bullet crashed through his living-room.

But, remember, the above are all dead thrills. And a certain percentage of them, to me, have long since become petrified regrets. The last thrill they produced for me was when I sold and loaded my whole mounted collection into a box-car to go to the Panama Exhibition.

For the last quarter of a century I have concentrated more on living thrills. One pair of barn-swallows, protected from their imported enemy (the English sparrow) multiplied to twenty-five nests, which produced two hundred or more young thrills the fifth year.

Three wild ducks, left alive, brought seven hundred duck-banding thrills to seven years.

Four years of careful study and anxious waiting, were rewarded by honking thrills when, high in the air, eleven migrating Canada honkers shut off the gas and, putting on their four-wheel brakes, thrilled the whole neighborhood with wonder and excitement as they lowered, steadily and cautiously, down-down, down-down-down, until they joined and rejoiced with the wing-tipped decoys in the mud-hole below.

But possibly the most blessed and far-reaching living, sporting thrill that ever set any man's heart to pounding came to me one night while at my work, burning brick. It was about two o'clock in the morning. I was sitting back from the kiln, waiting till it would be time to build the next fire.

I was studying the stars — stars that had guided me in my boyhood raccoon-hunting days; that have guided me hundreds of miles through the pathless wilderness, although I could not call one of them by name. There they were, all back in their November formation and in my simple way I seemed to want to know more about them. With my hands cupped, I tried to focus my eyes on them. Just in that moment my soul was thrilled to the extreme limit with what I firmly and conscientiously believe was "the still, small Voice" saying: "Stamp the Sunday text from among those Salvation Army calendar messages, on your goose bands, and make missionaries of your banded birds." Reader, in a flash I threw that old blanket off my shoulders and sprang to my feet as quickly — or more quickly — than I have ever seen a bull-moose rise out of his bed. How I could do it and its far-reaching possibilities, all seemed to be visualized or picked up in that one instant. Since that, I have caught, banded and liberated over ten thousand Canada geese.

Think of it! Ten thousand ten-pound honking thrills, tossed into the air to go and multiply.

Picture now, if you can, an aged, white-haired man reaping living thrills from his life-long study. He has fairly good hearing, he knows. And by the language and accent the geese are using, he knows that they are feeding on the shelled corn that is in the pool of water under the net. Clad in warm clothes and hip rubber boots, he slips quietly over the pine-needley carpet under trees planted by his own hand, in their direction. Soon he is in Job's library, with the trip-wire in his hand, ready for action. The remarkable spectacle of between two hundred and four hundred geese under the net, gives him such tingling thrills that his hand quivers more than it did when he shot his first deer.

Jack Miner about to liberate a tagged Canada goose to study its route of migration for scientific purposes. Besides Jack Miner's name and post office, each tag has printed on it a verse of scripture which is Jack Miner's unique way of spreading the gospel to the natives in the far North.

Soon a low, quiet trill, rising up to a shrill whistle, from his lips causes every goose to raise its head. That instant the trembling hand jerks the trip-wire, and gas-pipe framed trap-doors come down with a splash. Three hundred and eighty-four missionaries are in captivity, and not one hurt! Yes, that was a great living thrill, such as lives on and multiplies into other living thrills.

Black Ducks—*One Thousand Here on Christmas Day*

For the last three years we have had the most mournful reports about ducks being killed off by the drought in our western provinces; yet I am sure that all observant sportsmen and nature-lovers who have travelled our Ontario will agree with me that black ducks have increased here by leaps and bounds during this period. Now, there is a reason for this most welcome change. And I believe I have a fair idea as to what it is.

At the beginning of the century, the Ontario government had a one hundred per cent closed season on beavers. These most intelligent little denizens of the solitudes multiplied like rabbits. Dozens — yes, I might say hundreds, of swamps and pieces of low land through which my moccasined feet had quietly taken me

Jack Miner and a party of friends liberating tagged Canada geese on the Jack Miner Bird Sanctuary to gain scientific knowledge of bird migration.

while hunting moose, had, by 1912 and 1914, been converted into beaver ponds ranging in size from one to ten or fifteen acres, according to location and character of surroundings. When the beaver season opened in 1916 almost every small living stream in the wilds of Ontario had been dammed up here and there by the beavers. They even tried to dam the Spanish River, up between Stralak and Pogamasing, which is fifty or sixty miles northwest of Sudbury, in northern Ontario. In fact, only those who were there and saw it, can believe how abundant the beavers actually were. I am sure I could have taken fully fifty — possibly one hundred — occupied beaver houses in one day. Well, as I have stated, the beaver season opened in 1916; but the wholesale slaughter of them did not start until 1918. In that year the prices of furs started soaring, and every hunter, apparently, rushed to the woods to get rich. The beavers were trapped — yes, and massacred — by the tens of thousands. In many cases their dams were partly torn out and dogs used to drive the animals from their hiding-places into the shallow water, where they were clubbed to death. I counted sixteen sets of beaver entrails at one big dam. In seven years, the beaver was all but exterminated.

Today, their dams and remnants of dams are settled down, the scrub trees, killed by the high waters of their ponds, are blown down, and grass and rushes have grown up over the low lands where these were. The scene is entirely altered. The living stream is, of course, still running. No; it is not still. It is noisier than ever. For a percentage of these little, settled-down ponds or basins are alive and quacking aloud with black mallard ducks.

In November of 1930, my boy and I were hunting in such a region and came upon a high rock overlooking a vast area. All was silent. The only sound to be heard was the ticking of the watch in my pocket. The only living thing in sight was a goshawk in a dead pine tree about a quarter of a mile off. The boy allowed he could hit him, so I encouraged him to try it. At the crack of the high-powered rifle, up jumped over one hundred black ducks out of a little beaver pond off a little to one side and below us. Astonishingly, though, they flew only a short distance, then dropped down again into the partly burned-over country, where, evidently, were more black ducks in another such pond.

This is the condition; the extremely high prices of fur caused the hunters to forget all about tomorrow. The majority of them not only trapped, but poisoned everything that would take bait — that being almost everything except the timber-wolves, most of which were too shy and wild for these inexperienced trappers. They survived. All this means that the black duck has been left with only three surviving enemies, namely, the owl, the goshawk, and the timber-wolf.

This fall being wet, the black ducks fed all along our southern border, in the buckwheat fields and in the corn fields, especially where corn had been left standing in the field, not husked out. On Christmas morning, over one thousand flew out of fifteen acres of buckwheat I have planted and left standing for the geese.

In conclusion, let me offer a word of explanation to those who may not be familiar with black ducks and their habits.

The black duck is one of the largest, if not the largest, edible duck we have in America. It is extremely shy and cautious. The reason those ducks were so quiet when we came upon them, that day, was because they were evidently watching that goshawk, *and* a clump of green shrubbery prevented their seeing us. And the reason they lit again, so close by, was because they were mostly young ducks and had not yet been terrorized by the sound of a gun.

Black ducks are surface feeders. They tip up and reach down, but seldom dive for food. The farthest north I have had a banded black duck killed, is La Pas, Manitoba, Canada.

Mourning Doves — *Their Habits and Migration*

Among my earliest recollections of dear Mother is that of her gathering us children about her, and trying to teach us how to distinguish the different birds. Of course it was easy to tell the red-headed woodpecker from the blackbird. But to tell the wild pigeon from the dove was a different problem. Both were the same color and build. It is true the wild pigeon was fully twice as large, and migrated in clouds; but to tell one odd pigeon in the distance, from a dove close at hand, kept our childish minds guessing. Of course, as the years rolled on, all became an open book to us. We discovered that the doves nested close to the ground, while the few pigeons' nests that we found were in the tip-tops of the highest and thickest topped trees.

In 1878 we came to Canada, and found that the mourning doves were very rare here, but slowly increasing. From 1910 to 1915, I got the sanctuary fever and started planting trees in earnest. The delight of my heart was that the desirable birds seemed to know that this whole place was theirs. The shy, cooing dove came here, became as friendly as the robin, nested and multiplied, their numbers increasing by leaps and bounds. From 1927 to 1930, I had over one hundred occupied doves' nests on one acre. In 1931 and 1932, however, the starlings drove them out and killed their choice nesting trees. In January of 1933, we cut the dead trees down. And the touching, pitiful part of it is that several pairs of doves returned and nested on the ground where their nesting trees had stood. Previous to that, I had seen only three doves' nests on the ground.

How soon does a young bird recognize a friend? A dove built, very low, beside one of my pine-needle paths. As soon as the two young could raise their heads, I would stop and speak to them. This happened two or three times a day for nearly a week. Then, one morning, I reached to catch them and, to my surprise, one flew out. I watched through the evergreens and thought it had alighted near the edge of the big goose pond. So, after banding the one that remained in the nest, I went to catch this one that had got away. But it was not there. I saw what I at first took to be a sandpiper, paddling about among the ripples on the pond. A second glance and I saw that the piper was the little dove out, fully fifty feet, from the shore. What would I do! I knew that by the time I could go to the house and return with rubber boots, the dove would have drowned. I sat down at once and started to pull off my shoes. I would wade out and get it, I thought. But I looked again, and saw that this innocent little bird, seeming to know I was his friend, had started flopping and swimming toward me. I sat still and he landed within ten feet of me. His wet wings drooped. He toddled and staggered up the bank, the best he could.

I caught him, put both my warm hands about him and dried him off. Then I returned him to the nest and held my hands over the two. At last I went away. Returning in about ten minutes I found the mother bird had beaten me there, and was spread out with her warm breast over them.

In my excitement, I had forgotten to band him after all. I went back to the nest the following day to do this, and neither baby dove even flinched, but allowed me to catch and band the one that had, the day before, flown away.

Doves multiply fast. They return here in March and start nesting in early April. They nest from three to five times, and lay two pure white eggs that hatch in thirteen days. To hide and protect her first egg from their egg-eating enemies, the mother dove usually sets on it and lays another egg the next day; consequently, one of these twins is twenty-four hours the older. I have known them to fly in ten days, but usually in from twelve to fifteen.

This year we have found several nests on the ground in the cornfields. The dove's only protection from its many natural enemies is its speed and ability to select color-protection. I often see one hundred or more rise out of a cornfield when discovered and pursued by a winged enemy.

Last year I banded about five hundred and eighty baby doves. Sixty-seven of these were reported shot by sportsmen; Georgia, Alabama and Florida reporting forty-three of the sixty-seven. But the first one reported was killed near Kingsville, Texas, on September 27. And there were odd young doves in the nests here at that date.

Doves are gradually coming farther north. The pigeons' real home was the virgin forest, but the dove followed the farmer. I have seen odd ones in the southern part of our prairie provinces, but, strangely, it seems to me, have never seen one in Nova Scotia or New Brunswick. Three years ago I saw a bunch on that nice bit of farming country near Lion's Head, in the Bruce Peninsula. I have seen them on Manitoulin Island, and this year I saw a pair near Huntsville, Ontario. I have every reason to believe that the younger generations are going to see them as far north as James Bay.

In conclusion, I wish to state that the mourning dove is one of the best birds we have on the farm. He eats and digests more weed seeds, for the insignificant amount of grain he eats, than any bird in America.

Last year a young dove flew against the service wires near my home. I sent its stomach to be analyzed. The following is the report: this dove's stomach was not one-quarter full. If anyone tells you that one adult dove will eat and digest ten thousand small germinative weed seeds in a day, you can believe it. Professor L. L. Snyder of the Royal Ontario Museum, Toronto, examined one dove's crop and gullet which contained: 8,533 seeds of the three-seeded mercury, 30 seeds of ragweed, and 3 small gravels, and by weight the gizzard contained the same amount.

Professor M. S. Ferguson of the University of Western Ontario, examined one we sent him which contained the following: 1,854 green fox-tail seeds, 40 yellow fox-tail seeds, and 3 grains of wheat.

ASSISTING NATURE

During the past year I have read a number of articles both in magazines and newspapers, as well as many letters that have come to me, on the subject of "nature's balance," decrying actions or systems on the part of man which the writers described as "interfering with nature," "upsetting nature's balance," and so on. To all who adopt that attitude I should like to put myself on record to the effect that, personally, I believe the so-called "balancing" of nature was left entirely with man, and that I believe in assisting nature for the benefit of humanity. God created everything — every *thing* — and then He created man "in His own likeness, and gave him dominion over all"; that is, as I understand it, the power and authority to manage everything here on earth.

Look, for instance, at the animal world, with the livestock in the farmer's barnyard as example. Did God create the Jersey cow, and the Holstein, and the Hereford? No. He gave man the original stock and then God, through man's instrumentality, developed many breeds, some for the high cream content of their milk, some to produce the greatest quantity of milk, and some as the best beef cattle. All have been on the earth a long time, of course; but their differences are the result of man's management. And, remember, man had to interfere with nature to develop them.

Much the same thing is true of the horse, different strains being cultivated for particular purposes, such as the Clydesdales and Percherons for heavy draft work, and the blue-blooded descendants of original Arab stock for racing.

Recently I was in the southern United States where the character of the farm work to be done is too heavy for the common ass, yet where the climate is too warm to permit of the horse doing its best. In that part of the continent, therefore, man crossed the ass with our common horse and produced a breed that withstands the heat and is also strong enough to do the work of tilling the soil. Yes, he has developed the mule. But the mule kicked, and so far as I know, has gone no farther.

In poultry, if you trace back the various species, it is very easy to see that it has been the work of man that has developed the different breeds—Leghorns, Brahmas, Minorcas, Plymouth Rocks, and so on, some of which are especially valuable as layers and others as food. Our much prized turkey is nothing more nor less than the wild turkey, domesticated and improved.

Seventy-five years ago, our Canadian Northwest was grazed by millions of wild buffalo (bos bison). Then came the white man who, realizing the value of the fertile soil, established a park where a herd was placed to preserve the species from extinction, slaughtered the great, roaming herds, and turning the land upside down, made it into one of the largest and most valuable of earth's great wheatfields, with towns and cities and stately governmental buildings dotted here and there across its vast expanse. Remember, though, that in order to bring about this state of things, man had to "interfere with nature," as some would call it.

And speaking of wheatfields, wheat has been man's favorite food for centuries. Yet wheat, even as it was being grown in Canada in comparatively recent years, had certain weaknesses — it had to be planted in the fall and did not always survive the severity of the western winter; it was not producing as abundantly as seemed desirable; it did not mature rapidly enough always to escape the early autumn frosts. Then came to our aid such men as Professor Charles Saunders, of Ottawa, cerealist, and by study, experimentation and the rigid selection of choice grains, developed a wheat that could be planted in the spring, that would yield several bushels more per acre than had been the rule previously, that would mature within a certain period of time and that yet retained all its former qualities. We have today the Marquis and the Garnet and other species of wheat, developed by man. God created the original, the germ; but man was given — and has used — the power to develop, manage and control it.

Or if you will consider your flower garden, look at the iris. God gave to us, in America, a little, insignificant flower growing along the banks of streams, which we called, commonly, the "flag." From it man has devloped irises that grow three or four feet

One corner of Jack Miner's Bird Sanctuary. As long as the Jack Miner Bird Sanctuary exists, no one will need to build museums to save specimens of the Canada goose and other waterfowl.

in height, varied in color, and some giving out an exquisite fragrance. But man had to interfere with nature to accomplish this. Or take the rose. Did God create the American Beauty rose? No. He gave man brains and a little, old wild rose which served as the germ, so to speak. Today through the efforts of outstanding botanists, man has been given flowers of beauty and fragrance as the Creator intended.

But let us look at another side to the question. At the same time that God created the little wild rose, he created also the weed. Typical of this is the Canadian thistle. Still he gave to man the brains and the means of controlling these also, so that they may be restrained from predominating the plant world.

In your orchard are many varieties of fruit. Did God create the Stark-Delicious apple, the Northern Spy, and other varieties? No. He gave man the little wild crab and the hawthorn, which is a miniature apple or germ, and from these man developed what we have today. Yet according to some people's statements, if you kill the mice that girdle these fruit trees when they are small, you are "interfering with or upsetting nature's balance."

If you are raising poultry or other bird life, and hawks begin to destroy and live on the birds, and you fail to take a gun and shoot the hawk, then you are not using the brains God gave you.

If your clothing were to become infested with vermin, or your dwelling with rodents, you would destroy the insects or animals that were troubling you. Yet (if they were consistent in their argument) these people would have to maintain that in doing so you were "upsetting nature's balance," since God created all these creatures at the same time. Or how about the fly, carrier of typhoid? Do you control it, or, preferring not to disturb "nature's own" let it live? Personally, I am glad He gave man "dominion over all" these things.

Indeed one is moved to ask the question, what would our animal world, our farms and orchards and gardens — our whole world — be like if man had not assisted nature? Yet the very minute the white man discovered this continent, came ashore, cut down a tree and began to develop North America into a garden for hundreds of millions of people, that man, according to some, disturbed the balance of nature.

As for me, I thank God for all He made — for the raw materials He gave us with which to work; that He made us in His own likeness, after His own image, and endowed us with sufficient brains to develop those raw materials and keep on discovering and bringing within reach of us all the blessings He created. To illustrate my meaning, allow me to quote the following poem, written by Ida M. Thomas:

MAKING A GARDEN

Man ploughs and plants and digs and weeds,
    He works with hoe and spade;
God sends the sun and rain and air,
    And thus a garden's made.

He must be proud who tills the soil
    And turns the heavy sod;
How wonderful a thing to be
    In partnership with God!

In glancing over the many articles written about the crow in our Canadian papers, I have noticed that several writers fall back to this old wornout argument, "interfering with the balance of Nature." Now, dear readers, I would like a full explanation of the meaning. Does it really mean that no person should attempt to assist Nature?

Now, remember, I only have an A B C, Sunday-school education, but there are a few of His lovable promises I have been privileged to test out, and I know they are true. For illustration, I ask you to read Genesis 1 : 21-26 and 28, when He said, "Let man have dominion over all." Could anything

This Is a Common Mallow, Brought to Twice Its Usual Size.

be written plainer? Last summer our Nettie raised sixty bred-to-lay Plymouth Rocks. We killed and ate twenty-two of the twenty-five roosters. The pullets started laying in October. Now, if we had left the twenty-five cockerels with the thirty-five pullets, would we have had eggs all winter? Don't forget the fowls of the air are all ours and they will come to us for our assistance and protection.

On our first arrival here on our farm we were terrorized by the rattlesnake stories we heard and, really, I was expecting to see snakes as large as clothes props, that would strike at a distance of ten or fifteen feet away, and then all would be over except a brief report in the weekly town paper— "Those who knew him best, loved him most," and so forth. Well, in a few months, I got acquainted with those rattlers, but, believe me, they were only a little larger than our largest garter snakes and could only strike about a foot or eighteen inches. I have killed as high as six on one Sunday. In fact, I would hunt for hours to find a rattler, just to tease him and get him striking a stick. But in a few short years the danger was all over, for, where the snakes were, grew the fields of waving wheat and corn, but, mind you, in order to do this, we had to "interfere with Nature." Which was the best for humanity—a rattlesnake jungle or a productive grain field?

In 1898 I enclosed four acres with a wire fence seven feet high. There I raised English and ringneck pheasants for profit. This pheasantry was right alongside of my brick and drain-tile manufacturing plant. I could watch my machinery and overlook the pheasantry all from the same spot. In this way I made my hobby more than self-sustaining and gathered stores of knowledge about the enemies of our birds, and let me say to any young man, breeding game birds for profit is a lovable occupation and there is good money in it. The seven-foot fence is not necessary. All that is required is a dog-proof fence. But, remember, unless you educate yourself how to destroy their many enemies, you had better give up the job about two weeks before you start, for this little, innocent-looking weasel, that is no larger than a Northern Ontario chipmunk, will kill from twenty to thirty of your baby pheasants in one night and crawl through one-inch-mesh wire-netting to do it. But, remember, you are "interfering with the balance of Nature" if you kill him.

I believe the indoor naturalist calls him the mouse weasel because the greater part of his food is mice. Crows must be checked or they will steal every egg laid, unless your brood pens are under netting. But, after the young pheasants were hatched, I found hawks and weasels their worst enemy. But you say to kill one you are "interfering with the balance of Nature," for God put them there. Yes, I say, God also put the bed bug here, but He gave man dominion over them and the present generation would hardly know one if they saw it.

Crows! God did not put them here to control our poultry, nor our song, insectivorous and game birds. He did not even allow them the privilege of controlling themselves. He left all of this for man to do. Please think that over and look up what He says regarding this point.

In the spring of 1914, I drove to Point Pelee, a distance of about fifteen miles, where my intimate friend, Mr. Forest H. Conover, and I pulled three hundred and sixty little red cedar seedlings out of the sand. There were none of them over a foot in height. I brought them home and planted them in the clay on May 15, 1914. I cultivated them for five years and today fully ninety-five per cent. of them are over twelve feet high and have been bearing fruit for the last three or four years. Now, isn't that "interfering with Nature"? This is where the five robins that wintered here got their food and, oh say, this winter we have had a cardinal added to the songsters and there hasn't been a day when he has not sung for us. Now he has fairly set me cardinal crazy—or wise—and is going to be the cause of more of my "interfering with Nature," for I am going to import some of these winter and summer singers. I am going to put a pair in each cage. Then, in March, I will let the male bird out, but will feed him on the outside of the cage. Here he will stay, just flittering and singing among the trees, but will not go far from his mate, who is still in captivity. Then, after he has got well acquainted with the whole outside proposition, I will let her out and in this way I expect to have the whole place cardinal with song.

Dear readers, don't let me try it first. Jump in ahead of me. It can be done. Yes, if you are privileged to live in the country, you can make your home into a little earthly heaven by "interfering with the balance of Nature," as you call it, but, as I term it, "assisting Nature," for you can get seedling trees from our government forestry departments, free of charge. If you will

In the Middle of the Scotch Pine Forest Planted from Seedlings
Just Ten Years Before.

plant five hundred of them in the proper place and formation around your home, by cultivating them the same as you would hills of corn for the first five summers, which will not take you over one day a year, in ten years' time these trees will be from twelve to fifteen feet high and will break the wind off your home and, on a cold wintry day, will reduce your fuel bill. In addition to this, your assistance will double and treble the quantity and quality of the birds at your home every year.

On that beautiful frosty morning, which father used to call "the 17th of Ireland," I awoke before the stars had closed their eyes. Now how could I go to sleep again and miss such a musical feast, for that cardinal I had mentioned apparently had his voice focused right on my open window, saying in distinct tones: "Good cheer! Good cheer! Good cheer!" This is mingled with the low notes of the song sparrows and even the robins are trying to join in the chorus. The lovable mourning doves, one of God's chief mourners, in low voices, are saying: "Khoo-coo-coo!"

In spite of all this, I will admit I was about to doze back into dreamland again when, all at once, the honking of at least a thousand wild geese seemed to echo from every spot on the premises, saying: "Home again!"

Really, my thoughts drifted nearly one-half century back to the morning we left Ohio, when a dear old Yankee by the name of Calvin Pease said to me: "Good-bye, Jackie." Then, as he gripped father's hand, which I believe was for the last time, he said: "John, do you think you can make a living over in Canada for your big family?" Father apparently gripped his hand tighter and he looked him square in the face and replied: "Calvin, we are going to make more than a living—we are going to make a life."

More About
Jack Miner

JACK MINER

PLEASANT MEMORIES

THE DEEPEST SNOW I have ever seen in dear old Ohio was in January and February of 1878. I was then twelve years of age and the proud owner of fifteen muskrat and skunk-catching traps. However, owing to the deep snow these traps were all cleaned up and carefully hung up in an old one-horse stable. Father had gone to Canada to build us a log house on our 100 acres of woods for which he had agreed to pay. He wrote us stating that the deer were coming to browse among the tops of the choice trees they had cut for building logs. I became more anxious to go to Canada than I was to go to Heaven.

To bring cheerful thoughts closer home, Washington's birthday was in the air once more and the 'teen age Sunday School girls and boys of the Congregational Church were having a sleigh ride to celebrate the occasion.

Fortunately for me, I had one of the most fatherly brothers with which any red-headed, freckle-faced, crimson dispositioned boy was ever blessed. He and his life-long friend, George W. Cooley, were then seventeen years of age. The Cooleys were nearby, well-to-do farmers and a blessing to the neighborhood. Well, these two kind boys knew that I was not a bit worse than I looked and they invited me to come and help fill a high sleigh-ride box with clean, dry straw. They also gave me sealed orders how to proceed. Shortly after dusk I was all muffled up in a long second-hand overcoat. I had dug myself in at a side angle next to the tailboard of the high box full of straw. Oh, how musical those old-fashioned sleigh bells did chime out as we drove from house to house gathering up this and that Sunday School party!!! Soon the horses were jogging along. The well-beaten sleigh track and the starlit heavens echoed and re-echoed with the Sunday School hymns being sung by this packed sleigh load of clean, young voices. Well, there was nothing for me to fear as no person could tell the color of the other person's hair, and, fortunately for me, there was no cluster of electric lights to pass under. Well, soon these hymns were climaxed with patriotic songs as some voices began, "Union Forever, Hurrah Boy! Hurrah! Down with the Traitor and up with the Star." This was followed by "As We Go Marching Through Georgia." I well remember a young lady's voice leading out on "Nellie Gray" and the whole sleigh load joined in the chorus. These are the blessed, tender memories of the first and only sleigh-ride I ever was privileged to enjoy, and that was on Washington's birthday, many years ago.

Time rolled by, and my days became altogether too short, for they were so very full of accumulating interest on my heavily-mortgaged scant belongings that sundown was never welcome. Although I retired early yet

"Uncle Jack" Making the Leg Bands.

I only had time for one sleep before my eyes automatically flew open just about time to see the stars close theirs and I was rested, up and dressed with my battery charged ready for action. Really my heart was so young and so full of ambition that the days, weeks and months flashed into years before I was conscious of it. When I stopped to think as I looked into the mirror, the man facing me had become partially grey, but, thank God, he was quite active and strong and as well preserved as a wildcat. Yes, I was forty-five years old and homesick for scenes and trees and sweet songs of the birds of my boyhood days. There was a robin heard in the distance as they issued their challenge to all-comers but outside this bird life the summer was dormant.

My aged mother was still my adviser. "Jack," she said, "you can grow trees." Then she followed up by saying, "If you cultivate them the same as one does a hill of corn, nine out of ten will grow."

I took on a new life and started planting trees by the hundreds until I was planting a thousand a year and 95 per cent. of them grew. Bird-lovers and hunters, planting and growing trees, fruit-bearing shrubs and vines, is a pleasure and health-building exercise every man should seek to enjoy and in less than ten years you can surround your little country home with a melody of songs of thrushes, cat birds, robins, goldfinches, native song sparrows, and warblers. Oh yes, and dozens of others including hundreds of loving and cooing mourning doves. All this combined with the fragrance of wild grape and hawthorne blossoms, mingled with the good old lilacs that the gold finches nest among. People of America take this from me, to live in such a spot will cause you to cease worrying about what heaven will be like and the

A Bird's-eye View to the North from Jack Miner's Observation Tower. The trees around the ponds serve as a windbreak for wild fowl and also as a shelter and nesting-place for song and insectivorous birds.

beauty of it all. It is in reach of every country home financially. I am absolutely certain the 15 or 20,000 seedling trees and wild shrubs I have planted the last twenty years have not cost $500 and I doubt very much if they have cost me $300 in money. It has all been done by cheerful anticipation and exercise. Bird-lovers, it is your privilege to have all this. My trees are in borders and provide evergreen windbreaks around my duck and goose feeding fields and ponds. You see Lake Erie is their big bath tub and my home is their cafeteria, and this spring there are more geese here than ever I saw before. But how I am going to continue feeding them is a problem that should be left with the sportsmen of North America!

CROWS

IT HAS been proven that if a man writes an article stating what he knows about crows, he will get lots of people interested. I believe the same could be said if one wrote his experience in raising calves or growing tobacco. My father (the best man who ever lived) compelled me to split rails to make a recreation ground for our pigs. But now, let us banish all such insignificant side issues from our minds for a while.

My real reason, dear reader, for writing this chapter is simply to encourage you to take more interest in our great out-of-doors and to make a study of the so-called wild creatures that occupy it. Yes, and to ask you to study them closer for yourself, since at the present day there are so many indoor naturalists writing and misleading the public. Whenever you are driving, walking, running or flying keep both eyes open so as to gain more from personal observation, and when you see a crow pursued and pecked by smaller birds stop and ask yourself why. Why are these song and insectivorous birds putting in their valuable time chasing a dirty, black crow? Surely they don't want to eat him. Then, why are they chasing him?

Or you may see a killdeer or other species of bird fluttering and hobbling out from right near you. Immediately you are convinced that she is crippled in the back or her wing is broken, since she keeps falling over herself every time she attempts to get away. Of course, you are going to catch her and see just what is wrong. But soon you find you can get just so close and no closer and when you have run yourself out of breath you will get discouraged and stop, for you find the bird you are pursuing can fly fairly well and is five times further from you than she was when you started. Now please ask yourself why and go back where you first saw her. But be careful where you put your feet for you might step on her eggs or one of her babies. She was leading you away from them. And see how these God-given creatures, in the majority of cases, take advantage of color protection. For illustration: if it is a killdeer's nest, see how she has gathered pebbles, shells, bits of wood or fragments of anything the color of her eggs, and placed them all around her nest. Remember this is the mother's doings. And when you see a baby ruffed grouse (partridge) not over three days' old, hide among leaves the color of itself, what do you call this? I simply call it God.

In the spring of 1879, which was the second year we were in Canada, I put in every Sunday hunting for young foxes, to keep them as pets. With axe in hand, I would scour the woods for miles around and, when I heard something meowing and screaming, which sounded like an old Tom-cat making his last screech, instead of running for home to tell mother I was chased by a lynx or a wild-cat, I quietly pursued this pitiful, squalling sound, taking good care to mark the exact direction it took me. When about one quarter of a mile away, the squalling usually ceased. Now, I turned and, if the noise took me straight north, I went straight back south from where I first heard it, keeping both eyes open for hollow logs and so forth,

Something Frightened These Birds.

and for remnants of rabbits, ruffled grouse or turkey feathers. And in the majority of cases I would soon be using the axe to chop out the young foxes.

Sometime ago I read a nine-page letter sent to me from a gentleman explaining that "it was not the English sparrow that was driving the barn and eave swallows out, but that the systematic control of house flies by the human race was robbing the swallows of their food and starving them out." Really, it was a beautifully-written letter, and, if one did not know better, he might be induced to believe it. But the fact is, the English sparrow, or imported flying rat, is the direct cause of the decrease of fully ninety-five per cent. of our barn and eave swallows. I hadn't seen an eave swallow in Ontario for twenty-five or thirty years. In Alaska there are no English sparrows but in July, I counted forty-seven occupied swallows' nests under the eaves of a building we stayed in while there. In other words, they are there now, just the same as they were here in eastern America fifty years ago, and would be here now were it not for the devilish, dominating ways of this imported, undesirable house sparrow, a dirty bird that doesn't do as much good in a year as a swallow will in a week.

Some years ago, I saw an article in a sporting paper stating that canvasback ducks and Canada geese migrated at the rate of one hundred and twenty miles per hour. One hundred and twenty miles per hour, or, in other words, two miles per minute! Now a test I have been making recently is as follows:

Wild Geese Rising from the North Ponds.

My oldest son lives two miles south of me on a road running east and west, the same as the one I live on. The wild geese that make their home with me at least five months of the year all go out to Lake Erie to roost, returning early the next morning. Lake Erie is three miles south of my home. When I hear them honking and see them towering high before leaving the sanctuary, getting ready to cross over this three miles of no-man's land, I get my son on the telephone. As I say, he is two miles south of me, between the lake and the sanctuary. He holds the receiver with a watch in his hand and just as a big, distinguishable flock crosses the road at my house I call "Go!" He marks the exact time, goes to the road and, of course, can see the geese coming. Here are results of the last three tests: First, two and three-quarter minutes. Second—with a nice breeze in their favor, lifting them along—two minutes and eleven seconds. Third, as they were facing quite a stiff breeze, four minutes. Remember, these birds are from three to five hundred feet high before they leave the sanctuary, therefore they are not doing much climbing after they leave here.

Oh, but you sigh and say, "What has all of this to do with crows?"

Nothing at all. I have only unrolled these experiments to encourage you to study for yourself.

The first hunting I did in Canada was crow hunting. This was in May, 1878. We shot the crows because they pulled up our corn and from boyhood up, whenever I started to hunt my creature, I studied its habits. Soon I found myself practising how to imitate the call of a baby crow in distress, mingled with the hoot of a great horned owl, the creature that was causing the young crow's trouble. I would practise this quivering, cawing and hooting in the early morning, when all was silent, and let the echo from the forest speak for itself as to the perfection of the deception. Then I would conceal myself in the thick undergrowth of the woods, in easy range of a few dead tree-tops for Mr. Crow to perch on. I would then start giving these low, delicate caws of distress, just the same as I had heard the young crows utter, now and then giving the low hoot of the owl. Many, many of these black, old nest-robbers have come to protect me or have even brought me food but, to my surprise, they were not feeding their young on corn. As I held these old birds up by the tail as they gasped their last, they spewed up birds' eggs. I have seen as high as seven unhatched robins pour out of the mouth or throat of a dying crow, and the little bits of life were sometimes still squirming.

Dear reader, the above is only a flash of the cruel, wicked, murderous ways of these black, old nest-robbers. Fortunately, in those days there were not many crows. Really, I don't believe there were ten per cent. as many then as there are today. We must not blame the crows for their increase. This is man's fault. We have gone wrong. We have combined our force with the crow's and pointed all our attention at the game birds. Yes, and song birds, too, and left these organized nest-robbers to multiply by leaps and bounds.

My esteemed friend Mr. Thomas Baty, of London, Ontario, kindly says: "If Jack ever had a pet crow, he never would kill it." Really, this makes me laugh. Say, I wonder if there is a man in America who has gathered up more pets from the woods that I have. Crows, crows, why, bless your life, I have had them by the dozens, and I will admit they are just as cute as they are black. I once had one that would say "Look out!" so plain and sharp that he would cause you to flinch, but I never kept but one to be over a year old. Then he, like all the rest, died guilty of murder in the first degree.

My friend, Mr. Baty, says that if I had had a pet crow to study the crows' habit, I would know more about them. Let me reply to my friend and kindly say that when he has studied them enough to catch them by the thousands, he will know more about them. Personally, I have studied birds more than I have my financial obligations and I am glad of it. They have brought me closer to God and man. If my life's study hasn't taught me something about the habits of the crow, how did I catch five hundred and ten of those organized murderers at one catch? Will you please think that over? I do wish there was nothing but good in the ways of all birds, for I don't want to kill any of them; but how can I be humane and protect a baby murderer?

Fifty rods north of my engine-room door is an elm tree, and morning after morning have I seen a crow perched in the top watching my neighbor's turkey hen come through the line fence just ninety rods east of the tree. Mr. Crow would sit and watch and the very minute the turkey came out of the fence row and started back toward home, he would fly straight over and

It Surely Works! One corner of Jack Miner's Crow Trap after it has been sprung.

get the egg she had laid. This could all be seen with my field-glasses. Smart? I should say so. They are the shrewdest thieves of the bird family.

Now I am not contradicting a word which has been said about the crows eating a few wire-worms and grubs and so forth, but here is what I know about it. If he can find them, he will rob at least one hundred of our more desirable birds' nests in order to raise his family of four or five, while, if any one of these murdered song and insectivorous birds were left to mature, he would do twice as much good as a crow ever did.

Now, if a man wants to make money that man must study money. The prospector is more apt to find earthly gold than the astronomer. In other words, if a man concentrates on one line he is more apt to catch something on that one hook.

Thirty years ago no crows wintered in Ontario, but now they are with us the whole year around. In traveling from Windsor to Chatham, Ontario, a distance of less than fifty miles, I firmly believe I have seen over one hundred thousand crows in less than an hour. There is another reason for them multiplying so rapidly the last twenty years. Their worst natural enemy is practically gone—the raven. Forty years ago, ravens were just about as numerous in this country as crows. The raven is nothing but a big, powerful, overgrown crow in his habits, only he doesn't migrate. He will search for a crow's nest and rob it of its eggs and young, treating them just the same as the crows treat our robins, mourning doves and dozens of other species of lovely, desirable, song and insectivorous birds. The raven is an inhabitant of the more dense woods, but will scour the clearings for food.

The Crow Trap from the Side.

Up until the last few years, ravens fairly thronged in northern Ontario and Quebec.

Between 1895 and 1905, the very height of my sporting ambition was big game. I usually carried four ordinary two-bushel, twine sacks and when I shot a moose I would bag the meat up, carry it a few rods and cover it with boughs to keep it from looking suspicious to wolves. Then I would shoulder the head and go to camp. When the party of us would return the next day to carry out the meat, I have often seen as high as a hundred ravens fly up from around the running gear of one moose. But now, going over the same ground, I haven't seen a single raven for two or three years.

You see, the price of furs started soaring in 1904 and kept right on going up. The result is that in the last fifteen years the woods have been overrun with trappers and, although against the law, the majority of them used quantities of strychnine and, just as soon as the ice will carry a man about, every lake in our northern country has poison bait or baits upon the ice. Some trappers will shoot deer and moose for no other purpose than to make poison bait of it. By injecting the poison into the meat while warm, I understand, they make the most deadly kind of bait. Putting bait on the lake gives the trapper the great advantage of finding the fox, wolf, fisher, lynx, or whatever animal takes the least bite of it.

In January, 1905, I was with a professional trapper. On going to his bait on a lake, we saw that a raven had taken a few pecks of the bait, had flown about fifty yards and died. A fox had eaten part of the raven and lay stretched out within twenty feet of it. There was a fresh fall of snow and, as the fox had come from the direction we were going, I tracked him back for fully one half mile, and I am absolutely certain he did not get any other bait in that distance. Hence it is plain to see how the high price of furs has all but exterminated the raven. In fact, the crow's only enemies now are the fox, great horned owl and red-tailed hawks, but these three combined aren't one, two, three, with the raven. I have been asked by a great many people, "Why didn't this poison kill all the wolves?" In reply to this, let me say, the wolf is the shrewdest animal to poison or trap on earth. So many inexperienced people, carelessly putting out this poison, caused the wolves to be shy of any cold bait they saw, in fact, it is only experienced trappers that know what that means. The most experienced trapper gets them taking bait weeks before he puts any poison in it.

Before I go further, I want it distinctly understood that I don't want to kill any bird. This killing desire has apparently all left me. But how can I call myself humane and stand and see these black, highway murderers of the air—the crows—robbing the more desirable birds of their eggs and young, and hear the mother screaming and crying, "Help, help, help!" How can I be humane and hold myself when I know he is coming back to repeat this cold-blooded, murderous deed? Moreover, I know that if one of these insectivorous or song birds were left to mature, it would do more good in ten minutes than a dirty, old crow would do in a day. Think of all the good the descendants of this one insectivorous bird would do had it been allowed to mature and raise young. Oh, but you sigh and say, "Jack Miner, are you sure that you know what you are writing about?" Yes, I am. I have tested it out.

In 1910, I started reforesting near my home, in fact, nearly all around my home. I secured the majority of the trees from the Ontario Forestry Department. The fifth year I had one nesting pair of mourning doves and now the doves nest and roost among these trees so thickly that they are actually breaking the limbs down. During May, June and July, I can take you to at least three hundred occupied doves' nests in that many minutes, and, to-day, I would far sooner loan you my gun and permit you to go in there and shoot one hundred pairs of doves than to allow one pair of crows to nest there and murder and terrorize this whole bird haven. Remember, here in southern Ontario doves nest from four to five times a year. My intimate friend, Mr. W. E. Saunders, of London, Ontario, located a doves' nest here with young doves as large as sparrows on April 19th. Fully ninety per cent. of them cease nesting by September 1st. Why, bless your life, these doves have got so bold that last summer there were three pairs nesting at one time on the piles of drain tile at our drain-tile factory adjoining this little sanctuary. And remember, there were from five to eight men working there all summer, piling out and shipping away tile. But one-half mile north of here is a ten-acre wood, equally as inviting for any desirable bird to

A Close-Up of One Corner of the Trap. These crows will eat no more birds' eggs.

nest in, but there are no doves there, for the simple reason that there is usually a crow's nest in that vicinity. Remember, these doves are only one variety of desirable birds that nest in here under our protection from the crows, coopers and sharp-shinned hawks. Robins and catbirds are wise to this protected spot. Seeing them, isn't it lovely to think, yes, to know, that these sweet, lovable creatures are so ready and willing to come to us homely, human beings for protection?

A great deal has been said about the crows' diet, so let me add my testimony. Crows will eat most anything. Yes, and about everything. I have had enough pet crows to find this out. But shelled corn will kill young crows about as quick as any diet you can feed them. If you have a young one and are anxious to raise him, feed custard—one hen's egg to a half a cup of milk (no sugar)—and just watch him grow. I have fed them chopped up snakes and they always cawed for more snake. Old crows will even graze like a chicken. During the winter in this section of the country, their chief diet is corn, but if they can find carrion that is what will tickle their palates most.

As to the value of the crow, let me tell you this. A crow will do no more good on the farm than a Leghorn chicken that will lay a dollar's worth of eggs a month. And as for the grasshoppers the crow destroys, let me advise you to keep a flock of turkeys and condense these grasshoppers into fifty cents per pound.

And now to the sportsmen and bird lovers of the continent let me hand this boiled-down sentence: Don't expect our desirable birds of Canada to increase until the crows are decreased—to say nothing about the game birds they destroy by eating their eggs. I honestly believe, especially in Manitoba, Saskatchewan and Alberta, that, by eating the duck eggs, the crows are the cause of decrease of ducks more than the hunter and his gun. In Manitoba, crows are so thick I saw them nesting on the telegraph wires. This stark, naked fact is what caused me to study crows so much the last five years. To reduce them by shooting campaigns has been proven a failure. Thousands of men are trying that and, in spite of their many varieties of decoys, the crows are increasing. Here is where my life's study of them helped me out, for I know how shy and cute a little shooting will make them. At last the idea of catching them presented itself to me, and immediately I could see results. More study increased my faith until I simply had to try it out.

Since I knew I would have to have bait, I at once called up Mr. Art Brown, one of our Kingsville fishermen, and he agreed to let me have a truck load or so of fish heads, scales and entrails, providing I got them off the dock before the health officers put him off. Next, I secured a dead horse or so and was about all set for crow bait. Then I built the net on the same principle as I had built my net to catch and tag geese, but much smaller, the exact dimensions being six feet high, twelve feet wide and seventy feet long. I started building the net on a Thursday and finished it Saturday, doing practically all the work myself. And on the following Tuesday I caught 510 crows at one catch. While there may be dozens of other ways to control crows, yet I do know this method, if put into practise, would soon reduce their numbers to the same proportion as they were fifty years ago.

About the only fault I have heard about my crow net is that it is altogether too expensive. This surely must be a Scotch complaint, for I know two young men that built a crow net last winter and caught as high as 237 at one catch, and the net only cost them seven dollars. Of course, this one was built of junk material, such as poles from the woods and old fish netting, but it caught the crows just the same. To build a neat net as large as mine, and to use new one-inch gas pipe as frame, and new two-inch mesh netting, would cost from seventy-five to a hundred dollars. But it is not necessary to build the net as long as mine. A net twenty-five feet long, instead of seventy feet, would soon catch some crows.

The big thing to make the net successful is the attention given to it. That is, keeping it well baited. We bait for two or three days outside of the net and then, when we have a thousand or two crows coming, we draw the bait under the net. Of course, we never allow any shooting near the net, as that will frighten the birds, and we don't even go near the net or allow any one near it except toward evening, when the crows have gone to roost, at which time we take the bait out. I understand indirectly that some parties have built nets but had little success, which I think was largely caused by failure to bait the crows enough outside of the net to get them coming before the bait was moved under the net. Again, I have made all my big catches mostly during the winter, when snow was on the ground, and all the odd ears of corn in the open fields were covered with snow, and thus the crows went any place for feed. During the last three winters we have caught thousands of them in this one net and have made as high as two catches in one day. But this happens very seldom, because after they get a fright it takes the ones that are not caught two or three days to get over it. So, usually, after we make a catch, we bait well around outside the net for two or three days.

THE JACK MINER CROW TRAP

Editor's Note—A few months ago, after the publication of so many letters in the papers and two or three articles from Jack Miner on the so-called "crow controversy," there was a demand from various quarters for detail regarding the Miner crow trap. At that time Mr. Miner handed plans and specifications to the United States government, by which they were placed in the hands of the Biological Survey. This organization drew plans and prepared condensed specifications. These it seemed worth while incorporating here as below:

In preparing the drawing of the crow trap developed by Jack Miner, of Kingsville, Ont., the Biological Survey has made a few slight modifications that in no way affect the mechanical features, but which it is believed will simplify its construction and possibly reduce the cost. The dimensions conform closely to the original trap, which had a total length of 73 to 75 feet, a height of 6 feet, a bottom width of 20 feet, and a top width of 12 feet.

MATERIALS—The materials used in the construction of a trap of this size are 14 heavy posts (about 8 feet long and 6 or 8 inches in diameter) ; 2 posts about the same size but about 11 feet feet long ; 2 smaller posts, about 11 feet long ; 412 feet of 1½-inch iron pipe with elbows and T-joints ; 12 posts about 2 x 2 inches and 7½ feet long ; 340 feet of 2-inch mesh galvanized poultry wire, 1 foot wide ; 10 pieces of quarter-inch flat iron, about 1 inch wide and 18 inches long ; 10 pieces of quarter-inch flat iron, 1 inch wide and 10 inches long ; 10 pieces of half-inch iron rod, about

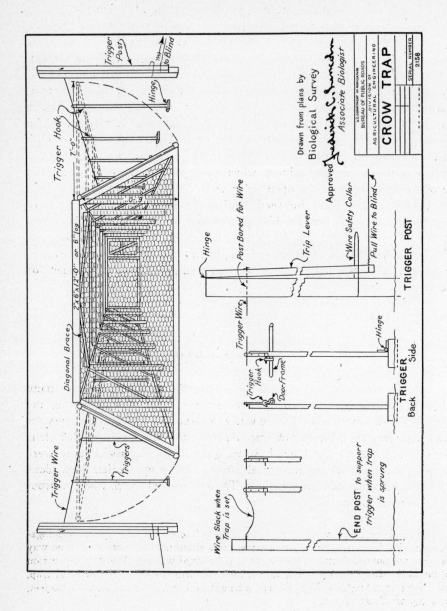

CROW TRAP

SERIAL NUMBER 2158

Drawn from plans by
Biological Survey

Approved _____
Associate Biologist

U.S. DEPARTMENT OF AGRICULTURE
BUREAU OF PUBLIC ROADS
DIVISION OF
AGRICULTURAL ENGINEERING

TRIGGER POST

TRIGGER
Back   Side

END POST to support
trigger when trap
is sprung

3 inches long; 12 flat or strap hinges, about 2 inches wide; about 300 feet of heavy galvanized iron wire; a quantity of old lumber to complete the framework of the trap; and the necessary tools for pipe fitting, forging, and carpentry.

CONSTRUCTION—After the site has been selected, the 14 heavy posts are set in the ground in two parallel lines 12 feet apart, so as to inclose a rectangle about 75 feet long and 12 feet wide. The posts can best be set by the use of a regular post-hole digger and should project 6 feet above ground. The opposite posts in the two lines are then joined together by heavy timbers (12" x 6" were used by Mr. Miner), and cross bracing added where necessary. *Note*—The ends of these timbers should not extend entirely across the tops of the posts, but should leave a space about 3 inches, which will be necessary in attaching the doors.

Two pieces of 6-foot wire netting will be used to cover the top. The details of the ends are best left until the doors are in place.

DOORS—The doors are merely frames, made from 1½-inch iron pipe, 206 feet being required for each door, which measures 75 feet by 7 feet. Six pieces of pipe are used as cross braces, parallel to the ends. Joints should be made with the usual T, or (at the corners) elbow joints. Having completed the frames, a piece of netting 6 feet long and 1 foot wide is used to cover them, the netting being laced together and to the frame as tightly as possible. The doors may now be set up against the posts, to which they are hinged by the simple expedient of heavy spikes driven into the tops of the posts and bent over the upper pipe of the frame.

With the doors in place, the ends may be completed on board frames nailed to the end posts. They also should be covered with wire netting, and a door should be provided to admit the operator.

TRIGGERS—By pulling each door out and up until horizontal, the place for the line of the triggers can be determined. On each of these lines five blocks are placed at equal distance apart. (Short sections of 4 x 4 timbers set in the ground will do.) These should be set so as to project an inch or two above the ground. To these the triggers are hinged. The triggers are 2 x 2 inch posts, 7½ feet long—(2 x 4 timbers, ripped longitudinally, will make satisfactory triggers), to the top of which are bolted pieces of quarter-inch flat iron, about 18 inches long. These irons must be drilled for screws or bolts before they can be attached and there also should be a quarter-inch hole near one end; the opposite end is forged to a piece of half-inch iron rod so that the latter will project as pins at a right angle about 2 inches. Great strain will come on this iron work, so the pins must be firm. In attaching the irons to the posts, the perforated end should extend several inches beyond the wood and when held vertically the half-inch iron pins should be approximately at the height of the doors when open; i.e., 6 feet from the ground. The triggers are secured to the ground blocks by strap hinges placed on the side toward the blind of the operator.

At the end of the lines of triggers and about 4 feet beyond, posts are set firmly in the ground. The end posts need not be large, but the trigger posts, which carry the operating levers, should be 6 or 8 inches in diameter. Also the end posts should be 2 or 3 feet higher. At the height of the tops of the triggers a hole is bored through the trigger posts and through each is passed a piece of heavy wire, which connects the triggers by means of the holes in the iron work, where a loop is made, and is finally fastened to the end posts. Each wire should be taut from the trigger post to the last trigger, but should have a few inches of slack between the last trigger and the end post. This is to prevent the triggers falling too far forward.

On each trigger post a trip lever (of the same material as the triggers) is attached by hinges across the tops. These levers should extend within about a foot of the ground, and to each is attached the ends of the trigger wire that passes through the trigger post. To prevent the levers from being pulled too far, wire safety collars are attached to the trigger posts a few inches above the lower ends of the levers. These should allow the lower ends of the levers to move about 2 feet. The pull wires are attached to the lower ends of the two levers, and after extending about 50 feet they may be joined together and continued to the blind as a single wire.

TRIGGER HOOKS—At points on the door frames corresponding to the position of the triggers, the trigger hooks are attached. These are made from pieces of quarter-inch flat iron about 1 inch wide, which are forged so that one end may be curled tightly around the pipe of the door frame while the other end is formed into a hook that will rest over the pins on the triggers.

OPERATION—As will be obvious from their size, the doors are very heavy and will likely require the services of three men to set. The doors are pulled out and up to the horizontal position and the triggers moved so that the hooks on the door frames rest over the trigger pins. It is well to attach the blind end of the pull wire to a short stick (such as a section of broomstick), so that it may be better grasped with both hands. A sharp jerk on this will pull the trip levers from 1 to 2 feet at their lower ends, which will pull the trigger wires in the same direction, 2 or 3 inches. As these wires are attached to all triggers, the action is simultaneous. The upper ends of the triggers move toward the operator, drawing the pins through the trigger hooks, and allowing the doors to fall.

BAIT—Unquestionably carrion is the bait for crows, and the carcasses of horses, mules, or cattle will be found effective attractions. If these can be obtained fresh, they should be cut up into sections *in* the trap and the pieces distributed through its length. It is well to allow the birds to feed unmolested for several days before attempting to pull the trap. A larger catch is thus assured. For the same reason it is not advisable to try to operate the trap every day. Probably once a week would be about the right interval.

Jack Miner himself notes that posts and poles from the woods may be made use of instead of trimmed lumber as the specifications above suggest, and also that old fish netting might be used to cover the framework in place of the galvanized poultry wire. This, obviously, would cut down the cost considerably.

FACTS ABOUT SOME HAWKS

AS A BOY I lived in the open 365 days in the year. Down in Ohio, hanging on to mother's hand, strolling through a little jungle near our humble buckeye home, I visited as many as nine Brown Thrasher's occupied nests in practically that many minutes. Both spring and fall back in the seventies, I watched passenger pigeons, not by the thousands, but by the clouds. Then in the first year of my teens we moved here to the sunny side of Canada where the woods and the few cleared fields were simply aglow with birds. I am sure I have seen as many as twenty-five Cardinals, I called them red birds, in sight at once. I wish the naturalist of today could have followed me for a few hours in the woods when the red bird storm came, as we called it, along about the 20th of May. He would have seen more warblers in an hour than I can find in a week right now. The long hours of a boy's life could not be made shorter and richer than all these God-given creatures made mine. I forgot all about my appearance—long red hair and freckles—and every Sunday in the summer would find me in my little hiding-places, allowing these creatures to come closer to me than I could get to them. Of course I knew no scientific names for them. I knew them and their habits but not their college-given names, and I am persuaded that today there are many with university degrees, who know their names but not their habits.

Let me give you the natural methods of our wickedest hawk's hunting system in his natural home, the virgin forest. He darts through the woods at a height of about six or eight feet from the ground, then noiselessly he shoots up at about a one o'clock angle where he perches on a limb as motionless as a statute about fifty feet from the ground, then in about five or ten minutes he comes darting down at a five o'clock angle, creating speed but making no more noise than a dart. If any bird moves in front of him, he is on it like lightning. When in the open field he travels high and I have seen a small Cooper's Hawk come down out of the air like a miniature aeroplane, and the Bobolinks and Meadow Larks dart and hide in the tall grass. So swift is this hawk coming from this elevated position, that I have seen him pick an adult forked-tail Barn Swallow right out of the air and go on. As for game birds here in Canada at that time, there were no Mourning Doves worthy of mention, but I have seen over 150 Bob-White Quail fly to the surrounding woods off of one settler's partly cleared farm. As for Ruffed Grouse, they were in the woods by the hundreds. I am certain that taking all classes of song, insectivorous, and game birds into consideration, there were ninety-five per cent. more than there are today. Of course, this includes the Passenger Pigeons that were here in the early seventies. I do not know when the Passenger Pigeon started dying but in 1885 they were practically extinct.

For the last ten or fifteen years "Uncle Jack"
has largely used field glasses rather
than a gun.

Now, with ninety-five per cent. of their food birds gone, which includes the Passenger Pigeon, the hawks are left here hungry, and the only way to restore a natural balance is to reduce the hawks to the same extent other bird life has been reduced. However the larger variety of hawks, which include the Red-tail, Red-shoulder and Broad Winged hawks do less damage. I do not shoot these big, clumsy varieties.

It is true the Sparrow Hawk's chief living in the Fall of the year is crickets and grasshoppers and he is a good little mouse-catcher, but years ago when I raised pheasants and quail in captivity, the Sparrow Hawk was one of my worst enemies, the first two or three weeks of the baby game birds' life. One Sparrow Hawk took ten baby pheasants in three hours.

The Great Horned Owl is one of the hardest, if not the hardest birds of prey we have to control, because he comes like a thief in the night and the darker the night the keener his eyesight appears to be. He will kill adult wild geese, turkeys, ducks, full-grown chickens and so forth, that the cat is hardly, if ever, known to kill. My greatest defense has been jump traps disguised on poles. I fail to find a successful game keeper, who doesn't control them. Once they take a bird of any variety, they will take more while food lasts. Common sense tells us, they are just as hard on the pheasants, Hungarian partridge, quail and grouse, that the governments are liberating in the wilds, as they are in the sanctuary or game farm from which the game birds were purchased. I have never seen a Great Horned Owl killed by a natural enemy.

Jumping down from the largest of our owls to one of the smallest, the most sickening and heart-breaking sight I ever witnessed was of the remnants of song and insectivorous birds I found at a Screech Owl's nest less than a half mile from my home.

Don't think I am one who wants to exterminate any variety of bird. My home is surrounded by the continuous song of insectivorous and lovable birds because I have controlled their enemies.

Knowing the depredation of the middle size and smaller hawks as I do, and have known all my life, I am completely bewildered to know why intelligent men will advocate the stocking of a country with song, insectivorous and game birds and make stringent laws to punish even a child for molesting one of them, and at the same time frame laws protecting the hawks that eat up these useful birds alive.

It is not the men and boys of our land who are depleting our song and insectivorous birds. Education has stopped that. It is the birds' natural enemies that are out of all proportion.

Many people write to me and say they like the action of hawks. But how can a man be humane and watch a hawk come down out of the air and catch and eat a song, insectivorous, weed-seed-eating bird—eat it practically alive? To me, it is more cruel than a Spanish bull-fight.

I have been opening hawks' crops all my life and know what they live on. Last September when hawks were migrating, I went a quarter of a mile east of my Sanctuary (as the hawks in this locality migrate from east to west), built a blind in a fence corner and used a cage eight feet square with twenty-five to fifty Bronze Grackle (Crow Black Birds) and Cow Birds for decoys. I got the hawks fully a quarter of a mile before they got to the Sanctuary. Each night, as the weather was warm, I would pack them in common salt and express them to the Biological Department of the Ontario Royal Museum at Toronto, Ontario, for examination. The accompanying report sent to me speaks for itself. The owls I shot at night at the Sanctuary.

Examination of hawks at Royal Museum of Zoology.

DATE	SPECIES	CONTENTS

August 20—Marsh Hawk—Remains of a young Mourning Dove.

September 5—Sharp Shinned—Part of remains of House Wren.

September 5—Sharp Shinned—Part of remains of a Song Sparrow.

September 8—Sharp Shinned—Nearly entire remains of an English Sparrow. Fragments from a Sparrow taken at an earlier feeding. Few oat grains from Sparrow crop.

September 8—Sharp Shinned—Remains of English Sparrow and also part of feet of another English Sparrow taken at an earlier feeding. Several oat grains from Sparrow crop and a few dry grass blades.

September 8—Sharp Shinned—Feathers and a few bones of a young Robin.

September 8—Sharp Shinned—Remains of English Sparrow, fresh, and part of feet of another from an earlier feeding. Four oat grains from Sparrow crop.

September 8—Sharp Shinned—Part of the remains of an English Sparrow. Oats from the crop of a Sparrow.

September 8—Sharp Shinned—Stomach empty.

September 8—Sharp Shinned—Stomach empty.

The following were taken latter part of September and October:

Marsh Hawk—Contained part of remains of Olive Backed Thrush.

Marsh Hawk—Empty.

Marsh Hawk—Feathers and bones of House Sparrow and Thrush.

Marsh Hawk—Feathers and bones of Mourning Dove and feet of a White Breasted Nut Hatch.

Marsh Hawk—Feathers and bones of House Sparrow and of small native Sparrow.

Marsh Hawk—Part of remains of a young (pinfeathers) Plymouth Rock chicken.

Cooper's Hawk—Remains of at least one Mourning Dove.

Cooper's Hawk—Trace of bird feathers.

Cooper's Hawk—Remains of House Sparrow.

Cooper's Hawk—Empty.

Cooper's Hawk—Feathers of Grackle.

Cooper's Hawk—Remains of domestic fowl. Two leaves, probably taken accidentally.

Cooper's Hawk—Empty.

Sharp Shinned—Empty.

Sharp Shinned—A few unidentified feathers of birds.

Sharp Shinned—Feathers of a thrush.

Sharp Shinned—Trace of feathers only.

Sharp Shinned—Feathers of a Maryland Yellow Throat.

Sharp Shinned—Feathers and remains of House Sparrow.

Sharp Shinned—Feathers of a Thrush.

Sharp Shinned—Feathers and remains of House Sparrow and a Warbler.

Sharp Shinned—Feathers of a Blackbird.

Sharp Shinned—Empty.

Sharp Shinned—Remains of a Chicadee.

Sharp Shinned—Remains of a Chicadee.

Sharp Shinned—Parts of remains of a Chicadee.

Sharp Shinned—Feathers of a Nut Hatch; parts of a small bird foot.

Sharp Shinned—Feathers of a Blackbird.

Sharp Shinned—Few remains of native Sparrow.

Sharp Shinned—Empty.

Sharp Shinned—Few feathers of small bird, perhaps a Warbler.
Sharp Shinned—Empty.
Sharp Shinned—Empty.
Sharp Shinned—Empty.
Sharp Shinned—Part of remains of a White Breasted Nut Hatch.
Sharp Shinned—Empty.
Sharp Shinned—Empty.
Sharp Shinned—Feathers of a House Sparrow.
Sharp Shinned—Feathers of a Thrush.
Short Eared Owl—Remains of at least two Sapsuckers, one almost entire.
Great Horned Owl—Part of remains of a young Ring-Necked Pheasant.
Great Horned Owl—Part of remains of a young Ring-Necked Pheasant.
Broadwinged Hawk—Empty.
Broadwinged Hawk—A few insect remains.
Broadwinged Hawk—Remains of forty-four crickets.
Pigeon Hawk—Remains of a Warbler.
Sparrow Hawk—Remains of a Dragon Fly; partial remains of nine Crickets.
Cooper's Hawk—Some rodent hair, apparently Rat.
Red Tailed Hawk—A young Blowing Adder.
Sparrow Hawk—Insects, mostly Grasshoppers, Crickets and Dragon Flies.
Red Tailed Hawk—Entire remains of a Bronze Grackle, gizzard of another bird
    (from former feeding) which was of the same size as Grackle, two gravels
    and some coarse grain chaff.
Sparrow Hawk—Remains of fourteen Crickets.
Sparrow Hawk—Remains of eighteen Crickets, one Moth, one Grasshopper, several
    feathers of a small bird, apparently an English Sparrow.
Long Eared Owl—Traces of hair.
Screech Owl—Six feathers of a small bird.

As I have said I do not shoot the three big, clumsy varieties of hawks, for while they kill a few rabbits, snakes, etc., I know they are not destructive to our small and lovable birds. Moreover, Mr. Redtail will kill Crows and the death of one Crow means more live songsters. But the Red-tail and Red-shouldered hawks are among the worst enemies the farmers' domestic fowl have to contend with. Hence, he gets the name of hen or chicken hawk. However the Marsh Hawk is worse on younger chickens. I have seen a Marsh Hawk take a young Wood Duck when it dived into six inches of water. Moreover, the Marsh Hawk is one of the fastest breeding hawks we have. He nests on the ground and if not molested, raises from four to five young. I have a motion picture of five young in the nest. Another nest I located through a neighbor complaining about his little leghorn chicks disappearing, had four young and was completely surrounded by remnants of white leghorn chicks.

The fact is that practically any one bird the hawks or crows kill will do as much good as one hawk and hawks of certain species kill an average of a bird a day.

THE DESTRUCTIVE STARLING

WHILE I HAD SEEN thousands of starlings in Southeastern Pennsylvania and the New England States, I had not seen one in Canada until 1924. In January, 1925, three came to our Sanctuary, and, to tell the whole truth, I rather welcomed them. But in 1927 and 1928 they began to wear out their welcome, for they ate up all the bob-white quail food I had about the premises. In 1929 and 1930 they drove out the five to ten thousand purple martins that roosted here in late July and August. I had over 100 occupied mourning doves' nests on less than one acre and these birds began driving them out. They had driven out over 90 per cent. of our beautiful red-headed woodpeckers in this locality. In every part of America they are occupying the woodpeckers' cavities in trees.

In July, 1931, we declared war on them and built a starling net or trap. By September 1 we had caught, drowned and buried over 17,000. But bless your life, there were a million that came to their funeral! Then the Italians of Windsor came down with a net and under our supervision they caught, smothered, and trucked to Windsor approximately 200,000. They were used to feed the hungry. In February our men hauled out of this starling-roost nearly fifty wagon loads of pine needles and starling droppings. To clean it thoroughly they had to take about two of the four inches of pine needles out with the manure. This left the other two inches of needles quite clean. Two weeks later there were at least five bushels to the acre of droppings—yellow, undigested, shelled corn lying on the ground. A portion of this corn was dropped where my son's chickens got and ate it, and over 100 of his John S. Martin strain of White Wyandottes died before we could check the deathly disease they contracted.

Starlings are edible. My sister scalded and cleaned twenty-four in less than an hour. I took them to Kingsville to weigh them and the twenty-four weighed exactly three pounds. My sister made a real English blackbird pie of them, and the only cheerful part of my story is they were fit to set before the King—that is if he got there ahead of me. If properly cooked, they are a treat on the table—one point of hope of controlling them.

Now, between two and three thousand of my choice white and Scotch pines are dead, dead, dead—killed by the slimy, poisonous droppings of the starlings. The beautiful nature's cathedral that I planned and planted in

1914 is a sight to look at. Yes, that lovely green canopy over head and carpet of fully four inches of pine needles below, where less than a year ago not a weed could be seen, is now grown up with weeds from four to seven feet high, grown from seeds carried there by these destructive starlings.

I can give you but a faint idea of what it is like to walk or, I might say wallow, through this tangle of noxious weeds with the wind moaning

One Thoughtless Visitor Drove Through
"Uncle Jack's" Pet Tulip Bed.

through the skeletons of the once beautiful trees. It seems like looking through the undertaker's show-rooms.

Here is something you can depend on right now. Starlings are not weed-seed destroyers but weed-seed distributors and killers of valuable trees.

Starlings! Why the last year I have spent one long, tedious hour after another lying on my stomach with a pair of high-grade field glasses, studying how to control them. At last I have built a net known as the Scotch Success Starling net or trap. It is Scotch because it catches so many starlings with such a small amount of bait and because it is a success. At present I believe we have them slightly checked. Fully 1,000 purple martins are coming again and roosting in the maples. During June and July we caught and buried over 25,000 starlings.

My personal findings of the starlings up-to-date are that they are driving out some of our best weed-seed and insect-destroying song birds, such as the Kentucky cardinal and lovable mourning doves, purple martins, and wood-peckers. They are the worst weed-seed distributors America ever knew. They carry deathly chicken diseases. They are very destructive to fruit and vegetables, and they are death to trees where they roost. Last and worst of all they are already lowering the general public opinion and appreciation of bird life.

THE UNWRITTEN LAW

PLEASE allow me to offer a brief wholesale reply to the constant written enquiries as to whom I am, what I am, why I am, and where I am. No, lady, I am not a preacher, but I thank you for the compliment; I am a brick-maker by inheritance and complexion. My first wife was my only wife, and I have three boys and two daughter-in-laws and, thank God, we are all on speaking terms and working harmoniously together. The last few years I have backtracked myself and I find that two of my great uncles on mother's side were outstanding gamekeepers 125 years ago, and my father was an underprivileged high-grade English sportsman, who delighted in sharing every shot possible and the last bird in the bag. And dear mother always had some little orphan wild bird in our small two by two weather-beaten rented Ohio home.

My long-neglected red hair and absolutely countless amount of freckles and scant clothing, combined with a crimson disposition, forced me out of school and I developed into an outstanding muskrat and skunk trapper and soon was wearing warmer clothes. At the age of thirteen when I was liberated on the sunny side of vast Canada, I took to the woods as cheerfully and as delightedly as a skunk in a hen roost and soon developed into a professional market-hunter and left a bloody trail behind me. Four years later when I was but seventeen years of age, my ability as a hunter and skill as a snap shot introduced me to some of the most sympathetic gentlemen sportsmen this world has ever known. I became the leader of the hunt, but the true manly influence of these big men gradually weaned me from the cruel market-hunting. My trigger finger gradually relaxed and I developed into a converted Jesse James to the fowls of the air. I am just a piece of crude, clean-born humanity, who unconsciously but ambitiously cultivated his inborn ability. Eventually it introduced him to the best, self-sacrificing, Godly-principaled humanity and now I only shoot the deathly enemies of our better birds.

Today I have absolutely proven that God and man can change the migrating route of the fowls of the air and cause them to come to sanctuaries where they can be saved from extermination. One man can care for more of them with the sanctuary system than ten game wardens can, chasing after them. The whole secret is protection from their natural enemies and a handful of feed instead of a thimbleful of shot.

In 1909, I was forty-four years of age and as busy as a cow's tail in the fly-time. On August 5th of that year I caught and banded and liberated my first wild duck. This bird was shot by Mr. W. E. Bray, of Anderson, South Carolina, on January 14th, 1910, and the band returned to me less than two weeks later. Since then we have banded at least 50,000 ducks. Some of these banded ducks have been reported from as far north as The Pas, Manitoba, as far west as Helena, Montana, and as far south as Venezuela, South America.

After waiting four long years for wild geese, on April 2nd, 1908, nine of these Canada honkers shut off the gas and glided down—down—down, and eventually put on the four-wheel brakes and splashed, feet first, into the

"A Handful of Corn instead of a Thimbleful of Shot" is the secret of this.

shallow, muddy water of one of my ponds. In 1909 thirty-two came. In 1910, fully two hundred. And fifteen years later (that being 1925), my three sons and I paid for the husking of more than 18,000 bushels of corn to feed the geese and ducks that (as we have absolute proof) have changed their migrating route to come to my artificial ponds and hand-planted groves.

In 1915 we had caught and banded only six geese. Up to 1922 we had been able to increase this number only to one hundred and nine. Readers, it was only my faith in His blessed promise that kept my personal power-house keyed up in the face of those discouraging results. But that faith was enough. My enthusiasm was just like a crude old freight-engine carrying two hundred pounds of steam and no damper! Then, all at once, I saw His promise fulfilled. One day I tripped the trap-doors and had two hundred and sixty-five of these wise old, ten-pound Canada honkers in captivity at one time. Since then we have caught over 32,500 of these lovely Canadians—they're really Eskimos by birth. About 150 *tons* of wild geese we have tossed from our hands into the air! Each one carries our post office address and a Gospel message to the hunter lucky enough to bring it down.

We now have reasons to believe that fully 25 per cent. of the honkers that winter east of the Mississippi river have found this International migratory bird cafeteria and almost wear their welcome out twice a year. Very true, our Government is helping us a little but at least 75 per cent. of the responsibility is carried by my boys and me. We now have one thousand five hundred of these tagged geese reported killed and fully one thousand of the tags returned, which gives us absolute proof of their whereabouts each month of the year. The Eskimos in the far, far north take the bands to the permanent fur-dealers for an interpretation. There they meet the Missionaries; the Eskimos dictate letters to me and the missionaries write them. Fully 500 of such bands are back in our possession from that part of the world.

I wish to say right here that we are very, very thankful for the co-operation of the Eskimos and of the hunters and sportsmen throughout North America for their kind assistance in this line of education. But I am compelled to believe there are hundreds upon hundreds of these tagged geese killed that are not reported. Now, brother sportsman, will you please sit down with your sincere thoughts and open up this blessed old book known as *The Unwritten Law*—this book, as you know, is read from the heart and not through the eyes. Now turn to the chapter known as consideration. Here is a man who has fed birds far beyond his means and who, please remember, is not your enemy, no, no, far from it. You got a good fat corn-fed Canada goose, a duck or a swift-darting mourning dove and a band on its leg asks you, as kindly as I can word it, to write me. Now, my dear sir, please take the Golden Rule in your hand and I have confidence that you will obey the *Unwritten Law* and write me and possibly return the band.

THE UNFINISHED MIGRATORY
BIRD TREATY

POSSIBLY one of the greatest steps ever taken towards the protection of the birds of North America was the forming of the Migratory Bird Treaty between Miss Canada and Uncle Sam. But, when that treaty permitted any province or state a three and one-half months' open season, I am sure all thinking conservationists will agree with me that it was unfinished. Now, dear reader, I feel fully qualified and justified to have a heart-to-heart talk with all classes on the above important subject.

As I was born in Ohio and made in Canada, God forbid that I should say one word that would cause even a thought of friction between the people of these two countries that are so near and dear to my heart. My only purpose of writing this article is to create a deeper consideration among the shooters.

Now, without the vast breeding grounds of Canada for our ducks and geese or without their winter home in the Southern States, all thinking humanity knows these beautiful birds would soon follow the passenger pigeon and become extinct.

Therefore, it is compulsory that we must work heart and hand together. But, don't let us use that word "compulsory." Let us say, lovingly together. Yes, for God's sake and for the sake of the rising and unborn generations, let us work lovingly together. Now, do you know, dear brother Yankee, that you have as many shooters as we have population? Have you ever stopped to consider the vastness of the Dominion of Canada and that we have less than nine million people? Do you know that the Province of Ontario alone is more than eleven times larger than the State of Ohio, with less than one-half the population? Ontario borders New York State to the east, and, coming west, it borders Pennsylvania, Ohio, Michigan, Wisconsin and Minnesota, yet Ontario is only one out of our nine vast provinces, saying nothing about the hundreds of thousands, yes, I might say a million or more square miles of unsurveyed territory still farther north. This fact will surely give you a glimpse of the vastness of our breeding grounds for the water-fowl that are forced to congregate by countless thousands in your warmer states during the winter months.

Just recently one of my highly esteemed Yankee friends and I were discussing this migratory bird question. When I told him that, taking North America as a whole, wild geese were fast decreasing, he looked me in the face and said, "Jack, who has been talking to you along this line?" Now, I don't know as I took it as a compliment, for it sounded as though I had no knowledge of what I was saying and was easily influenced. You will note that in the beginning of this article I said I felt justified and qualified to express my views. I feel justified because of my birthright and qualified by personal knowledge and experience.

In addition to the above facts, let me say I have been privileged to cross our continent four times during the last three years, on one occasion going

A view from the Observation Tower at the Miner Home showing birds rising from the North Ponds.

to Alaska, and the last three Octobers have found me lecturing in our prairie provinces, the greatest wheat field in America. During that time I visited over one hundred cities, towns and villages, often motoring over fifty miles a day across the prairies. When traveling by rail, I always ride in observation coaches and try to keep both eyes open, for, like Zaky of old, I want to see for myself. And will you believe me, I didn't see one thousand wild geese. The most I heard of any hunting party killing was fourteen. But every place I lectured persons were asking. "What has become of our wild geese that used to come here by the tens of thousands? Where are they? Have they changed their migrating route or what has happened to them?" I answered them by saying, "Automatic guns and systematic shooting is where they are migrating to."

Why do I answer this way? Because of the number of letters I receive enquiring for wild geese to use as decoys. One letter reads as follows: "So many geese came in to decoys and we killed them all. Among them was this one with a tag on." Another letter reads: "We killed thirty-seven this morning." Some of these letters are accompanied by snapshots showing a car literally covered with geese. Snapshots don't lie.

I also receive letters from persons living along the Mississippi River, enquiring: "What has become of the sandhill crane—a large bird that stood nearly five feet high? They used to come here by the hundreds, but we don't see them any more." Yes, what has become of the sandhill crane, brother sportsmen of North America? Wake up, or in less than twenty-five years the same question will be asked about our wild geese.

Now I am convinced that a bag limit as a law is a failure, as it seldom can be enforced. Its principal motive and advantages are to educate the people that slaughter is unsportsmanlike, but what kind of education is this—a lawful privilege for any individual to shoot twenty-five hundred ducks and eight hundred geese in one season? What will our children's children think when they search our records and find that grandfather could lawfully shoot six tons of ducks and geese in one year? I say to all classes of humanity, a law like that is worse than no law at all. Yes, we all know that no sportsman will kill that amount of game in one year. Then, why in the name of common sense do we leave that lawful privilege open to those who will?

Yes, we know that when these ducks are forced to pile up for four months in their winter quarters they cannot be estimated by thousands but by millions—millions of ducks on thousands of acres. But, when they are scattered over the northern states and Canada, it is hundreds of ducks on millions of square miles. Five hundred house flies in a little six inch balloon fly-trap make it black with flies and, if we are short-sighted enough, we will think flies are increasing by leaps and bounds. But, liberate them in a big barn and you will find them few and far between.

Another trigger-finger excuse advanced by the thoughtless shooter is that the southern marsh lands are drained and the ducks' food supply is destroyed. Is it all true? Forty-five years ago, I am absolutely sure, there were five ducks migrating through Ontario where there is one to-day. In other words, they have decreased eighty per cent the last half-century and at that time artificial feeding was not even thought of. Is eighty per cent of their original natural feeding grounds destroyed? I cannot believe so. Who hasn't been duck hunting the last ten years and seen thousands of acres of green marsh with more guns than ducks?

I have had some of my friends write me and fully agree that ducks have decreased fully eighty per cent in the last forty-five years, yet they go on to say ducks are not decreasing now. All I wish to ask these friends is—if they agree ducks have decreased eighty per cent when did they decrease? I say they have gradually decreased as the hunters and guns have increased.

Now, I am not complaining for the sake of doing so, nor have I any personal motive in view. No one is paying me to do so or even suggested or even knows I am writing this. Moreover, there are no government strings attached to me. But I want to cheerfully devote the balance of my life to conservation, and I have some carefully thought-out and a few tested-out plans of improvement to offer.

There They Go!

But before I go further, I want to apologize for my lack of scholarship, for neglected red hair, freckles and the fragrance of a young skunk catcher, and mother necessity all combined their forces and kicked me out of school. The result is I was educated for ditching, splitting rails and market hunting. But, since I was not able to read until after I was a gray-haired man, I was compelled to go to the forest, field and marshes and let these so-called wild creatures teach me their ways and it was they that melted the heart that controlled my trigger finger and caused me to stop and think. And while I don't want the readers to take me to be one of those old religious cranks that wouldn't boil a tea kettle on Sunday, yet I do want you to know that every one of His lovable promises I have been able to test out I have found it to be true. I want to mention three:

First. If man will take God at His word in harmony with Him, that man can change the migrating route of the fowls of the air. Second. Any bird that is intelligent enough to fly one-half mile from humanity for self-preservation, will fly clear across the continent back and forth to us for food and protection. Third. Civilization does not necessarily prevent us from knowing birds and they can be taught to know our voice and will come down out of the air when we call and, with a little patience on our part, they will actually eat from our hands. "Let man have dominion over all."

Knowing these facts, we must no longer treat these birds as wild, but as migratory chickens, and let each county establish a small Federal sanctuary of not less than twenty-five nor more than one hundred acres near the centre of the county. This should have a dog-proof fence around it and no shooting allowed within a mile of this fence. I just mention the above as an outline, but local conditions are, after all, the determining factor and, if you have no local conditions, do as I did—make them. Plant a forest border of evergreens from four to ten rods wide all around the outside. Now erect a small observation tower beside the public highway, but just outside the sanctuary fence, where

Wild Whistling Swans Resting on Lake Erie, in Front of the Miner Sanctuary.

all classes can go up with field glasses and kodak and enjoy the sights. But remember, the public must be kept outside of this fence. Now liberate a few pairs of wing-tipped pinioned wild ducks and geese in there, and feed and protect this haven of rest and watch results. In a few years you will find your sanctuary a stopping place for thousands of our migratory chickens, with many other species making their home in the evergreens.

Brother bird lover, the plan is not a joke. It has been tested out and the opportunity is pounding at the door of every county. We can bring these honking V-shaped waving lines of birds down into our little lakes, rivers or even in artificial mud holes and have them with us for at least two months twice a year, or we can let them continue to migrate over a mile high. This is left entirely with us.

Last April, Mr. Henry Ford and I stood on the north bank of Lake Erie, just three miles south of my home, and twenty-six miles south-east of Detroit, and there, about one-half mile out was the sandbar, fully one mile in length, literally covered with wild geese. A little closer in were thousands upon thousands of canvas-back ducks and there right near the shore, in the calmest of the water, by actual count, were over three thousand of these beautiful white angelic birds—our whistling swans. Some had their necks curved and their heads lying on their backs resting, others were tipping up, leaving their black feet out of the water. They were feeding. Some were hovering and making love to their sweethearts. Their cooing could be heard for miles inland. Mr. Ford pushed his hand through his hair and, turning to me, he said, "Jack, I never saw a more beautiful sight in all my life."

Don't forget brother bird lover and shooter, we are now overlooking a hunting ground where I hunted for thirty years of my blood-thirsty life and never shot a wild goose or ever saw a swan on the water. The swans

We know of no other Whistling Swans in captivity. And these birds are happy.

coming to our country have multiplied the public interest in bird life fully tenfold. The little town of Kingsville, with two thousand population, boasts of having fifteen thousand people there in one day to see the birds and, let me again say, to any county bird society, the opportunity to duplicate what I have described is rapping at your door. But now, the latest report I get is —the swans are eating the duck food in a southern state and we are going to shoot the swans. How can such a report be true?

Now the first flag I ever knew was the Stars and Stripes and I was taught to believe that each of those forty-eight stars represented a state. Then, when I got to Canada, I was told that our Dominion was larger than all of these forty-eight states combined. Such being the case, we have the equivalent of one hundred states or more in the United States and Canada and these swans belong to all of us and, just because they are eating a small portion of the duck food in one small state, should the other ninety-nine per cent. be

deprived of seeing them alive? I say, "No—No—No—let's feed them." Why
do I say this? Because of personal knowledge and experience.

A few years ago the elk in Wyoming were starving. The Izaak Walton
League of America, of which I am proud to be a member, sounded the alarm
and big-hearted Yankees rallied to the cause and saved the situation. Now,
if you can give thousands of dollars to save the elk for a few thousand people
to go and shoot, surely to goodness you can give a few hundred to save
the various water-fowl for millions of people to see alive and thousands of
people to shoot.

Oh, I would to God that all of us had more of that dear old Abraham

Here's the Rose Arbor at the Miner Home.

Lincoln spirit, when he stood up and said: "I stand for what is best for the
most people." As a further illustration I refer you to my own twenty-five
acre mud hole experience where there is absolutely no natural food at all.
If one man, with no natural advantage and no money (the biggest bank
account I ever had was an overdrawn one), can do what you are compelled
to believe has been done here, what might the organized effort of one hundred
and twenty-five million people accomplish. Dear North American people,
from sunny south to the North Pole, this all depends on the desire of our
hearts, for as soon as I allowed my heart to love the birds, it stayed my
bloody hands. My trigger-finger relaxed.

I started planting trees in 1910 and today I am one of the richest men
on earth because there isn't money enough in the world to buy my home
and compel me, in my old age, to leave this sacred spot and go somewhere
else and reestablish. In the spring of 1926 I fed over four thousand bushels

of corn to our migratory water-fowl that had been educated to come to my home. I am thankful to say our Canadian governments are helping me a little, and some big-hearted Yankees give me good donations, which are very acceptable. In fact, I wouldn't be able to carry on this work to the extent I have had it not been for their help, because it now costs me nearly $6,000 per year to feed the birds which stop at the sanctuary on both spring and fall migration trips. The balance of this expense is derived from my lectures.

Now let me offer a few suggestions. Let us call and call and call until every hunter and bird lover in America is aroused and let us have the biggest international meeting of sportsmen and bird lovers that ever got together on this continent and let us get close together, so we can talk low and avoid friction. Let us go prepared to talk kindly and plainly and to listen to plain talk. Let us put on the soft pedal and point out to the shooter that the fall of one bird out of the air from his deadly aim can give pleasure to one only, while thousands are deprived of seeing it alive. On the other hand, we want the bird lover to be reasonable. We cannot say that the ducks and geese are of any particular value, only to see them lined up in the air and here and there cheerfully honking and quacking.

Ducks and geese multiply very rapidly, and what reasonable man can be opposed to shooting a limited number any more than taking the surplus of our domestic fowl? Shooting takes thousands of men away from the grind of life, gives them an appetite to eat and a desire to sleep and they wake up rested and are better husbands and fathers in their homes. Such being a positive fact, what reasonable man can oppose it? But we must curtail that federal open season of three and one-half months and either have a uniform smaller federal-controlled bag limit or none at all. Yes, I said federal-controlled bag limit, because the migratory birds are federal property since they know neither state nor international boundary lines. Therefore, federal property can only rightly and justly be controlled by federal laws.

One of the complaints I have heard is that the ducks' breeding-grounds are destroyed. Such nonsense! There are breeding-grounds in America for many times the number of ducks that we have. The only reasonable complaint for us not having ten ducks where we now have one is hinged on their winter quarters. We can overcome all of this by feeding. In this way we can move them from all polluted streams and stagnant lakes, which at the present time are killing our ducks by the hundreds of thousands. Feed them in marshes and lakes where the water is pure. Any person that knows the letter A about birds knows this is true. We feed to bring them to our guns; then why not feed to protect them? Oh, but you sigh and say, what an extravagant suggestion. But if our hearts are with the game it isn't. Remember, good sensible bird protection pays over two hundred per cent. dividends. We paid two million dollars to see a prize fight. Scatter the price of that half-hour's punishment over two years, with the addition of the natural feeds we could grow, and see how many ducks it will feed. Or, take one per cent. of our automobile expense. We all know that, if necessary, we could impose a gun license of one dollar. In fact, I am sure, if put to a vote, fully seventy-five per cent. of the sportsmen of America would vote for such a license.

Let me again say, the whole proposition rests upon the desire of our hearts, and every thinking person in America knows that the day is past for having something for nothing. Remember, the birds know no boundary lines, so don't let us conservationists know any in affording them food and protection.

Now, just another word re the three and one-half months' open season, I say, No, it is six months, as it starts in Ontario, September 1st, and ends

Shelter in the Time of Storm—Wild Geese on the Miner South Pond.

in the Southern States six months later. Another point I want all to take into consideration: Why do we want three and one-half months' open season on the migratory birds in each country when we only allow fifteen days on those that winter with us, such as quail, pheasants and other non-migratory birds? It is pure unadulterated selfishness; that is why. We are afraid the other fellow is going to get them. We should all be old enough to know that selfishness will not protect our birds, reforest our waste lands, nor erect educational buildings for the unborn generations. Selfishness will not take us any place where we would care to stay. Surely selfishness will not take us in the direction Jesus Christ went.

I don't care what line we take up, its success and enjoyment will depend upon the amount of real heart love, enthusiasm and education we put into it. Yes, love and education are the hope of the world.

And education does not end with the human race—not at all. Every one of our so-called wild creatures I have studied, from the chickadee to the lordly moose with the five-foot spread of antlers, all expose how they educate each other for self-preservation. Wild geese have often been known to nest in trees where foxes and prairie wolves are patrolling the ground. Crows never wintered in Ontario, Canada, thirty years ago, but as soon as the corn-binder came in and knocked off five per cent. of the ears, these black, nest-robbing murderers found, when they could get plenty of corn to live on, they could stand the winter. They all educate others to stay, and now they winter here by hundreds of thousands, and I know that our wild geese can be educated to winter in every state where the thermometer doesn't go over twenty below zero.

In 1924 fully five hundred wintered here and they would stay with me every winter only for being disturbed by my catching them. Wintering them here and in the northern states would relieve the south from having so many to feed. Moreover, as I said before, it would distribute them more evenly throughout the nation. As caring for them brings one so much more enjoyment than shooting them does, it is easy to see how this plan works out. For illustration, in 1922, I let Mr. Henry B. Joy, of Detroit, have seven of my domesticated, hand-raised, wing-tipped, wild goslings which I raised, and he started a sanctuary on the north shore of Lake St. Clair, about thirty-five miles, as the goose flies, north-east from my home. He got geese coming the first year and last year he fed over a thousand bushels of corn. Now he is so enthused over his success he has added a fifty-thousand-dollar addition to his Joy Ranch, as he calls it, and just leave it to Henry whether the ducks, geese and swans that visit this Lake St. Clair sanctuary will be fed. He can and will feed all the birds in North America if they stop there.

Mr. Joy is only one of many I could name that have visited here and have gone home, copied and improved on my plan. There is Mr. Henry M. Wallace, of Detroit, who came here about 1920 and today has one of the most promising sanctuaries in the State of Michigan. Also Mr. W. K. Kellogg, of Battle Creek.

Who reaps the benefit of such controllable sanctuaries? As I have already stated, the sanctuary does not take anything from the shooter, but constantly increases his chances.

CONSIDERATION, JUSTICE, AND PREVENTION

FAR FROM BEING a menace to the birds, the Eskimo, I believe, is our greatest assistance. Let me call your attention to the almost unbelievable way our swans have multiplied the last fourteen years in which the swans have had protection south of Eskimo land. Remember, these angelic white swans that winter along the southeast Atlantic coast are all Eskimos by birth and by being given absolute protection from the hunter's gun, they have multiplied from perhaps less than one thousand, when the Migratory Bird Treaty went into effect, to perhaps 50,000 or more now. This is absolute proof that the Eskimos in the far north with their bows and arrows are not keeping birds from increasing. Furthermore, it is proof that drought, pollution, and other menaces of the present day have not kept them from increasing, but the protection from the hunter's gun has allowed them to increase. We all know that ducks and geese multiply faster than swans.

Now, if you will please allow me, I want to pour my heart out to all Canadians. Remember, I am a Canadian and, as I said before, my home isn't for sale at any price, for I love the people of Canada, especially the Canadian-born, and I love our fertile fields of the south, the rolling hills and pathless woods of the north, the home of such a variety and abundance of big game and fur-bearing animals, and our thousands of deep, inland lakes, teeming with the choicest of fish, and the sparkling streams where the speckled beauties are leaping the rapids every day. Since I have been privileged to camp out in our Northern Canada on hunting trips for forty-one Falls in succession, I feel qualified to say we are territory-poor but millionaires in our outdoor privileges and future prospects.

But such a large percentage of Canadians, after visting my home and taking in the situation, look at me as if I wasn't all there and very often remark: "Jack, you are only feeding and protecting these birds for the Eskimos and Yankees to shoot." This statement has been repeated so much I have got so it doesn't annoy me in the least, for I feel it comes from the lack of knowledge and consideration. Do you know, brother Canadian, the Eskimo is our Northern Canadian? He was here long before you and I were thought of and today we Canadians are sending thousands of dollars to foreign fields to civilize, educate and assist the needy, and I am in favor of it. But when I fatten a flock of wild geese and harness them up with a gospel message and let them go over the top to the needy Eskimos, I feel I have assisted them in securing meat for the body and bread for the soul and have upheld my slogan, "Do the Duty closest to me."

Readers, you can rest assured that our Eskimo land contains at least a million square miles of breeding-ground for our migratory birds, with a few scattered Eskimos dotted here and there trapping the enemies of our geese, swans and ducks and trading their furs to the fur dealer for existence. What sane person with a heart can object to these natives taking a few geese?

In April, 1915, I caught six wild Canada geese. In October one was reported killed by an Indian in Hudson Bay. In April, 1916 and 1917, I

The Goose Trap, from Above.

caught, tagged, and liberated a few more geese. One was reported killed by an Eskimo in Baffin Land. This got me more and more interested and I sent a few dollars to the far-off Hudson Bay fur-dealers along with some printed literature with the request that they pay one dollar for each tag brought in. This plan worked O.K. and letters reported some Eskimos bringing tags in for five hundred miles and more.

Finally, I found I had bit off more than I could chew, financially, for instead of catching geese by the dozens, I started catching them by the hundreds, then by the thousands and, of course, the more geese I caught the more it cost me for feed. Then I had to get out more printed pamphlets than ever and this time I mailed them to the missionaries and fur-dealers to explain to the natives that my ambition was big but my finances small and that I would thank the good hunters in advance if they would send tags back free of charge and I would try to continue sending more geese. Readers, just think of it, those kind, conscientious Eskimos often send me the hour along with the day, date, and place they killed the goose. This has caused me to have a real gnawing desire to meet these kind, co-operative Arctic Canadian North Americans, and some day in the near future, I hope to go up there and grip their honest hands and thank them face to face.

Fully 90 per cent. of the first 4,400 geese I tagged were caught in April when they were on their way to the Eskimos to have first chance at them, when they flew north for the summer. Readers, you can bank your last dollar that those Arctic citizens have sent in the tags every bit as conscientiously, according to the number gathered, as we citizens have to the south of them.

Do these gathered facts say that the Eskimos are such a handicap to our migratory birds?

Now, as for me feeding the birds for the Yankees to shoot, just let me unroll this fact. Nearly seventy per cent. of the money it costs me to feed these birds comes from the United States; it does not come from those who want to shoot the ducks. It is given me for lecturing in schools, churches, before bird-protective societies and in good donations. These Yankees are the biggest-hearted people you ever mixed with and we Canadians have the best neighbors of any country in the world.

Now just a word to you Yankees who often say to me, "It is of no use for us to try to protect the geese and ducks while the Eskimos are robbing their nests and slaughtering their young and molting birds and feeding them to their dogs." I will admit that there must be Eskimos of this kind, for there are undoubtedly outlaw Eskimos the same as we have outlaws further south. But, I am sure, the great, great majority are not that way. I am in constant communication with the fur traders of that country, especially the Hudson's Bay agents, and, while it is true I have more goose tags returned from Hudson Bay than I have from any two states in the Union, yet it must be understood these Eskimos shoot to sustain life. Yet, I doubt very much if the average twenty Eskimos, with their bows and arrows, kill as many geese in a season as the bag limit allows one man in some of our states and provinces.

The Rev. W. G. Walton, Anglican missionary, who has been a missionary on the east side of Hudson Bay for thirty-five years, has visited my home three times, and I would that every man that complains about the Eskimos could hear this reverend gentleman tell the story of the starving conditions these natives often experience and how he has actually known cases of cannibalism to take place. And, right here, I want to reproduce the last letter received from this reverend gentleman, which speaks for itself. This territory he speaks of is the nesting-grounds of about all the Canada geese which winter east of the Mississippi; that has been proven by my tagging system. By the way, I am sure it will interest the readers to know that the geese that winter east of the Mississippi River never go west of the Rocky Mountains. The same may be said of the ducks, although they wander farther west than the geese. Yet the farthest west I have ducks reported is Montana and Alberta. The following is Rev. W. G. Walton's last letter to me from Hudson Bay territory:

"My Dear Jack:

"Yours of the 15th inst. has just reached me and in reply re the census in the territory east of James and Hudson Bay. We had 797 Eskimos and about 1,000 Indians when I took the last census. Last winter about one-third of the Belcher Island Eskimos died through sickness and many along the coast from Great Whale River north and, in the recent summer, when my last letters were being written, some deaths among the Indians were taking place through a cold that was laying the people up. Some thought it might be the 'flu.'

"I took the census in 1911 and since that year there has been a high death rate, for the people are sadly neglected and the food is extremely scarce, hence why I have agitated so strongly in Ottawa for the introduction of the domesticated reindeer into that territory. It seems to me that in a few years we shall have few, if any, Eskimos left alive, for tuberculosis is playing havoc with the people, through lack of suitable food, clothing, bedding and tents. Tents are always used in the summer season, and now, through lack of skin clothing, in winter, too. I must confess that I am somewhat pessimistic with regard to the protection of my people, the Eskimos, for little or nothing has been done in an adequate way after my years' appealing. Those who have seen the conditions and have any interest in these helpless people realize the urgency of the need. A trader with many years' experience wrote the government that 'things were getting worse each month.' Yet nothing that will adequately meet the situation is done. I am not leaving a stone unturned in seeking to arouse public interest in these people, but we lack concerted action.

"The Right Hon. Arthur Meighen in his appeal for those people said, on June 26th, 1925, in the House of Commons: 'I do not know any trust we have more sacred than seeing to it that some means of keeping up the Eskimo race is provided and that they are not simply allowed to die right at our doorstep as mere dogs.'

"I certainly appreciate your kindly interest.

"With all good wishes, I remain,

> "Yours most sincerely,
> "W. G. WALTON."

To you Yankees who are not well acquainted with the Canadians let me introduce them. A real North American Canadian is the same human being that you have in Ohio, Michigan or Minnesota or any other state. He has neither split feet nor antlers and if his body was built in proportion with his heart he couldn't crawl in a box-car. Our accent may differ a little from yours, the same as the accent of people in one state differs from the accent of people in another state.

While hunting and trapping in our far northern wilds, fifteen or twenty-five miles from any human being, I have often gone in an old deserted lumber camp or a trapper's cabin and there, hanging from the highest peak of the ceiling, is a wire that deer mice cannot get up or down. This wire is holding a loaf or two of bread, out of reach of animals, ready for a brother human being who might lose his way and fall by the wayside hungry. You may find a big telescope tin pail that contains a knife and fork, a baking-pan and a few hard biscuits and enough flour to sustain life for a week or so. I am only using these backwoods rough-and-ready facts to illustrate to you the principles of a real Canadian and, as to our conserving ideas, I will give you this fact. Mourning doves nest in southern Ontario by the thousands and are given absolute protection on account of their vast value as weed seed destroyers, yet there are several states which have an open season on them.

Oh! both Yankees and Canadians, let us quit complaining and go to building, or else we will wake up and find we have no birds to build for. Very few Yankees appear to know that way back in the early eighties this vast but thinly-populated province of Ontario prohibited the shooting of ducks in the spring of the year.

This law was a step in the right direction, but on account of no co-opera-tion, it was very unpopular and extremely hard to enforce. Today a whole lot of us Southern Canadians look upon the present Migratory Bird Law as unfair, for the Northern-bred ducks do not arrive here until about October 20th and are gone on farther south by the 15th of November. While they are all hatched in Canada there is a big doubt if 5 per cent. of them are killed here.

In the prairie provinces we may get a few more than that, but I doubt it. I am now referring chiefly to the Canvas Backs, Redheads, and Blue Bills. Oh! Yankees, let us carefully consider, at least 85 per cent. of the ducks and geese are hatched and matured in Canada. Remember, we Yankees are allowed to use automatic guns giving us six shots in five seconds, which is entirely prohibited in Canada. The United States has more hunters than Canada has population.

Can you blame me for being a little irritated at some of us Yankees condemning us Canadians for the scarcity of ducks and geese? Especially when you consider the fact that I have more goose tags returned from one Southern state than I have from the whole of Canada, including Eskimo territory—yes, and more than I have from all the Northern states in the United States combined.

Now, let me again repeat to you my plan. Let the leaders of every conservation association in America get in touch with each other and arrange a time and place for a grand gathering. Then let each association take the responsibility of getting their members there, and I know we can do things.

During the eight months the birds are gone from their winter home, we can replant their natural feeding-grounds and make them five times as productive. We can move them one hundred miles in one year and take them to pure lakes and marshes where we can have many vast sanctuaries, financed and controlled by the federal government, with plenty of game guardians to feed and protect these birds. These to be the same as the county sanctuaries only on a larger scale. But, you must remember that there must be no shooting within the sanctuary nor within one mile of its borders, for a sanctuary where birds are fed and shooting is permitted even one day a week is only a systematic slaughter house. What could I do here on my sanctuary with a gun one hour a week?

Wild Geese in the Miner Trap. These will be tagged and released.

We can amend the bird treaty by shortening the unreasonably long open season and providing for a small, federal control bag limit that will give justice to all and favor none. In fact, if we will work harmoniously together and take God at His word, we can distribute these migratory fowl over every county in America. As proof of this statement, today we are having one of the worst blizzards I ever saw in southern Canada and, during this Christmas holiday, there were between two and three thousand wild geese resting within gunshot of where I am sitting. As soon as it fairs up, they will again be all over the county, and just and right they should, for they belong to the people of North America, just as much as the free air that we breathe belongs to us all. But, if it was not for the established home here, when they left Hudson Bay eight or ten weeks ago, they would have gone right on over the top and piled up with the rest, in the southern states, where they would stay till the last of February.

Yes, dear people of America, if we will only allow our hearts to control, we can have wild life and have it more abundantly.

Let us have an international migratory bird commission, composed of fifteen men. Five from Canada, five from the Northern states and five from the Southern states. Let our meeting-place or places be near the international boundary line. The first thing to be considered should be the birds, not the hunters, and the long open season should be cut down to a month and a half for any one state or province and this month and a half to be chosen by each state or province between September 15 and December 15.

Let me close asking all to consider these three words, Consideration, Justice, and Prevention.

DEER AND WOLVES

AMONG the editorials in the Toronto *Mail and Empire* of December 26th appeared the above words—"Deer and Wolves"— and, as I read and reread this most important article, I couldn't help but wish that all the editors in Ontario could be better posted on the destructiveness and cold-blooded, murderous acts of these timber wolves. Just to think that in Algoma District a doe was seen stumbling her way back and forth to a little stream and, when put out of her misery by a bullet, she was found to have one ham over half eaten away, and the shredded skin showed the marks of a devilish timber wolf's sharp teeth! This, of course, is an exceptional case, but it can be readily understood by men that know the letter A about sheepdogs and wolves.

Now, who is chiefly to blame? I say, from personal knowledge, we so-called sportsmen are to blame. We meet in convention and the decreasing of the deer is discussed. The still hunter condemns the dog hunter. The dog hunters claim it is the still hunters and also the settlers who kill them in the summertime, and I stand up and move that we recommend a buck law, so that only those with antlers be allowed to be shot. This apparently only increases the friction that is rapidly growing warmer, until the chairman can hardly keep two or three from talking at once, and, finally, we go home sorry we ever went and wishing we could recall every sharp word we have said. Meanwhile, the skulking timber wolf is gorging himself on our wild mutton, then coiling up in the sun or under the drooping boughs of the second growth pines, licking his chops and laughing at our calamity.

Now, just a word about the nature of some of these so-called wild animals. The moose, the caribou and the snowshoe hare are all creatures of the solitude or virgin forest, while the red deer, white-tailed deer, or Virginia deer, which is the same animal, as well as the cotton-tail rabbit, follow up the pioneer's axe. Yet we Ontario sportsmen, in our innocent ignorance, condemn the settler for the scarcity of the deer when, right down in our hearts, we know that where the country is partly settled we get our best deer hunting. Why? Simply because the settlers keep the wolves in check and allow the deer to multiply far faster than the settlers kill them —that is why.

Let us turn the leaves back twenty-five years and take a look at the old
trail that is grown up with personal knowledge. At that time, deer were very
plentiful and as far north as Bisco, which is one hundred miles northwest
of Sudbury on C.P.R., there was a good sprinkling of deer right through to
Fort William. But any novice of a hunter could get his two bucks as far
north as Bisco. The caribou, for some unaccountable reason, were fast dis-

Taken on "Uncle Jack's" Forty-Second Annual
Hunting Trip in Northern Ontario.

appearing or moving farther north. At Stralak, which is about fifty miles
west of Sudbury, I saw seventy-five deer the first two weeks of November,
1904. I saw twelve in one day and never fired a shot because I did not see the
buck I wanted. Five Kingsville tenderfoot hunters whom I directed there
killed ten bucks that averaged over two hundred pounds each, but, in 1907,
we saw the tracks of wolves and, in 1910, fully eighty or ninety per cent. of
the deer were gone. In fact, we saw the remnants of more dead deer than
we saw live ones. There is a great percentage of people who claim wolves
can only get the deer in winter, when the snow is deep. This is absolutely
wrong for, as long as there is a live deer left where there are wolves, you
will see deer hair in the wolf stools all summer. This is only one of the

many proofs of their dreaded ability to kill our deer. Remember, deer are only wild sheep and wolves are wild dogs and it is not because wolves are so abundant but because each wolf is so murderously destructive. Let one sheep dog go unchecked in your township and see how many sheep your council will have to pay for. There is one thing you can best believe—you will have more to pay for the first year than you will the second. We all know it would be far pleasanter for our government officials to report deer increasing, but they frankly admit they are decreasing, for ten years ago our two-dollar license permitted one to shoot two deer. Now, we pay four dollars for the privilege of shooting one deer—that is, providing you see one to shoot. But please charge your memory with this, especially when you have your rifle in your hands, you are not supposed to shoot at something you don't see.

Why have these wolves increased so the last twenty years? To us backwoods men this is easier understood than the alphabet. I can trace it back to January, 1905, when I spent three or four weeks trapping with the Phillips family, who lived on Pansy Island, which is about ten miles north of Bisco. I arrived there on the evening of January 6th, 1905, and Grandpa Phillips, who was then sixty-three years of age, entertained me nearly the whole evening telling how he had poisoned three big timber wolves and found two of them and taken them to Bisco, for the thirty-dollar bounty, fifteen dollars each, and how sure he was that he and I could find the other wolf. And that was only part of the rejoicing, for furs were going up. Mink were bringing as high as one dollar and fifty cents, and Mrs. Harry Phillips and her two oldest daughters, who were twelve and fourteen years old, had a short trapping line out and came home with a beautiful fisher and took it to Bisco and got five dollars and a half, which was fully one-third more than they had ever got for a fisher. Harry Phillips got as high as three dollars for foxes he got while I was there. This, of course, was fully one-half more than foxes had been selling for, and still Grandpa Phillips, Harry and I would go fully fifteen miles to some of their poisoned bait, anxiously looking for another fifteen or thirty-dollar wolf bounty haul. At that time there were eleven in the Phillips family and they killed all the deer they required within one-half mile of their home.

What happened the next fifteen years? Furs continued soaring. Think of it, fisher selling for as high as one hundred and twenty-five dollars; mink, twenty dollars; beaver, thirty to fifty dollars; muskrats, four dollars! What is the result? These same fellows that were making five to ten trips to their wolf bait in order to collect fifteen-dollars bounty were getting five hundred dollars worth of furs with less exertion, and the wolves multiplied and ate the deer up alive.

I believe the Hon. E. C. Drury Government raised the wolf bounty to twenty-five dollars, but what temptation was that when the fact is one trapper could and did catch as high as a thousand dollars worth of furs in one month—(but not wolf furs). The beaver season opened in 1916 and our north country was overstocked with them, for in places they had become a nuisance. The above are all facts of the past twenty-five years. Since the Drury administration, the bounty has been set back to fifteen dollars, as it was in 1905 and other years. Now is the time, I say, to start anew, for if we could pay fifteen dollars wolf bounty by charging a two-dollar license to shoot two deer, surely we can pay a thirty-dollar or forty-dollar or even fifty-dollar wolf bounty by charging the sportsmen five dollars or seven dollars to shoot one deer. As the editorial referred to says, "the hunters are good sports—they won't kick as long as they can get rid of the wolves." Now that the fur-bearing animals are gone, the trappers will gladly turn to the wolves, if they are financially induced to.

This last fall, I camped for three long weeks on the same ground where I have hunted for the last twenty years, where fur-bearing animals were so extremely abundant, and I did not see a sign of a living fur-bearing animal except one muskrat and a few fox tracks. There are a few foxes left, their pelts bringing the trapper more than he can get for a wolf. The deer are practically gone. One trapper told me he had not seen a deer for over a year. Please don't say that Jack Miner killed them, for I have not killed a deer since 1921 and I never expect to shoot another. I shot my last moose in 1917. I want my grandchildren to see five times as many deer in Ontario as I have seen and they will if we kill off the wolves.

What about the future, dear readers, especially the hundred per cent. Canadians? Please give this most important proposition every heart-beat of your attention for at least five minutes and, above all, do your own personal thinking. Right here in Ontario we have at least three hundred thousand square miles of the best deer country ever laid out-of-doors, practically lying idle because of the timber wolf. Deer are only wild sheep. Exterminate the wolf; then, for example, one pair of deer on each square mile—how many deer will we few scattering hunters have to select from in ten years? How many bucks would our five-dollar or seven-dollar license permit us to kill? Again, let us ask you to please do your own personal thinking and figuring. I say this is not an idle thought. It is not a worthless dream. It is a suggestion that sooner or later will bear fruit. The wolf will be controlled, and, although he is the slyest, shyest, shrewdest, strongest-scented and most cunning four-footed animal in North America, remember *God gave man dominion over all* and the human brains of Ontario are going to work harmoniously together and beat the wolf to death. One point we will all agree on. That is the same glittering thing that has practically exterminated our choice fur-bearing animals will treat the wolf in the same manner, the glittering price. Jesse James was the shrewdest outlaw the world ever knew, but the price got him.

Please let us take one more glimpse at our vast north playground. We board our fastest west-bound train at Ottawa and in less than two hours we are in the deer country and we are going west and north-west two days and a night before we reach the Lake of the Woods, and from my home to Hudson Bay it must be eight hundred miles north, as the goose flies. In

"Birds and animals are only wild," says Jack
Miner, "because they have to be."

the summer of 1922, I camped for two weeks near Minaki Inn, Lake of the Woods, with one hundred and twenty-five Winnipeg boys, and the second morning we were there three boats set out fishing with hooks and lines, and returned inside of two hours with so many choice fish that the chief cook gave orders not to catch another fish for a week. I travel quite a lot in the United States, and I tell you Ontario Canadians the eyes of eastern North America are turning towards our vast summer playground and, if properly managed, we have a Klondike ahead of us. I say, compel these pure-air seekers to leave their fire at home, but let them come in and inhale our climate. They are good people and we need their good money to develop our unlimited resources. While they are doing a little fishing during the summer and seeing the deer as plentiful as they could be, there is no limit to

At "Uncle Jack's" Front Door.

the non-resident license fee they would pay for the privilege of coming back in the fall and being sure of their one buck. One thing we all know, their fifty-dollar non-resident license would pay more wolf bounty than our five-dollar or seven-dollar one—to say nothing of the hundreds of dollars they will leave in our country when they have a good taste in their mouths to come back.

Now, with all due respect to our present leaders—they are evidently doing the best they can alone; but, sportsmen and all respectable citizens of Ontario, our leaders need our support. When our game protective associations meet in convention throughout Ontario and get back to them, we can make them powerful enough to organize national wolf bounty regulations. Why was our beloved, self-sacrificing, Christian-spirited Sir Wilfrid Laurier such a powerful leader for good. Not all in himself. No, no; but because the best thinking people of Canada got behind him and helped him carry his cross. How we love to refer to our Sir John A. Macdonald, one of the best and most powerful leaders Canada ever knew! How this wonderful man, in spite of the sneers and jeers of the opposition, connected Canada together so that Halifax can shake hands with Vancouver in a few days instead of that many months. But this was accomplished through the fact that the best and most foresighted people in Canada stood firm behind him with willing hands.

I now come to my closing point. Today we are more anxious than ever to keep our boys in Canada. This appears to be our national problem and I say to fathers and neighbors, in the name of God, take your boys on an annual outing. Introduce them to our northern wilds and the ways of the creatures that occupy it. Let your boy take his fishing tackle and catch a few speckled beauties or a few lake trout. Warn him never to get in a canoe until he can swim at least a quarter of a mile. Let him take his compass and learn to pick his way in and out of the big woods while you follow with him. Teach him how to hunt against the wind and when he approaches the tops of the hills to stop and peep carefully over. And, before you can realize it, this big boy will develop into a successful hunter and realize he is a millionaire in out-of-door privileges and he will become a healthy and stronger man to face the world through the fact that his enjoyment is out-of-doors recreation. And that boy will stay in Canada.

In closing, let me quote the following poem, written by my esteemed friend, Rev. E. C. Hunter, of Toronto:

WHERE THE NORTH BEGINS

You tell me you're a stranger
  From lands that lie afar;
You ask me where the North begins
  And what its boundaries are.

The North is not an area,
  It's not a piece of land;
The North's a spirit and a life,
  Which you must understand.

Up where the handclasp's stronger,
  Far from the city dins,
Up where the smile lasts longer—
  That's where the North begins.

Up where the sun shines brighter,
  Where worries easily end,
Up where the snow lies whiter—
  You're in the North, my friend.

Where every man's a fighter,
  And no one quits the game;
Where the bond of friendship's tighter,
  And honor's more than fame;

Where you feel the fresh wind blowing
   From pine woods clean and pure;
Where you find the trout streams flowing,
   You're in the North, for sure.

Where fewer hearts are aching,
   And fewer men walk broke,
Where the world's still in the making,
   And all hearts carry hope;

Where fellows don't mind giving,
   And we ask not creed or name;
Where the fun of life is living,
   For life is worth the game.

Have you left the camp at daylight,
   As dawn was breaking forth,
Carried back your deer at twilight?
   Then you've really known the North.

Have you smelled the bacon frying
   By streams where the big trout swims?
Made friends without half-trying?
   That's where the North begins.

For the North is not a country,
   Measured by terms of land;
The real North is a spirit,
   Which you must understand.

Dorothy Perkins Roses which "Uncle Jack" has
"improved" to this stage.

EDUCATIONAL CONSERVATION

OF ALL the home-run hits in the first inning I have seen the best was that made by Father Crowley, of Algoma, and published in *The Globe* of March 17th, when at the game conservation meeting this reverend gentleman suggested an educational conservation campaign.

The fact is that our game in Northern Ontario is in the eleventh-hour stage, and fining a man for blood that he has already spilt will not allow that animal to multiply, but, rather, in many cases, it will make that man a worse outlaw. For illustration: You are a settler in our undeveloped North, and you are doing a little trapping in order better to clothe your family. Now the law says you must not take beaver or otter, but allows the Indian to come for one hundred miles and tear the dams out and destroy every one on your trapping ground. Would the men that framed that law observe it? No!

Now, reader, you will please pardon me if I am a little partial to the settler. It is experienced poverty and need that have molded my heart. My father moved his big family from Ohio here to Canada, and all the money he took in the first summer we were here was four dollars and a half ($4.50), for one hundred and fifty bushels of wood ashes that we sold for three cents per bushel. We gathered these ashes where we burnt the log-piles to plant our corn. My brother, Ted, was seventeen and I was thirteen, and I am absolutely certain that we two older boys made more money with our traps and guns to purchase warm clothing the first three years we were in Canada than father and all of us got off the wet, newly-chopped-out farm.

Brother soon ceased market hunting, but I followed it up every fall until I was twenty-one years of age and the murder I committed in my uneducated, innocent ignorance privileges me conscientiously to speak to the other fellow who might also be standing in his own light. For illustration: There was a long-whiskered farmer who lived about five miles from town. He owned fifty acres of land, and had a rail fence all around it. He was just good enough a farmer to allow the weeds and brush to grow about six inches higher than his corn. This made a perfect winter harbor for bob-white quail. This man would not allow shooting on his premises. I went to him personally and asked permission, but he stoutly refused. Now, he was an enthusiastic politician, and when he went to town on Saturday morning with a basket of eggs on his arm you could best believe he was going to talk politics the rest of the day, and would not return home until night. If there was no snow on the ground, in less than an hour I would be knocking his quail right and left, and would not leave a track because I would wear moccasins. I was the only market hunter in this township, and

"Uncle Jack" Works with Flowers as Well as
with Birds.

whose quail was I shooting? Why, bless your life, when I gave the matter a second thought in the right direction, I saw that I was shooting my own brood stock for next year. In other words, in my bloodthirsty ignorance, I was closing an account that gave me over two hundred per cent. dividends.

In July, 1925, I spent two weeks in Alaska and Northern British Columbia. One evening I strolled into a butcher shop where a man was selling the hind quarter of a young bull moose to the butcher. I inquired of this gentleman as to where he got the moose. He stated that he went down to the lake about twelve miles to mow wild hay, and near where he was working he saw five moose feeding in a small lake. He shot the young bull and let the two cows and calves go. The next morning two motor boats, loaded with four native hunters, started out to mow the rest of the hay. These men then killed the biggest living financial proposition that ever rapped at their door of need—more moose. They could have gone to other shallow lakes and gathered lilypad roots to feed the moose, and in less than two weeks they could have been taking in tens of dollars every single day, and left the moose alive with their pictures scattered over North America as an advertisement for this summer resort. But they killed them and sold their hind quarters for five cents a pound, and that opportunity is gone forever.

Now, I will admit, there are extreme cases of ignorance; yet we are

Wild Geese Headed for the Breeding Grounds in the North.

all stumbling along more or less. But what is the remedy for such blindness? As I see it, there are three hopes: education—first, second, and last. Remember, education isn't all gathered with one's nose between book covers. I think Pat worded it right when he said: "Get all the education you can and then add the learning."

I want to admit I have no knowledge concerning fish propagation, but only want to say: What other people are doing we can improve on, for I am absolutely certain that there is no state or province in America that surpasses Ontario for game fish possibilities.

One Sunday morning when I was in Northern British Columbia, I drifted over to an Indian camp. While there I saw a man come along the shore in a canoe. I approached and asked: "Have you been hunting?"

"No, just fish," was the reply.

"Any luck?"

"Not much, just little," and as he stepped ashore he took a two-bushel bag fully two-thirds filled with fish from his canoe and poured them out on the green, green grass in front of me. Reader, my eyes almost struck fire and my heart leaped with the thrill, as this bag of beauties wriggled and flopped there in the sun on that green sod. My first words were: "Mister, I never saw fish like those before."

"No," he replied, "I don't guess likely you ever did, 'cause dem is grayling trout." If my memory serves me right, these fish were about fifteen inches long, and would weigh about two pounds each, and they were as uniform as silver dollars.

We may have grayling trout in Ontario, but I have never seen one. Yet I firmly believe we can have them here by the millions. Another interesting sight for me was when I visited a game fish hatchery near Portland, Oregon. Here a little river came spouting over the high rocks and fell into a spray fully one hundred and fifty feet below, where the river took another short tumble into a small lake. This lake appeared to have hundreds upon hundreds of big rainbow trout that were so tame they would actually follow you. These, I understood, were their brood fish. Then I was shown some large cement vats, about eight feet in width and fully one hundred and fifty feet long. The water, which was from three to five feet deep in these vats, automatically came in at one end and out at the other, and I know I am not exaggerating when I say there were tens of millions of fingerling trout there, all ready for distribution over the state. But what interested me most was that only one man and his wife were required, apparently, in caring for this wonderful success. This gentleman manager told me that those baby trout, that were then about the size of one's finger, grew to weigh two pounds and over in two years.

Now there is one great mistake that fully ninety per cent. of our people are making. They are looking upon this conservation question as a sportsman's proposition only, when the fact is it is the biggest undeveloped commercial opportunity our vast and beautiful Ontario has to offer us. Yes, conservation, as I see it, has got every citizen of Ontario by the coat collar, holding on with both hands, begging us to help ourselves.

In closing, let me make a suggestion that I trust all readers will consider carefully. Let us all line up and hold the biggest national educational conservation convention that ever was held in North America, and let us hold it at Sudbury, Ont., where it will be in easy reach of the trappers and guides, or, in other words, close to the men who know; and let every sportsman's organization in Canada be represented, and let us hold this great convention between the 15th and 30th of June. By holding such a convention in late June we can have outdoor meetings. All of us that have tents can take them with us, and, if necessary, camp out in the suburbs in order to help out hotel accommodation. Now, to one and all, if you think this suggestion worthwhile, get behind it with your pen points at once. I am sure the press will help us. Let us send a special invitation to every member of Parliament. Now who will take the lead? There are dozens and dozens of names I would like to suggest, but for the present let us all be leaders.

(The following was written two weeks after the above article appeared.)

Since making the statement that I stood for educational conservation, my mail has been flooded asking for a full explanation, and, in brief, I will say, that during the last fifteen years I have been lecturing, I have no doubt spoken to a million or more school children in North America, where I emphasize to them and encourage them to build a bird house. If I can get a child to build a bird house he becomes a conservationist. He becomes a better citizen, because of the love kindled in his heart, because he, himself, will not kill the bird that is going to build in a house he made, nor

Bird Houses Built by Boys of One City after a Jack Miner Lecture.

will he allow any other person to destroy any bird in his vicinity. This I call educational conservation. But we must not lose sight of the fact that we have got to have laws, and strict laws, for experience and personal observation have taught me to know that kindness without firmness is a total failure and we must have qualified game-wardens to enforce the laws, because there is a small per cent., less than five per cent., who are outlaws, and this small percentage can upset what has been accomplished by the majority of people.

Ontario needs conservation. Between Sudbury and Fort William there are thousands of square miles which have been stripped of valuable timber and at present are practically only good for their minerals and big game hunting, as well as game fish fishing, in the multitude of small fresh-water lakes and rivers. No state in the United States or province in Canada has such a vast sportsman's paradise and such opportunities knocking at its door. If we take out wolves and let deer increase, we will be richer not only by the money paid out for licenses, but also by the money left in our country by tourists and hunters who can be attracted to our vast northerly playground. Think of the places the tourist leaves money: railway fares, gasoline for automobiles, hotel expenses, grocery expenses, taxis, boat fares, rent of cottages, rent of boats. Best and most encouraging of all is the money he leaves, or would leave, with the guides and settlers. The license is a small fee in comparison to the outlay of money spent in our country.

We all know that one hundred dollars brought in by tourists has just as much purchasing power as if it were for one hundred dollars' worth of wheat shipped out. Are our fresh-water lakes worth more to us than if the country they cover was a wheat field? Let's get together and educate each other how to make it worth more than a productive wheat field. I was told by one of Wisconsin's government officials that their lakes in Wisconsin and Minnesota were more valuable to their state, that they brought in more money into the state, than that much cleared agricultural land. We all know these states border Ontario. Such being the case, what is the value of our lakes when up to the present time they are free of pollution. Think it over. Don't let us get together to talk laws. Let us get together and do something.

WHICH ARE WORTH MORE TO CANADA: LIVE OR DEAD ATTRACTIONS?

WHICH ARE worth more to the people of Canada, living or dead attractions? I say without hesitation that one family of our big White-tailed Deer bounding across the highway, and possibly stepping into range of the tourists' kodaks and movie cameras, is worth more, to more people of Canada, than twenty-five dead deer hanging in the woods or in sight of the same tourists. And, remember, the White-tailed Deer is not to be compared to our lordly Moose, which the majority of hunters would shoot first. Those living sights and pictures are as valuable to us as golden wheat-fields: they are actual dollars and cents, scattered through that rocky, picturesque country.

Best of all, live attractions are self-advertising. As illustration, tens of thousands of people go to Yellowstone Park, in the United States, and they spend tens of thousands of dollars; and all they get for their money are the pictures of the bears and other living attractions. Yet such photographs cause thousands more to go there and spend their money. On the other hand, our innocent Black Bear of Canada has hardly ever had any consideration. He is, however, one of the most attractive animals Canada has today and if given a chance would be the most pictured animal we have in this country.

These common black bears in Ontario are practically harmless to other game, such as deer and moose. As proof of this, moose were so scarce in the Province of Ontario that the Government did not allow an open season on them until the fall of 1900. Ontario hunters, like myself, were compelled to go to Quebec to hunt them. The fact I want to point out is this: The bears have always been here; the moose came in afterwards and have multiplied and increased in the midst of the bears by hundreds of thousands. There may be odd cases where a bear kills a calf-moose or a sickly, weak cow-moose in the spring of the year; but these are few and far-fetched.

It was estimated that there were 20,000 American cars at my home last spring bringing people to see the geese. I have no proof of the exact number, but we do know there were over four hundred cars parked here at one time. How many carloads of sightseers, do you think, would come to see a pile of dead geese?

ONTARIO THE GREATEST PLAYGROUND IN AMERICA

NOW THE QUESTION comes to you, why is Jack Miner so interested in Ontario? Well, over fifty-six years ago Ontario opened her doors, took me in, and eventually adopted me, and today my Ontario home is not for sale or exchange for the rest of the world. My burning desire is to help develop our Ontario's God-given advantages that are already planted-to-start so that tens of thousands of other under-privileged boys of today will see the time they can conscientiously say, "My Ontario home is not for sale."

Now, why do I call Ontario the greatest playground in America? Not just because it is practically twenty times as large and only one-third as thickly populated as our beautiful Nova Scotia. No, no, but because of its almost unbelievable amount of unpolluted inland fresh water lakes and crystal streams, thousands of which are teeming with fish almost undiscovered. Ontario is great for a playground because of its favorable location and extremely lengthy southern border. In the six States at our side doors, there are between thirty-seven and forty million of the wealthiest people in the world raring to come to our playgrounds with fishing tackle, kodaks, and guns in the Fall. We have far, far more game fishing opportunities in Ontario than there are in all the United States east of the Rockies and possibly east of Alaska. Today our Ontario playgrounds have five times as many moose as there are in all the United States east of Alaska. And please remember, moose are the largest antlered game in the world. In 1907 I shot a moose near Fort William, and as he lay on his side he measured seven feet four inches from the point of his two front hoofs to the top of his shoulders. Moreover, the moose is the easiest wild animal I know of to glide up on with a canoe or call to the kodak.

There were no moose in Ontario sixty-five years ago. In the early 80's odd ones appeared in Nova Scotia. The first antlered head of a moose I ever saw was killed by a Mr. Goldie, who kept the post office at Dwight, Ontario. This was in the Fall of '85. During the 90's my brother and I hunted moose in Quebec because there was no open season for them in Ontario. In 1900 the season opened in Ontario and the wilds of our north was almost overrun by them from Mattawa to Fort William. In November

1917 I counted forty-four quarters of moose meat hanging on poles near the door of one resident hunting-party's camp. These eight or ten hard-working resident sportsmen were rightly and justly securing their winter's meat right near the railroad. Remember that moose are of the deer and sheep family and multiply fast. Owing to their size and strength they have very few enemies. I have reasons to believe that 90 per cent. of the moose that live to be a week old die of gun shots.

"Uncle Jack" in Northern Ontario on One of
His Annual Hunting Trips.

Now we come to the black playful clown of the north, the black bear, that the commercially-written Red Ridinghood stories call dangerous. Let me leave the thickly-populated country and say a few words to you fathers of the far north, who are possibly situated as my dear father was fifty years ago. Put up a few tons of ice and in May beat the bears to the sucker creeks, catch and take home 500 or 1000 or more of these so-called worthless suckers. Keep them as best you can on this ice. Now pick out a setting for a picture not over one-half mile from your home and bait the bears with the suckers there, as you are now going to trap them. Build a movable blind or picture gallery of natural material about two hundred feet south of your bait. Hang a little glass bottle or pieces of tin so the wind will swing it right where the lens of the kodak or movie is to be taken. Soon you have one bear coming, then two, and soon four. Day by day gradually move your blind toward the bait until you are within one hundred feet of it. Now arrange with some picture-taking tourist and when the wind is north, four or five of you go to the spot where the glass or tin is. All but two of you must leave. Then put the lens of the machine where bears are used to seeing glittering moving glass. Now, Mr. Settler, these tourists will buy and bring you honey for bear-bait. Bore some inch holes in big old logs and pour warm honey in and watch results. Just study live attractions as you have studied dead ones and you can be the germ of a wild bear fight, that will go on the leading screens of the world. Then the wealthy tourists will make a beaten path to your door. Your harvest will last all summer and your boys, who have never seen a wheat field or a barber shop, can become leaders of leading men.

Yes indeed, our game is worth millions of dollars alive and only thousands of dollars dead. We can have both but let us consider first things first. Won't someone please publish the value of the bushels of wheat harvested in our three Prairie Provinces the last three years and compare it with the estimated value of Ontario's tourist trade for the same period?

WALTONIANISM

ALTHOUGH THE Izaak Walton League did not originate until 1920 or 1922, yet I am, and have been, a 100 per cent. Waltonian since 1904, when I started my sanctuary and conservation movement in Canada.

During the last three years I have crossed the continent five times on lecture tours, on one occasion going to Alaska, having audiences of not less than 500, and on several occasions 5,000 and more. Never have I failed, no matter what class of people I was addressing, to urge them to join the Izaak Walton League, and not only to join, but to back up the movement financially. I have repeatedly said and I have demonstrated what one man can do without the advantages of money. What can the 100 million well-organized people of America do with their wealth and streams and marsh lands to start sanctuaries? You can readily see how happy it made me to see such an active organization as the Izaak Walton League come into existence.

A whole book and many a helpful Christian sermon could be preached on the good the Izaak Walton League of America is doing. But to me the good it is doing all centers around the word *others*, not only *others* in this generation, but *others* in generations to come. The following incident will illustrate more fully what I mean. A few springs ago my good friend the late Jim Heywood, a true Waltonian, arranged for me to come to Chicago and accompany him and his Waltonian brothers on a week's fishing trip to Northern Wisconsin.

At the appointed time, I went. They met me as agreed, and on a Saturday morning we arrived at their fishing reserve. Poor Jim rowed me out and I caught the first speckled trout, and the last one, I ever caught. The next morning being Sunday, I put on my rubber boots and went for a stroll up the bank of the stream, above their two or three occupied beaver houses, and I flushed several pairs of mallards that were evidently nesting in or near that vicinity.

When fully one-half a mile above the line of their reserve I went to cross the stream on an old log bridge, evidently used by the settlers of that country every winter. The bridge, I should say, was about fifteen feet wide and the clear water fully three feet deep. As the sun was hot, my rubber boots were extremely warm, so I sat down on this bridge and pulled them off, and soon I was listening to the songs of the migratory birds that were flitting among the scattered trees in the swampy ravine.

The sun beamed down nice and warm, and I stretched out like a black snake. I was about to drift off into dreamland when the corner of my eye was attracted by a glitter in the clear water. Now in my younger days I have enjoyed seeing five different varieties of ducks in my decoys at once. In Northern Quebec and Ontario I have time and time again had a carload of moose at the mercy of my rifle. During the last fifteen years I have seen the wild geese fly up so thick and close to my little home that the vibration

Studying Tree-Growth in Northern Canada.

of their wings has actually shaken the windows, but never in all my un-dreamed-of, eventful life have I beheld such a thrilling, glittering, over-flowing, beautiful sight as I did for the next hour. I had hard work even then to break away, for I saw a real horde of fine speckled trout going up stream. Before leaving I took particular notice, and here was a public fisherman's path beside this trout stream.

Now, who was the cause of these speckled beauties glittering their way up and up this stream? Why the very same class of Izaak Walton, self-sacrificing men who paid my way, and were the cause of my being there to see them.

Yes, dear Jim Heyworth, has passed to the beautiful beyond, but fish that he helped plant in the lakes and streams of North America are still going on up stream for *others, others,* and *others.* This is the spirit of true Waltonianism.

In closing, allow me to quote C. D. Meigs' poem *Others.* It so nicely brings out the thought of Waltonianism.

> "Lord help me to live from day to day
>   In such a self-sacrificing way,
> That even when I kneel to pray
>   My prayer shall be for—OTHERS—
>
> Help me in all the work I do
>   To ever be sincere and true,
> And know that all I'd do for you
>   Must needs be done for—OTHERS—
>
> Let self be crucified and slain
>   And buried deep, and all in vain
> May efforts be to rise again
>   Unless to live for—OTHERS—
>
> And when my work on earth is done
>   And my new work in Heaven begun,
> May I forget the crown I've won
>   While thinking still of—OTHERS—
>
> OTHERS, Lord, yes, OTHERS,
>   Let this my motto be:
> Help me to live for OTHERS
>   That I may live for Thee."

FISHING ON THE WRONG SIDE
OF THE BOAT

NOT SO LONG AGO I noticed an article in the press stating "that all ditches must be railed or filled in to protect the motorist." This I am strongly in favor of, but what about our country children on their way to and from the little red schoolhouse? Have they been considered at all? I am compelled to say *"No."* I don't believe they have.

Just recently, my boy drove me to Windsor, a distance of twenty-six miles, and I counted eighty-five school children dodging their way to school along our cement highway and, to me, it looked pitifully wicked. One little fellow actually fell into the ditch in his effect to escape these dodging gas-burners that came upon him from east and west. To our people of Canada, let me frankly say, I would sooner see a bunch of our children using the railroad track for a school path than to see them on our automobile highways where their rights have never been considered. And, if we were fishing on the right side of the boat, I am sure they would have first consideration, for what will Canada profit if we gain the whole world and lose the rising generation of our boyhood and girlhood? Yes, you may be riding in your big limousine with your own darling boy at the wheel when you meet or pass this self-neglected, long-haired, bashful little fellow with his dented, little dinner pail in his hand and a bunch of handed-down books under his arm. Yet, you have no proof that your boy will be a greater asset to Canada than he will be.

In speaking of Queen Victoria, my father once said to me: "Jack, if you had known her, you are a man that would have dearly loved her. God bless her." He said: "I well remember the day she was crowned," and then he went on to say that one day she was passing a bunch of under- privileged children. She stopped and spoke to them and some of the royalty chastised her for doing so, but father said the dear soul wrung her hands as she replied: "I like to speak to them *all,* for we don't know who the coming men are."

Now please don't understand me to say that all country school children are under-privileged. No, no, no! But I do say that in building our get-me-there-quick highways the safety of our school children has not been considered and the paths they did have, in the majority of cases, have been destroyed and no provision made for them whatever. Personally, I don't like to hear a man complain unless he has a carefully-thought-out plan of improvement and, first of all, let us stop and consider the amount of material

"Uncle Jack" built this walk beside the highway
in front of his home for the safety
of the children.

it takes to build a highway from sixteen to twenty feet wide and eight inches thick. Then let us consider the insignificant amount of practically the same material it will take to build a school-children's path two feet wide and four inches thick, six feet or more from the rolling traffic, with a nice piece of green sod separating the two. Please figure it all out and ask yourself if this really is an extravagant suggestion when five per cent. of the material used for the twenty-foot road will build our little loved ones a path in the safety zone. Again let me ask, have we become so penny wise and pound foolish as to allow our hearts to be completely crowded out and silly, speedy recreation scare the foundation of our future hope into the gutter?

In closing, I have this request of my readers. If through personal observance or experience you have reason to believe that what I have outlined

Jack Miner and His Grandchild
in Front of His Residence at
the Sanctuary.

above is true and we are fishing on the wrong side of the boat, will you please help us cast our nets to the right by having a close-up, heart-to-heart talk with your government representative? If possible, take him for a drive where he can see for himself. At the same time, let each of us do our bit, for "how can I go up to my Father if the lad be not with me?"

SUNDAY SCHOOL INFLUENCE

MY FATHER was a brick-maker by inheritance in Leicestershire, England. My mother's people had been prominent game-keepers for generations, back in the same county. Therefore, they were both as English as roast beef and Yorkshire pudding combined—that is, when they could get roast beef and Yorkshire pudding!

My mother's parents and their six children all migrated to America in 1848, and settled in Cuyahoga County, Ohio. My father followed them and married dear mother in 1855. There we kiddies, nine of us, all were hatched. I happened to be the fifth to arrive and was such a disgusting-looking sight that father called me his "fifth calf." Since Abraham Lincoln was shot when I was four days old, mother called me her "Little Lincoln boy." This gave me a ground-floor chance of becoming President of the great United States of America.

I trapped and skinned my first skunk and sold the pelt, before I was eight years old. This did not give the school-house any peach-orchard fragrance nor help qualify me for the presidency!

Oh, yes, I was a good fighter. But, too, I was a mighty poor judge of fighters. So that's that.

Well, in spite of the much-needed, helpful kindness given to our big family by those dear people of Ohio, father took another irresistible desire to migrate, and loaded up all his belongings on two wagons. (His family was by far the largest load.) We drove to Cleveland, took the boat from there to Detroit, crossed the river by ferry and arrived in Canada at about seven a.m., on April 23rd, 1878, when I was thirteen years old. I was the proud owner of a beautiful Irish setter bird-dog, fifteen skunk-traps, and a little cotton-tail Yankee rabbit (pregnant, of course) which mother and I liberated here the following morning, April 24th, 1878.

When Fall came I started market-hunting. In spite of my outward appearance, I won the confidence of all classes of out-of-doors sportsmen. And let me say—and I do it with head bowed in gratefulness—that no family could move into a strange country and be trusted more completely or be treated with greater kindness than we were by the old-fashioned, honest-to-goodness Christian people among whom we settled. The tenth year we were here I married one of the best Christian girls this world has ever known.

Jack Miner Surrounds Himself with Natural Beauty. This Rose Arbor Is at His Back Door.

Let me now skip ahead about ten more years, when my dear little boy sweetly pleaded with me to go to Sunday School with him "and Mama." And, will you believe it, in a very few short months I was looking forward to each Sunday School hour. I did love to sing with the children.

Soon a cloud of sadness piled upon us; but still I clung to the Sunday School. And one day Kingsville's godly grand old man Mr. Watson Coatsworth, our Sunday School superintendent, kindly invited me to take charge of a very-much-alive class of teen-age boys. I protested that I could not teach Sunday School but assured him I could keep them from putting chewing-gum in each other's hair. In less than a month the class grew to fifteen and they were the best boys (at singing) I have ever heard.

A very few years later the same Mr. Coatsworth invited me to come to the platform and lead the singing for the whole school. Here I had promised that dear, aged man that I would do anything to help him, but the fact was I didn't know a musical note from a bear-track and had no more grammatical education than a sideshow ape! Yet the influence of that godly Sunday School enabled me to walk right up on the platform and face the proposition; and the smiling faces and cheerful voices of those 300 or more young people just seemed to lift me heavenward.

That first Sunday afternoon procedure was followed by at least fortyseven similar ones every year for the next fifteen years. Yes, and that fifteen-year period was, for enjoyment, the cream of all my life.

At the end of that time I faced the responsibility of lecturing throughout the whole of North America. I was called upon to speak from the most distinguished platforms from Florida to Alaska and from Seattle to Newfoundland. And whenever the 1000-watt bulb in my portable motion-picture machine would happen to blow everything into darkness, did my audience get away from me? No. Because in less than three seconds I would be leading them in the community singing of such familiar favorites as *Pack Up Your Troubles in Your Old Kit-Bag,* or *There's a Long, Trail A-winding* or *Let Me Call You Sweetheart.* And when, in a minute or two, the lights would come on again my audience would feel closer to me than when the blackout occurred.

Readers, please let me roll the pages back to the germination of that blessed Sunday School class of mine. Those dear, mischievous boys did the reading. And what they read out of this blessed, good, old historical Book corresponded so exactly with my life-long, night and day discoveries of the ways and doings of the so-called wild creatures of our North America that it thrilled my very soul with delight. The A.B.C. education I had brought from Ohio was unconsciously cultivated and in a very few years I, too, could read, though even today I would not attempt to read in public.

To make my meaning more clear let me refer you, one and all, to His promises in Genesis 26, 27 and 28; and Job 12: 1, 2, 3, and 7.

Such facts as these, thoroughly tested have established a firm belief in my heart, body, and soul; and my God-guided accomplishments have introduced me to the people of the world, more especially to the deep-thinking of them. Therefore let me stop once more and thank Almighty God for the Sunday School influence of that mischievous bunch of smiling Sunday School boys.

Dear Readers, as I glance over this, my own hand-written, toggled-together bunch of facts, my dear mother's gentle face comes before my mind's eyes, and again I can almost hear her loving voice as, over sixty-six years ago, she looked into my eager, freckled face and, smiling said, "Jack, some day you will find that *I* is the first letter in Ignorance." Yet what can I do?—I have no literary education to draw from. Nothing but a few tested facts taken from God's blueprint. Yes, even to this day, as I slowly stroll about in the pathless woods of some part of Canada for my recreation, the twenty-third Psalm of David comes to me—only in different words:

> The Lord is my Guide and Teacher, I will not get lost.
>
> He makes my heart a receiving-station for His wireless.
>
> He sits down beside me in the pathless woods and opens His book of knowledge.
>
> He makes the trees I plant to grow, and flowers to arch my path with their fragrant beauty, gives me dominion over the fowls of the air, and they have changed their migrating route to honk and sing their way to and from my home.
>
> Yea, He has brought me up from a barefooted, under-privileged boy to a man respected by millions of people, and I give Him all the credit and praise, whenever, wherever, and forever.

HAVE BIRDS AND ANIMALS BRAINS?

IT IS AN undisputed fact that when God created this universe He made man supreme in every way, "Gave man dominion over the fish of the sea, the fowls of the air and every living thing that creepeth upon it." Thus, He made man's brain supreme but that does not say he didn't give the bird or animal kingdom brains and knowledge in some way superior to ours, which I will try to explain.

Take a dog for instance—if a cruel-hearted man comes on your premises and kicks your dog in the ribs, you can rest assured that that dog will from then on keep out of that person's way. But if another person comes on your property and pets and speaks kindly to your dog and perhaps brings with him a bone, the dog's attitude is more kindly towards that person. Thus a dog has knowledge enough or brains, if you wish to call it that, to know a friend from an enemy.

You can train a team of horses which stall is theirs, or which side of the tongue to go on and other common things you want them to do. One only needs go to a circus and watch animals perform to see that they can do things which are unbelievable. While I do not agree with some cruel ways of training animals for a circus, yet it proves that they have brains to learn.

In the beginning I said that in some ways birds had brains superior to ours, so let me try and explain. The ponds on my Bird Sanctuary are so small in comparison to the North American Continent that even the point of the finest needle pressed on the map of this continent would represent several square miles whereas these ponds cover only a couple of acres on my Bird Sanctuary. It is a well known fact that since 1909 I have been tagging ducks and these same birds have come back to my mud holes year after year for the food and protection and kindness which I try to give them. It proves they know a friend from an enemy, proves they know a place of safety and rest—where to go for a breathing spell. But the big thing it proves is that they have been given brains, knowledge, or sense so that, without the aid of compasses, instruments, or such aids, they start during early October at the Arctic circle with their family following in single file and in a short time come circling down on these little artificial ponds of mine, where they know they are safe. In the early part of March, the ones that have escaped the deadly aim of sportsmen along Mississippi Valley and the

Atlantic seaboard rise up out of range of shot and shell and keep at that great height till they land back to this spot of safety.

How many of us human beings, either with an airplane or on the ground in these above-mentioned localities, could, without the aid of compass or other instruments and only depending on our own brains, come anywhere near

Wild Geese will stay in the North through the Winter, if food is available.
This photo taken at the Miner North Ponds, January 1st, 1927.

finding our way to such a small spot. And if we did, how long would it take us? I am afraid we would be glad to have some duck or goose brains to bring us out of such desolate places in northern regions to civilization.

Take the robin that nests year after year on your window sill or on your verandah. Since tagging birds has become common, many know the same robins come back year after year. Although a robin's brain is small, yet that little bird, and even the little humming-bird, is given brains, instinct, sense, or knowledge, or whatever you choose to call it, to find its way even on the darkest of nights back to its nesting-place. Again, I say, could man do this by depending on his own brain power and not use a compass or other instrument which it took several human brains to perfect?

GEESE
(Different Varieties)

I WAS VERY much interested in the article entitled "Blue Geese" written by Mr. John Towsan, that appeared in the Toronto *Globe,* but that Blue Geese were ever considered rare was news to me. I was also surprised to read that it took six years for a white man to locate the nesting grounds of this "Blue Goose."

My reason for this is as follows: In 1915 and 1916 I started getting letters from the Indians and Eskimos of this far north of ours. This correspondence was in reply to requests I had stamped on the goose tags. I soon discovered that those far Northern natives were as honest as pure gold and I began asking questions re the condition of this almost unknown land. Many letters spoke of the "Wavies, white and blue wavies" and how the big Grey Geese nested as far south as Hannah Bay, which is the south arm of James Bay, and how these big geese could be seen flying around in pairs long before they started to nest, and so forth. The wavies stopped around James Bay for only a few weeks, then they went further north to nest. Letters from further north stated that the Blue Wavies nested in Baffin Land and that the big white wavies, which were the Greater Snow Geese, all went to Greenland to nest and come back with their young about October 1st. Later correspondence explained that the Blue Wavies were Blue Geese and the White Wavies the Snow Geese.

Another reason for our not knowing more of the blue geese is that they are often called Brant, especially in our Prairie provinces. The first Blue Goose that ever came to our sanctuary arrived here in 1912. We called her Dolly Whitehead. Now more and more seem to be coming each year and always a stray Lesser Snow Goose mixed with these white and blue Wavies. In fact we have a scattered few of six or eight different varieties of geese coming here now. They have taught me enough of their language so I can tell them in the dark of night from the other varieties. For the last twenty-five falls I have camped at the same spot in Algoma district. This spot is just 100 miles due north of Manitoulin Island and I carry the very best pair of field glasses my friends can buy me and I also carry the best pair of ears I have left. I am absolutely certain that fully 70 per cent. of the geese I see and hear coming south over that piece of the wilds are Wavies, blue and snow. These birds seem to follow the same line until they strike Manitoulin Island, then they swing to the right and follow the southeast and east shore of Lake Michigan, then into the Illinois River, and on and on to Louisiana and Texas. Mr. W. K. Kellogg's Bird Sanctuary is just half way from Detroit to Chicago and the very first year he had a protective zone set aside, sixty Wavies dropped in but no Canadas, because the latter, when they get to Manitoulin Island, come straight south down the east side of Lake Huron and gradually worked on here to the Sanctuary.

Just a few words regarding the different geese I am not intimately acquainted with. The Canada Goose is king, queen and prince and president of them all in every way, especially in principle, purity, character, and intelligence. The Greater Snow Goose comes next and, by the way, I have never had one of these white beauties come here of his own accord. Mr. Hayes Lloyd of the Department of Interior in charge of Dominion Game Laws sent five in April 1923, which, judging by their slightly scarred feet had been caught in rat traps. They winter near the mouth of the St. Lawrence and, according to Eskimos, hatch in some inaccessible swamp in Greenland.

Next is the White Front Goose. I have seen only one of these here in the wild state. I have a pair I bought in Minnesota. They are very fond of each other, but I don't see why they are called White Front Geese unless it is their moustache or forehead that gives them their name. If I were naming them I would call them "Orange Geese" because of their orange feet and legs. I believe they migrate up and down the Mississippi and breed in the Arctic Circle. They seem to be getting quite rare.

Next comes the prettiest little goose of all, a tiny pure white one, not a bit larger than a wild duck. I don't believe they would weigh over three pounds, but they are as white as snow and as trim and pretty as a painting. They winter in California and I believe they migrate along the west coast. I never saw one in the wild state, only in wealthy men's private parks.

Next is the Brant Goose. I have seen only one here in the wild state. They look more like a Mallard Drake than a goose. These Brants are very thick in Nova Scotia and around Prince Edward Island and come as far west as North Carolina and Virginia. They very seldom venture far inland but are tide water birds.

Next is a miniature Canada goose. He weighs about four pounds. Quite a few of them drop in here—six in one family once. I keep one with my wing-tipped flock which I caught, in fact I have had it for over ten years. One is all I want. They are called cackling geese. When alarmed they sound like a tiny fox terrier dog yelping.

Then there is another variety that comes here called the Hutchins Goose, this little mongrel, yes, I said "mongrel" because no two of them seem to have the same accent, weighs about four and one-half pounds.

Marking is exactly like that of the cackling goose, but he uses a different variety of language.

And now we come to the Wavies, the Blues and the Lesser Snow Geese. It would not surprise me in the least if these two varieties outnumbered the Canada honkers east of the Rockies. These Blue Geese and the Lesser Snow are exactly the same birds in size, build, and habits. Yes, and in language. In captivity they cross just as readily as Wyandotte chickens will, and I have never seen a flock of any size without the two varieties together. Last spring nine dropped in here, six Blues, two Snows, and one Mongrel, a cross between the Blues and the Snows. They often cross in their wild

Liberating a Honker After It Has Been "Tagged." Note the corncobs
on the ground.

state. One year two hung around here for nearly a month, a Blue and a Snow. I have no proof that they were a pair, but as Scottie says, "I would like to see the mon that could convince me to the contrary."

Moreover I caught one of these hybrids and I have had it over two years and it is still a hybrid. Remember, neither the Snows nor the Blues get their full plumage the first year. Often we see these young Blues all slate color, others have a dabbled white head with orange color from the beak nearly to the top of their white heads. Their face is all orange color. Now this orange is not a goose color at all, it is a stain, possibly a rust stain, gathered from the marsh where they have wintered. I say "wintered" because I never see it on them in the fall. It washes off in almost a month. These Blues and Snows, Wavies as some call them, weigh about five pounds.

WILD GEESE

ALTHOUGH I am a busy man, I feel it my duty to answer an article entitled "Wild Geese," written by Mr. W. R. Tighe, of Manitoulin Island, and published in *Rod and Gun*.

First, Mr. Tighe's letter:

"Editor, *Rod and Gun:*

"Having read Jack Miner's article in *The Detroit Times,* regarding the decrease in numbers of wild geese, I am taking the liberty to write you on the subject.

"Last fall, about the tenth of November, there was a heavy snow-storm on here. At that time the wild geese were in flight South and they settled in the bay of our town, Gore Bay, Manitoulin Island. There were acres and acres of geese. People standing on the bluffs looked down on them and old timers here said they had never seen the like in their time. The fish tugs coming into port at dusk had to plough through them, and the fishermen said there must have been millions of geese. That same day, out in Gordon Township, the field was black with their flight, which lasted nearly all day, passing overhead nearly two miles wide. They also flew over Gore Bay all night and kept citizens awake with their honking.

"This does not look as if the wild geese are being shot and getting scarce. If Mr. Miner had to tag all of these he would have some time.

"I can verify the above statements with the names of prominent citizens of our town and farmers from the surrounding country, and our farmers' boys, who went West on the Harvesters' Excursion, tell me that they saw wild geese last fall in Alberta and Saskatchewan by thousands, in the parts of the provinces where they were working, and all over the West they were plentiful.

"Yours very truly,

"Gore Bay, Ont.
W. R. TIGHE."

Now, it is true wild geese are decreasing in our Western provinces, and ninety per cent. of the early settlers, whom it has been my privilege to meet and who were there when the geese were really plentiful, have asked me: "What has become of the wild geese? They used to be here by the countless thousands, but we do not see them any more."

From Portage la Prairie, Manitoba, where twenty-five years ago geese were extremely abundant, the Park Commissioner of that progressive city wrote our government and secured a permit for Jack Miner to catch and ship them two pairs of wild geese for their park, and, although I do not like this kind of transfer, yet under such circumstances I did give way, and did catch and express them six wild geese.

Just recently the following item appeared in one of our local papers and I think it is worth reproducing:

"The four thousand sportsmen who made returns to the Saskatchewan game-keeper's department last year secured a total bag of 100,000 ducks, 26,000 prairie chickens, 6,000 ruffed grouse, and 3,200 geese." Now, it will be noticed, these hunters did not average one wild goose each. Does that say geese are increasing?

Now, why were these geese so thick at Manitoulin Island on November 10th, 1926? The story is quite a lengthy one, but as interesting as a piece of fiction.

About thirty-five years ago, my chief out-of-doors studies were, "Will a thirty-two-inch barrel bring 'em down farther than a thirty?" "Will Nitro powder ever drive a ball as accurately and as effectively as my old .45-70 black powder rifle puts 'em?" About that time, my brother, Ted, subscribed for *The American Field,* a sporting paper published in Chicago. A few years later, some kind friend mailed me a copy of the little sporting magazine known as *Rod and Gun in Canada,* published at Woodstock, Ontario. In this magazine, I read a short article on our decreasing game. "Would our children have anything to shoot?" I really thought it was intended for such men as I, so in 1902 or 1903 I sounded the alarm in our town and tried to organize a game protective association, but made very little progress, for the sneers and jeers almost got my goat.

But, remember, I am of a determined make-up and nothing knows this better than the game I pursued in my younger days. Finally, the annual meeting time arrived and I was cheerfully greeted by a bunch of real live, determined gentlemen, chiefly from Leamington, Walkerville and Windsor, and in less than two hours the leadership of this little existing association was in the hands of some real live, educated gentlemen, whose hearts and souls were all of one accord. The Essex County Game Protective Association was thoroughly organized and, while our association never has had a large membership, this little bunch of us have worked harmoniously together. There are usually about six from Leamington and the same from Windsor and Walkerville and only one from Kingsville, my own home town. There have been meetings where we have had between thirty and forty, but I am speaking of the average get-together bunch. For the last ten years we have held our meetings in our community club-house at my home. Yes, and I am sure God in heaven has been present with us, for today we have absolute proof that this little band of determined men, working heart, hand and mind together, have actually changed the migrating route of some of the fowls of the air and have caused the old timers of Manitoulin Island to say they have never seen the like in all their lives.

They're thick, aren't they? Wild Geese Rising from the North Ponds.

Now, how did all this come about? Why, about the time this organization was first thought of, I started harboring the geese at my home and these men backed me up with their brains, pen-points and influence. Finally, in 1910 or 1912, feed for these geese became a financial problem for me, so I went before our County Council and asked if they would recommend that the government assist me financially, and they passed an unanimous resolution requesting that our Ontario Government give me a grant of one hundred dollars per year to help feed these birds.

I kept on feeding the geese and the geese kept on coming, but not till 1915 did any come in the fall. Then two families came. But last winter there were fully five thousand that stayed until January 15th. The snow was over a foot deep, my corn pile sinking so fast that I quit feeding, and the geese went further south, where they evidently found bare ground. So you see I now have them with me for two and one-half months in the spring and as long as I will feed them in the fall and winter. Fortunately for me, the influence of this little organization I have already mentioned brought to my home Mr. J. B. Harkin, Commissioner of Dominion Parks. As Mr. Harkin stood before thousands and thousands of these dear old Canadian honkers, he apparently grasped the situation, and since then the Dominion Government is assisting me financially, as well as the Ontario Government. While these small grants are cheerfully accepted, yet both combined wouldn't pay twenty per cent. of the expense that I have been put to the last six years alone, for we have proven by my tagging system that we are now drawing the wild geese to my home for food and protection from all the southern states in United States east of the Mississippi, as well as from the states which border the Mississippi. I often put out one hundred and twenty-five bushels of corn in an evening and it is all gone by ten o'clock the next day.

Distributing Corn to Feed the Geese.

It will be interesting for you to know that when we first started feeding the geese in 1908, we carried the corn out in our pockets; the next year we used a basket. Then we used bags and now we haul it out by the cart and wagon load and scatter it with the scoop shovel.

The three maps show where the geese have been killed and the tags returned to me. The hub of the maps show where the geese were tagged and dots show where they were killed. The following day or two after they were seen at Manitoulin Island, there were four or five of this bunch that had my tag on killed along the east side of Lake Huron, on a direct line between Manitoulin Island and here.

Now, to the far-off readers who are not familiar with the map of Ontario, please let me say that Manitoulin is a large island near the north shore of Lake Huron, on a direct air line from my home to the nesting-grounds of these geese. They have been gradually educated to come and spend at least one-third of their time with me, and on going to and from their nesting-grounds they pass over it twice a year, usually at night. I have wired ahead of them time and again and know that geese leaving here about one-half hour before sun-down cross over near Cochrane, Ontario, between six and eight a.m. This, of course, is on their northern flight. Cochrane, I believe, is about two hundred miles south of James Bay, which is the south arm of Hudson Bay and two hundred miles north of Manitoulin Island, and both are in a direct line, as my charts show, between my home and James and Hudson Bay. Thus, as Mr. Tighe says, it has caused the old timers to say they never saw the like.

Now, Mr. Tighe, possibly my grey hairs of experience will permit me to sound one kind word of warning to you where in your article you say, "if Mr. Miner had to tag all these geese he would have some time." This, you know in your own heart, is intended for a little slam. Please let us not do this. Slamming will not protect our birds or make Canada a more cheerful place to live, but, in closing, I just wish to say that there is not a shadow of a doubt but what at least five hundred of these geese that you saw or heard on November 10th, 1926, were carrying my tag, and, if you could possibly arrange to come to my home between next April 1st and 20th, any day except Sundays, you and I could have a heart-to-heart visit and be glad we met face to face in the presence of the fowls of the air that introduced us. Here is for more game for the rising and unborn generations!

MAPS SHOWING THE MIGRATION OF CANADA GEESE

The dots on the maps below show the places from which tags have been returned to Jack Miner, and hence give exceedingly good evidence of the direction taken by the wild geese which have alighted on the Miner estate at Kingsville, Ontario, on their way north and south.

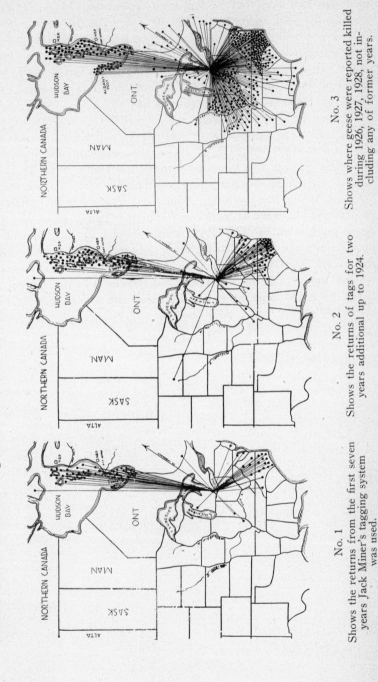

No. 1

Shows the returns from the first seven years Jack Miner's tagging system was used.

No. 2

Shows the returns of tags for two years additional up to 1924.

No. 3

Shows where geese were reported killed during 1926, 1927, 1928, not including any of former years.

THE CANADA GOOSE AS CANADA'S EMBLEM

IN REPLY to many requests as to my opinion of the white-throated sparrow as our Canadian national bird, I have said that the white-throat is a lovely bird, but not a bit more so than the white-crown sparrow, bluebird or some of the warblers, or yet the rose-breasted grosbeak. My, what a beautiful, lovely, musical variety we have to select from! And, I say, by all means let us have a Canadian national bird, but let it be the Canada goose, the noblest creature that ever lived on land, in the air, or on the water—yes, and on the ice or snow he is perfectly at home.

I was born under the protection of the eagle's wing, and I respect that great bird as much as it is necessary for any man to, but our Canada goose is far superior. When in captivity he will wash himself up and keep clean and respectable, and, in about three years, with his mate, will settle down to raise a family of from four to eight, as all Canadians should. Wild geese pair off for life. I never knew them to even make an application for divorce. The male guards his mate on the nest. As soon as the young hatch, he protects them from the side opposite the mother, keeping the babies between the parents. He will leave his family for her and for her only, but he will die in the front ranks for any of them.

I have placed their bushels of corn around one of my mating pairs, and, of the thousands of hungry geese that come here, none would interfere with these little plots to take even one kernel.

When traveling in the air, the male Canada goose leads the way, breaking the air for his sweetheart, who is quartering behind him, and his family travels next to her. In brief, he is one of the most self-sacrificing, godly-principled leaders the human eye ever beheld, and to know him is to love and admire him.

About one year ago I was interviewed by many reporters from our Canadian papers wanting a statement regarding our proposed national bird. After such requests had been made to me repeatedly, I wrote to the Canadian papers requesting that our already-established Canada goose be chosen as our national bird. I said, in brief, he is one of the most self-sacrificing, Godly-principled leaders the human eye ever beheld, to know him is to love and admire him, and there is not a human being on earth so good but that personal acquaintance with our noble Canada goose will give him a desire to live better. And now I come to you again and ask one and all to think for yourselves, and if Canada is to have a national bird let us revive the discussion. This lovely bird is already established throughout this continent as the Canada goose. Why hesitate to choose the noblest bird in the world as the emblem of the best and most promising country in the world?

A most unusual picture—the Nest of a Canada Goose. Note the goose on the nest. Photo taken in Wainwright, Alberta, National Park.

I want all fair-minded Canadians to read and re-read a letter I received last week. The writer doesn't know whether I am a man, woman or child, my name not being on the tag. The bird he shot was tagged in April, with four hundred and fifty others that I caught, tagged and liberated here at my home to study their route of migration. The letter "S" denotes spring and "27" the year, all my fall tags being stamped with a letter "F."

"ENGELHARD, NORTH CAROLINA, U.S.A.,
"November 2nd, 1927

"Dear Sir or Madam,
"At Kingsville, Ontario, Canada.
    "I had the good fortune of meeting one of your neighbors yesterday on the first day of the hunting season, and think he was the most remarkable goose I have ever seen. A flock of twenty-five or more geese lit to my decoys just out of gunshot, of which he was the leader, and as the flock started in he seemed to realize there was danger near my decoy geese, and tried hard to keep them back. He swam to and fro between the flock and the decoys, fighting at the flock, trying to drive them away, and when they persisted to come in he would fly off and circle around, hollering as hard as he could, and, when he saw the flock was coming in, anyway, in spite of warning, he came and lit between them and the decoys, as much as to say,

if it must be done, take me and let these children go. He being the largest goose in the flock, I took him first, the others got away, and, after the excitement was over, I brought him in the blind and saw his tag, and realized how nobly he laid down his life for his friends, my conscience hurt me. My companion and myself talked about the splendid traits of character the goose had shown, and we imagined him some pet that a little boy or girl had found and raised until he was grown, and

A Close-Up of the Same Nest.

carried and put with other geese to choose a mate and fly away to the safe, sunny South to spend the winter. Many will go back, but this brave gander was the first to fall, but in falling displayed such nobility as to convince me of the sin of killing game just for the sport of it, and if ever I go again it will be because I want a goose to eat and not to shoot them down just to see them die. On the tag, besides the address, was Ps. 37-3, 'Trust in the Lord,' which is the first line of the third verse of the 37th Psalm. '27,' I suppose, was the year. There was an 'S' off to itself, and I imagine the gander was named Sam or Sallie. My wife is putting dinner on the table now and I can smell the baked goose, and the sweet potatoes, collards, cranberry sauce with oyster dressing, so I am just now consoling myself with that passage of Scripture when the Lord said, 'Arise, Peter, slay and eat.' I really wish I could have killed an untagged goose and let old Sam go back home. I feel like you will look for him when the others come north again. I wish you would write me, tell me your name, and how you and old Sam became friends.

"Yours very truly,

"(Signed)   BILLY HARRIS."

THE WEIGHT OF OUR WILD CANADA GEESE

WRITING IS FAR harder work for me than splitting rails, ditching, or packing out moose meat, but having heard so many different stories about the weight of wild Canada geese, I feel it my duty to pass along what I actually know about it. During the last twenty-five or thirty years I have fed hundreds of thousands of Canada wild geese here at this Sanctuary. These birds hatch and mature in far, far northern Canada and start congregating here the last of October. They would stay all winter if I could afford to feed them. There are from three to four thousand here right now in January. They don't average over eight pounds each when they first arrive from the north but it is surprising how fast they put on flesh. We feed them the very choicest of American corn, 90 per cent. of which is fed on the cob.

About sundown they tower high and pass over three miles of no man's land and from one hundred to five hundred shooters. The geese land out about two miles in Lake Erie and at night swim or fly ashore to the big sand bars which are from one-quarter to one-half mile out and fully two miles long. At daybreak they either swim or fly a short distance into the blue water then just about sunrise they again tower high and string after string is seen passing over this same territory three miles back to their cafeteria, where they find twenty acres of alfalfa clover and acres of wheat sown three to four bushels to the acre about September 1st. All of this feeding-ground is bordered with an evergreen wind-break from ten to thirty feet high. Here they feed, drink, rest, and sleep, play and sun themselves, as contented and happy as we were on November 11th, 1918. Now and then a few hundred or a thousand will fly over the forest border and alight on the fall ploughed fields, but it is amusing to see how careful they are not to go within one-quarter of a mile of No Man's Border. Really they shun that line as the most intelligent human being would strychnine, dynamite, or nitro-glycerine.

Readers, I mention these details to show that conditions could not be more favourable to produce fat, heavy wild geese. Remember these birds all have to be handled individually and any extra heavy ones are brought to the house and weighed. Not one in a hundred weighs over eleven and three quarters pounds and not one in a thousand weighs a fraction over twelve pounds. Sportsmen and bird lovers, I am now speaking of the geese that winter east of the Mississippi River, for, out of the 1600 or more bands now reported to me, 99 per cent. have been killed east of the Mississippi river. Another interesting fact is that the pinioned young, hatched from these same wild birds, will eventually become so fat that at eight and ten years of age individuals will weigh thirteen or possibly fourteen pounds but they could not fly even if they had both wings. Indeed these geese that are here right now are so fat they will waddle back fully fifteen rods, when not

A Catch in the Goose Trap, from the Side.

frightened, in order to rise easily over the forest border thirty feet high. Remember these geese are not all babies. We recatch dozens that have carried their tag from five to twelve years—one killed in North Carolina lived to carry the tag thirteen years and eight months. Now what I actually know about the weight of the geese, that rise up and migrate north and south year after year east of the Mississippi River, is that they range in weight from seven and one-half to possibly twelve pounds when good and fat.

I don't pretend to know much about the wild migrating geese of the west, but the hundreds upon hundreds I have seen in captivity appear to have a trifle larger bone. A Mr. Yeager of Owatonna, Minnesota, has the largest pair I have even seen in captivity. If good and fat I believe the gander would weigh fifteen pounds, but how many generations these big birds have been reared in captivity I do not know.

BIRD NEWS

About 10,000 geese wintered here this year. I am sure I have been asked hundreds of times, why? When we eventually found we had an extremely mild winter, I was better equipped to answer this question, to which I am compelled to believe the silly old goose knew the answer the fall before.

Until the last day of February, we did not notice the flock getting any larger, but one warm Saturday morning the place fairly echoed and re-echoed with their migratory honks. Any person that has become slightly acquainted with these wild honking Canadian geese would say, "The geese are coming." Yet night came and no geese until 2 A. M. Sunday, March first, the honking of descending geese came drifting into my open bedroom window and they were coming by the hundreds. Daylight came and the geese continued coming, the wind was now blowing very hard from the North but still the geese came on. At 10 A. M. we drove three miles south to the shore of Lake Erie. A heavy wind caused the lake to be fairly wild, in fact the water was white with foam. With my high-power field glasses I could see Pelee Island sixteen miles straight south and two or three small flocks of geese apparently struggling in the air tacking against the heavy wind. Someone has written that "wild geese migrate at a speed of 120 miles per hour." I am from Missouri. We turned our Ford toward home and set the speedometer and these geese were not making a bit over fifteen miles per hour. No, they did not light in the wild water nor did they alight in no-man's-land, but they glided down into the safety zone and lit within half a mile of the border and rested for an hour or so. Then they rose up and came the other half a mile to their cafeteria back of my home and by 2 P. M. four or five thousand had arrived and, while I have no proof of it, I believe these geese came through from North Carolina and Virginia.

Well, by March 15th the flock seemed to be 20 per cent. larger than we had ever seen it before. We broke all catching records. In five catches we tagged 933 new ones and I am sure there were 70 or more that were previously tagged. We call the latter re-catches. The oldest tag had been put on eight years before. One outstanding fact to me about these noble Canada geese is that we had been catching them for seven years before we made a single re-catch. Now, at least five per cent. are re-catches. Yes, it is plain to be seen that these silly old geese have found where the choicest food is and know that even if they are caught they will not be hurt. Just the same, this is a fascinating sport. Catching geese is something like Pat catching fleas. "And sure," said he, "when I took my hand off him he wasn't there." For illustration, once all was shaping up fine for a big catch—there were fully two hundred under the net and more feeding towards it. I was on my tip-toe in anxiety, uttering imaginary whispers. "Go on under, the rest of you hungry honkers, go on under. I will give each of you a bright aluminum remembrance." Sure enough they all seemed to hear my heart whispers and started going under as I wanted them to and

A Close-Up of One Corner of the Trap.

I was about to slip back and pull the trip wire. Suddenly a young gander apparently looking for a mate arrived from parts unknown and when about 200 feet straight above the net he shut off the gas and put on the four wheel brakes and came straight down. Apparently he did not notice the nineteen-gauge two-inch poultry netting, for he struck right on top of the net above the 200 or more geese that were quietly feeding under him and under the net. Well, the spring of the loose netting tossed him back into the air and, believe me, I never saw a more frightened lot of geese in my life. They went out of there on both sides honking, flopping, flying, and not a goose could I decoy back under that net for over a week. Yes, readers, no person but those that have had experience knows the tingling thrill there is in the catching and tagging of wild geese.

One morning about April 10th I was all smiles over a big catch I had made. Soon I had six or eight boys and men helping catch and tag them. I was on hand like a sore thumb, giving the orders and assuming all responsibility of seeing that the four corners of the net were tied down and the catching-pen door closed and so forth. Here were the boys in hip rubbers, wading through the shallow water corralling the geese, a bunch at a time, marching them up the corrugated cement stairway unto the alfalfa hay cushion in the catching-pen. All at once as if in one voice a shout rose above the honks "Shut the door! Shut the door! Father, shut the catching-pen door!" Sure enough I had forgotten to close this door and eighteen wild geese walked right out. For all I know they are going yet without a tag. I haven't heard the last of that "Shut the door."

Do dreams come true? Well, visions often do. I have often said the time would come when others would be catching geese and then catching geese the other fellow had tagged would be still more interesting for me. This spring we caught a goose tagged by the other fellow and about the same day this gentleman, Mr. W. Ferguson, Route 4, Muskegon, Michigan, caught one with our tag on. This makes Mr. Ferguson and me partners. He writes me that he has caught, tagged and liberated fourteen, but remember I was seven years with my little single cylinder brain catching the first 109. Right here I want to take the opportunity of thanking the sportsmen of North America for their hearty co-operation. Believe it or not, 81 of these 109 tags were reported and 73 were sent back to me. One tag we received came from North Carolina. This goose was tagged in April, 1917 and killed on December 19th, 1930. Yes, he lived to carry the tag thirteen years and eight months. The 109 geese were tagged between 1915 and 1922. The tags from the south came from four states only, but from 1922 to 1930 the tags came in from twenty additional states.

Now, as to the smaller desirable birds, they are back keeping house as usual. Young horned Larks flying, young Killdeers running with parents, Kentucky Cardinals, Mourning Doves, and Robins nesting by the hundreds.

A MERRY CHRISTMAS TO YOU,
YOURS AND THEIRS

Yes, I say, "Merry Christmas," but does it come from my lips only? Let me assure you it comes from my heart, and I wish all a merry, merry Christmas. As I say this my gray hairs fairly twitch as my heart melts with thankfulness to Almighty God, for by far the greatest of the riches I have on this earth is my sincere appreciation of His loving kindness toward me.

If you will please pardon my personal reference I will give you a flash of my meaning. Near Dover Centre, Ohio, a little suburb of Cleveland, lies a small piece of land that is sacredly near to my heart. Often I drift back to the land of my birth, and after meeting a few old tried and true friends, I find myself stealing away alone. And time and time again I have gone and stood on this Memorial spot. Oft loving memories almost blind my sight, for that is where the first Miner home of which I have any distinct recollection stood. Again this little old rustic, one-story weather-beaten house comes before me. Yes, it only had one door and three windows, yet it was one of the most lovable homes God ever blest, and in spite of our scant belongings and poverty, old Santa Claus gladdened all our hearts. There were six children in the family, the baby slept with father and mother. Father had built a homemade trundle bed that was pushed under their bed during the day to make more play room. This was Christmas of 1868.

Finally the anticipated Christmas eve arrived and we children went to bed early, and closed our eyes tight to hurry the morning on. Although father was not considered a Christian man, next thing we would hear was his deep mellow voice, as he sang:

> "Come, Thou Fount of every blessing,
> Tune my heart to sing Thy Grace;
> Streams of mercy, never ceasing,
> Call for songs of loudest praise."

Well, we are all awake at once, but not dressed. One is blowing a little trumpet, another has a little five-cent jack-in-the-box. Sisters have nice pieces of ribbon to tie their long braided hair. The whole house is leaping, shouting, and tooting with so much delight that the strange noises awake and frighten the baby into loud cries. Later on, dear mother got breakfast ready, and will you believe it, we had oysters! Once a year on Christmas morning we had them. Yes, one whole pint tin can of oysters, cooked in water, for we did not have any milk. But mother had a way of seasoning water and oysters that made up for all that was lacking.

Now, father was a great rabbit-hunter and would bring home five or ten rabbits in a day. On Sundays and holidays we had only two meals a day, and about two in the afternoon mother would have two Cotton Tail Rabbits stuffed and baked. Oh, the fragrance of the dressing, seasoned with her home-grown savories! How we children would eat, but under such hungry conditions we were so Merry Christmasly happy, that it was hard to keep us quiet.

I am sure that the whole day's feast and toy happiness did not cost one dollar. Yes, my dear friends, we were poor financially, but multi-million-aires in harmony, love, and appreciation.

My hope is, that nothing will be big or small enough around or about you to mar your Merry, Merry Christmas.

Let us all rejoice, for if there had been no Christ, there would be no Christmas, and yet He, the dear Lord, had not where to lay His head. Yes, "foxes have holes, and the birds have nests, but the Son of Man hath no place to lay His head."

Let sunshine and cheer banish sadness and fear, and everlasting life start right here.

THE END